Date Due			
'05.8 Feb May 24 95			

I SAW POLAND BETRAYED

ARTHUR BLISS LANE

I Saw Poland Betrayed

AN AMERICAN AMBASSADOR
REPORTS TO THE AMERICAN PEOPLE

by ARTHUR BLISS LANE
UNITED STATES AMBASSADOR TO POLAND, 1944-1947

"They enslave their children's children who make compromise with sin." —JAMES RUSSELL LOWELL, *"The Present Crisis"*

THE BOBBS-MERRILL COMPANY
Publishers

INDIANAPOLIS   NEW YORK

COPYRIGHT, 1948, BY ARTHUR BLISS LANE

PRINTED IN THE UNITED STATES OF AMERICA

To the Memory
of Peggy

Foreword

IMMEDIATELY following the elections of January 19, 1947, in Poland, I determined to resign my position as American Ambassador. My mission—to ensure that "free and unfettered elections" should be held—had been a failure. To remain in Warsaw would be interpreted as tacit acquiescence in the fraudulent methods employed in the elections.

Furthermore, I felt strongly that the facts which had brought about the tragedy of the Polish situation should be placed publicly on the record. This could not be done so long as I remained an official of the United States Government; for the facts would indicate not only the intellectual dishonesty of the Soviet and Polish Governments, but also the grievous errors which our own government had made in following a policy of appeasement in its dealings with Stalin. My resignation was accepted, to take effect on March 31, 1947, with the understanding of President Truman and of the Acting Secretary of State (Dean Acheson) that I would tell the story as I had seen it.

The Department of State kindly allowed me to refresh my memory on the happenings during my Ambassadorship by putting at my disposal the pertinent documents dealing with that period. But the views expressed in this volume are solely my own and are in nowise to be interpreted as those of the United States Government, with which I am no longer connected.

If I have seemed to make excessive use of the first personal pronoun in this volume—as well as in its title—it is because I have wished to emphasize that this is a first-hand and personal account of what I have seen and experienced: the consecutive steps in the formation of a puppet police state.

Where I have not given the names of informants still resident in

Poland, the omission is due to my desire to protect the safety of the individuals.

I wish to express my heartfelt gratitude to the members of our staff in the American Embassy in Poland during my incumbency who unconsciously aided me in the writing of this book. The remembrance of these loyal public servants, whether Poles or Americans, has served as an inspiration to me in my effort to bring to the world the tragic story of Poland's present fate. My gratitude to them cannot be adequately expressed in words; but I shall never forget their courage and devotion to the cause of freedom.

In my concluding chapter I have stressed the essential importance of keeping the public informed as to international relationships before those relationships reach a critical stage. Yet, if the public has been kept insufficiently advised of our foreign relations, the reader may well wonder, as he follows my experiences in Washington and in Poland, why it was that the United States Ambassador to Poland was not advised by his own government of the commitments which had been made and were being made with respect to Poland. Such oversights—whether deliberate or not—are inexcusable. For no American ambassador can effectively represent his nation abroad unless he is acquainted with all the facts dealing with the situation in the country to which he is accredited.

Although I received close and sympathetic co-operation from all officers in the Department of State charged with the handling of the details of Polish affairs, the reticence and apparent indifference of some of the highest officials of the United States Government in this vital question are inexplicable. Nothing can more effectively ruin the morale of the Department of State and of the Foreign Service— as well as the very foreign policy which these bodies are required to carry out—if high officers of the government ignore the reports sent by observers abroad and withhold from them the information without which those representatives cannot properly carry out their functions.

Apart from the importance of the Polish question to the American people—due to the historically strategic geographic position of Poland in Europe and to the fact that millions of American citizens are of Polish descent—the fate of Poland is tremendously significant to all the world because it is parallel to the fate already suffered by Albania, Bulgaria, Hungary, Rumania and Yugoslavia and, in a lesser degree, by Czechoslovakia. In Estonia, Latvia and Lithuania, even nominal independence has been eradicated through the incorporation of these Baltic States into the Soviet Union. The Soviet technique in Poland—as in all these other nations—has been, through the imposition of the police state, to stamp out all political opposition, all nationalistic elements, and virtually all freedom of speech.

The execution of this policy, however inhuman in its methods, embraces more than the suppression of democracy in Eastern Europe. Inherent in the policy of dictators such as Hitler and Stalin is the aim for world domination, accomplished through the conquest, one by one, of the states of Europe until the turn of the United States is reached.

The American people has therefore a vital stake in the fate of Poland—and of all Europe. We cannot close our eyes to Communist imperialism without endangering our own existence.

As I write these words, the news has come of the escape from Poland of Stanislaw Mikolajczyk, head of the Polish Peasant Party, former Premier of the Polish Government-in-Exile, as well as former Vice-Premier and Minister of Agriculture in the Polish Provisional Government of National Unity, and of his safe arrival in London. It is a source of great satisfaction to know that this great democratic leader—who courageously returned to Poland in 1945 in spite of his conviction that the elections would be fraudulent, and in the full realization that he was running the risk of his own judicial murder—is safe on friendly soil.

He told me when I was in Warsaw that he would remain in Poland—regardless of the physical danger—as long as he might accomplish something on behalf of the Polish people. From my intimate association with this sterling patriot, I feel convinced that only the knowledge that nothing more could be accomplished by him within Poland would have led him to the decision to seek a haven of safety abroad where his work could be continued.

The paradoxical tragedy in Mikolajczyk's successful escape is that the police-state tyranny in Poland has reached such a high state of efficiency and ruthlessness that not even a leader of the indisputable majority of the electorate can further struggle for the cause of freedom within the borders of his own country.

After the grimly farcical elections of January 19, 1947, Mikolajczyk and I discussed the results which he had foreseen even at the time when he left London for the Moscow conversations in June 1945—on the urging of the British and United States governments. Those governments had also been responsible for Mikolajczyk's public adherence to the Yalta decision, much against his better judgment. Mikolajczyk said to me, "I was able to accomplish nothing in effecting free elections in Poland. But I have accomplished one thing: I have shown to the whole world that nobody can believe the promises of the Soviet Government."

Those broken promises of the Soviet Government and of its Polish puppet government are the basic causes of the Polish tragedy, the story of which is told, as I saw it, in the chapters which follow.

ARTHUR BLISS LANE

CONTENTS

LIST OF ILLUSTRATIONS

List of Illustrations

I SAW POLAND BETRAYED

CHAPTER ONE

Unhappy Landing

OUT OF leaden-gray skies, on the last day of July 1945, our three United States Army planes, C-47's, circled down to a landing at Okecie airport on the outskirts of Warsaw, capital of Poland.

Across the plains of Poland in September, six years before, had roared the planes and the tanks of Hitler's ruthless might, starting the war which spread from Poland over the entire world.

Ours were the first American planes to land in Poland since that unhappy year.

The war, as far as defeated Germany was concerned, had come to its end three months before our arrival. Now, around a council table in the Cecilienhof in Potsdam, the heads of the three chief nations which had brought Germany to her knees, "the Big Three," were putting the last touches to the Potsdam Declaration.

Across the neglected landing field, which was knee-deep in grass and pitted with weed-filled holes, and whose runways and hangars had been destroyed, our plane rolled to a stop. For the third time in twenty-six years I was in Warsaw. On the two previous occasions I had come, first as a junior secretary of legation, then as a visitor returning to my post as United States Minister to the Baltic States. This time I came as the newly appointed Ambassador of the United States to the Polish Provisional Government of National Unity.

But my mood, as I once more felt the ground of Poland beneath my feet, was not one of elation. Rather, it was one of hopelessness—a hopelessness resulting from the disquieting warning signals which had been repeating themselves month after month during the year preceding, as I bent myself to the study of United States policy toward Poland. More accurately, it was a study of our policy toward Russia, in so far as Soviet policy affected Poland. For I soon learned that the Polish Government was not sovereign, in our understanding of the term.

At the airport our only welcome was wind and rain.* Without leaving the shelter of the plane, we sat wondering what had gone askew. Presently in that wasteland there materialized a solitary human figure—an unkempt and taciturn soldier, who had heard nothing of any plans for receiving the American Ambassador's party. (We learned later that the telegram sent from Paris, five days earlier, announcing the hour at which to expect us, had not yet arrived. In fact, for eight days our arrival had been expected and a guard of honor had been at the airport daily to greet us. Finally, after so many delays, plans for the reception were abandoned.) The soldier plodded off.

Almost an hour later a welcome sight, an American jeep, came splattering through the puddles. From it emerged a tall and handsome young American in Navy uniform—Lieutenant William Tonesk, who was to be assistant naval attaché at our Embassy. Lieutenant Tonesk, American-born, was of Polish descent and had spoken Polish from his infancy. Before the war he had attended the famous University of Kraków, and had a wide acquaintance with leaders of Polish thought. Most recently he had been sent to Moscow as an aide to our Ambassador there, W. Averell Harriman, in the sessions of the tripartite commission (consisting of Mr. Harriman for the United States, Mr. Molotov for the U.S.S.R., and Sir Archibald Clark-Kerr for Great Britain), which had been given the responsibility, under the Yalta decision, of inviting representative Poles to Moscow to set up the new Polish Provisional Government of National

---

* In addition to my wife and me, our initial party consisted of the following: Gerald Keith, Counselor; C. Burke Elbrick, First Secretary; Edmund J. Dorsz, Second Secretary; Oscar W. Frederickson, disbursing officer; Stephen Jenkins, radio operator; Eugene J. Cronin, administrative assistant; Ben Jacobs, guard; Miss Iona A. McNulty, my private secretary; Miss Violet Hille, stenographer; Major Michael G. Hresan, medical officer; and Major Lawrence Treece, United States Signal Corps, on temporary duty to Warsaw. Thomas P. Dillon, Third Secretary, arrived a few days afterward in charge of our first automobile convoy.

Unity. Lieutenant Tonesk had attended all the sessions of that commission. He had come to Warsaw from Moscow, with a jeep lent by Ambassador Harriman, and luckily arrived in time to meet us at the field. As my aide and acting as my interpreter, he was to prove of inestimable value to me throughout the coming year.

Hardly had we exchanged joyful greetings, when a second car lumbered across the rain-swept field and came to a stop beside our plane. It was a dilapidated green car, a former Berlin taxicab, a relic of the German occupation of Warsaw, and the only car which the present Polish Ministry of Foreign Affairs possessed. Out of it stepped the tall, spare figure of the Minister of Foreign Affairs himself, Mr. Wincenty Rzymowski, huddled in an overcoat. We invited him into the shelter of our plane. His scholarly-looking face lighted with a shy smile as he welcomed us, in excellent French, to Poland. The acting Chief of Protocol, Mr. Wyszynski, also graciously extended to us good wishes for a happy stay in Poland.

Soon still another vehicle drove up. Out of it sprang a man of massive frame, whose broad face was topped by a tremendous shock of light curly hair. The strength of his features was softened by the pair of tortoise-shell glasses which masked his eyes. He strode toward us, beaming with cordiality. This was Mr. Lebedev, the Soviet Ambassador to Poland. He, too, welcomed us to the country. I was yet to appreciate how fitting it was that such a welcome should come from Marshal Stalin's representative.

Through his interpreter, who spoke excellent English, Mr. Lebedev smilingly reproached me for not having known him when we had both been in Belgrade, the Yugoslav capital. He had been, he reminded me, Soviet chargé d'affaires in Belgrade during the last year of my assignment as Minister to Yugoslavia from 1937 to 1941. It was true that we had not met; but I could scarcely reply that on his arrival in Belgrade, after the establishment of Soviet-Yugoslav relations in 1940, the official call should have been paid by him, rather than by me. The fact was that during those years, when the Nazi and Soviet honeymoon was at the full, the Russian diplomatic representatives took pains to see little, if anything, of the representatives of the Allies or even of those reputedly misguided friends of the Allies, the Americans.

Mr. Lebedev graciously informed me, however, that I had once done him a favor while in Belgrade, for which he would remain forever grateful. This had occurred in 1941 when, after the bombardment of April 6 and 7, German troops took over the city, and all foreign representatives were told that it would be "convenient" for them to leave without delay. On receipt of this word I had managed to reach Budapest by car to communicate by telephone with the Department of State and obtain authority to evacuate our staff, as well as the American colony. We were obliged to cross the Danube and the Sava rivers by rafts and pontoon bridges, all permanent bridges having been destroyed by the Yugoslav forces. After arriving in Budapest, I had sent word to the Soviet Legation, as I had been asked to do, that the staff of the legation in Belgrade was marooned there and, all communications having been cut, was unable to notify Moscow that they, too, had been ordered out by the Germans. In short, implied Mr. Lebedev, if it had not been for my kindness, he might not now be having the happiness of welcoming me to Warsaw!

As we drove the seven miles from the airport into Warsaw, I sensed the chill of deep depression. I was remembering the Warsaw I had known and loved in years long gone by. I had seen Warsaw first in 1919, when Poland had just arisen as a free nation, after one hundred twenty-five years of subjugation. One then sensed on the streets of its capital a gaiety of the soul, an intoxicating sense of freedom never felt before. I had seen Warsaw again in 1937, when it was one of the most beautiful capitals of all Europe. But now my heart grew heavier with every mile. I could see only a handful of houses left unharmed; all others were bombed or gutted by fire. The smoky smell of long-dead fires hung in the air. The sickening sweet odor of burned human flesh was a grim warning that we were entering a city of the dead. A part of the destruction had been caused by the

Nazis' artillery and the aerial bombing of the city when they first attacked it in 1939; but the major part of the city's devastation was due to the leveling of the Ghetto in the spring of 1943 and the vengeance which the Nazis wreaked upon a far greater area after they had suffocated the desperate insurrection of the Polish Home Army which emerged from the underground in the last quarter of 1944. At that time the infuriated Germans, acting under the Fuehrer's personal instructions, drove all the inhabitants of Warsaw out of the city and herded them in a concentration camp at Pruszków, a suburb some fifteen miles distant. They then destroyed the city methodically, block by block and house by house. Almost every building was gutted by fire from incendiary bombs set off from the ground; a few were destroyed by explosive bombs. The only buildings left standing were those housing the Nazi High Command and the barracks of their troops. Among these was the Polonia Hotel which had been headquarters of the Wehrmacht; and it was in this hotel that our Embassy was to be housed. My eyes searched in vain, as we drove deeper into the city, for any familiar square or building, until, in the center of the city, on Jerusalem Street, I saw two blackened towers of twisted metal and suddenly realized that these were all that was left of the once luxurious railroad station.

The day before I had been in Berlin. The destruction I saw there had impressed me greatly. A Polish acquaintance had shrugged his shoulders. "It is nothing, compared to what was done to Warsaw," he said. I had thought that he must be exaggerating. Now I saw that he had spoken only the truth.

Our little procession of cars drew up at last before the Polonia Hotel. The flags of all the Allied nations were displayed upon it; it was obvious that the hotel was diplomatic headquarters. We went in by a side entrance. The elevator at this entrance no longer functioned, but as we had only one flight of stairs to climb, this was of little consequence. We were ushered into an apartment which to us seemed luxurious, for we had been led to believe that only the most primitive accommodations could be found in Warsaw. I had been warned before leaving Washington that the housing shortage in Warsaw was so acute even the President and the Premier of Poland's newly created government had on their arrival been able to find one room only, which they shared, and which served as office as well as residence. Ambassador Harriman had, on the recommendation of the Poles in Moscow, cabled to me in Washington that our staff should at the outset consist only of the minimum essential personnel, perhaps half a dozen.

Happily for us, conditions had improved in the last few weeks. The suite prepared for my wife and me consisted of a double bedroom and bath and a large living room which was to serve also as my office. With its modernistic, overstuffed chairs, its metal, circular Turkish table, its imitation fireplace and its very fine antique pieces as well, it was ornate, rather than homelike, but we thought ourselves fortunate indeed. The manager of the hotel had gone to great trouble, Lieutenant Tonesk told us, in collecting furniture for the apartment, visiting distant parts of Poland to obtain suitable pieces.

One of two small rooms adjoining our suite was immediately put into use as our Embassy file room; the other was to be the office of four members of the Embassy staff.

The hotel had also put two servants at our disposal. One was Stanislas, a venerable, distinguished-looking factotum, with a carefully trained gray mustache. I later discovered that Stanislas had served as our butler for a few weeks when my wife and I were in Warsaw in 1919. Evidently both he and I had changed in the years since then, for neither of us at first recognized the other. The other servant they gave us was a maid. She was an intelligent-looking girl who, as we eventually made out, understood a very great deal more English and French than she professed. She knew little of the duties of a maid, but she kept a close eye on all of our visitors, and she displayed a remarkable diligence in emptying the contents of our wastepaper baskets—a task which she performed many, many times daily. Unfortunately for the Polish secret police, no confidential material was ever consigned there.

As we had not eaten since early morning and it was now midafter-noon, our little party descended to the garish dining room of the Polonia. Despite rumors of famine in Poland that had come to us in Paris, we were offered a plenteous bill of fare from which to select. The prices, however, were exorbitant, according to the rate of ex-change then prevailing. The Polish monetary unit, the zloty, was quoted at five and three-tenths to the dollar, giving the zloty a value of about nineteen cents, equivalent to that of the Russian ruble. For the diplomatic corps a rate of twenty zlotys to the dollar had been established. At this rate of exchange, our meal for four persons, con-sisting of cold smoked salmon and cheese, bread and butter, amounted to twelve hundred zlotys, or one hundred dollars. Fortunately the hotel permitted all of us to live on credit for some weeks!

After finishing our belated luncheon, my wife and I, accompanied by Burke Elbrick, went for a stroll through the streets of Warsaw. In particular we wanted to see what, if anything, was left of the building which, before the war, had housed the American Embassy. This build-ing, owned by the aristocratic Czartoryski family, had been situated on the Aleja Ujazdowskie, the boulevard famed for its trees and its beautiful buildings, and stretching from the Belvedere Palace at one end to the heart of the city at the other. We found the streets leading to the Aleja still heaped with rubble remaining from the burning of the city by the Nazis. The building was still standing, but gutted by fire, and there was nothing to show that it had ever been occupied by our government, except the fire-blackened shield of the United States, fastened to the side of the house facing the boulevard. Elbrick, who had been Secretary of the Embassy at the time of the German advance upon the city in September 1939, and who had now been again assigned temporarily to the Embassy pending his assumption of the Polish desk in the Department of State, led us to the ruined garden at the rear of the building and pointed out to us the trenches which he had helped to dig for shelter while the German bombers were roaring overhead. It was apparent that the building could not be rendered fit for use again unless completely reconstructed, and we decided that the best solution would be to continue in the makeshift offices in the Polonia Hotel until the Polish Government could provide us with a suitable building. Slowly we walked back to the Polonia, my wife and I sadly comparing the misery we now saw on every hand with the bright hopes of Poland in 1919.

In 1919 President Wilson had appointed Mr. Hugh Gibson to be our first Minister to the new-born Republic of Poland. It was my good fortune, at the age of twenty-five, to be assigned to serve under him. He was generally considered to be one of our ablest career officers, with a tremendous capacity for work. It was an inspiration to serve under his guidance and in the ever cheerful atmosphere which his keen sense of humor created.

In 1919 the feeling of gratitude toward the United States was universally expressed in Poland. First, everyone knew that it was President Wilson and his advisers who had been chiefly responsible for the resurrection of Poland as an independent nation. Secondly, the American Relief Administration, under the able direction of Mr. Herbert Hoover, had given to the Poles a practical demonstration of American friendship. The reception which Mr. Hoover received from the Polish people in August 1919 was spontaneous and real. Unlike demonstrations which I was to see in Warsaw in 1947, it did not require the prodding of government agents to evoke cheers from the children or from their parents. Because of these memories I had always cherished deep affection for the people of Poland and I had followed Polish events, especially during World War II, with the greatest interest.

The memories of April 30, 1919, when Mr. Gibson presented his credentials to General Pilsudski, then Chief of State, were still vivid to me. Preceded by a detachment of Polish cavalry, we were driven to the Belvedere Palace from our legation offices, then in the Bristol Hotel. Mr. Gibson and Mr. Frederick R. Dolbeare, First Secretary of Legation, who occupied the first open carriage, were greeted by cheers from onlookers as we made our way through the famed streets of Nowy Swiat and Aleja Ujazdowskie (the latter in 1945 appropriately renamed Aleja Stalina). The carriages were drawn by white horses which had been formerly owned by King Albert of the Belgians. Mr. Gibson, as a former Secretary of the American Legation in Brussels, had seen these famous horses on previous Belgian state occasions. After the German occupation of Belgium they had been removed to Warsaw for the use of the German governor-general there. As we approached the Belvedere Palace, a military band in the courtyard rendered the two national anthems. Immediately thereafter General Pilsudski, in his characteristically austere manner, received Mr. Gibson and the members of his staff. Official relations had commenced.

Rarely had I experienced such unbridled enthusiasm on the part of a people as when the Warsaw crowds celebrated Polish Constitution Day on May 3, 1919. At last the Poles were no longer under the subjugation either of the Russian, the German or the Austro-Hungarian empires. In keeping with the Polish custom, the open windows of the Warsaw houses on that warm sunny spring morning were draped with carpets to indicate the spirit of festivity. Thousands of people shouting "Long live independent Poland!" thronged the streets. The crowds flocked to the Citadel, which had been used as a Czarist prison for the incarceration of Polish patriots. In front of this building General Pilsudski reviewed detachments of Polish troops which had fought in the Russian, German, Austrian and French armies and in the German Navy. These detachments marched by the general, each with its characteristic gait, the German Poles even employing the goose step which they had been taught to perform when in the Kaiser's army. All of the troops wore their former uniforms, but there was one significant addition. On May 3, 1919, each hat or cap bore the emblem of the crowned Polish Eagle. Although Poland was no longer a monarchy, the crown was symbolic of the glories and traditions of the past and of the democratic principles of the Constitution of May 3, 1791. Pilsudski may have made enemies during the time when he and his associates ruled Poland. They were

Poles, however, and were masters in their own house. They took no orders from Moscow, Berlin or anywhere else.

When the offices of the American Legation were moved shortly after, in July 1919, from the Bristol Hotel to "the Blue Palace"— the property of Count Maurice Zamoyski, then Polish Minister to France—my wife and I were hospitably invited by Mr. Gibson to share the palace with him. Here, the then Premier of Poland, Jan Ignace Paderewski, was a not infrequent caller. Once he inscribed in our guest book a bar of music, composed extemporaneously, by way of signature.

Little did we dream then that on our return to Warsaw, twenty-six years later, we would find that this architectural gem, the Blue Palace, with its exquisite furnishings, had been reduced by Germany to a mass of ruins.

The view from our windows in the Polonia, westward across the railroad tracks, was a study in despair. Rows of shells of houses on the other side of what was once Warsaw's railroad center were mute testimony to the barbarity of Nazi policy, unjustified by any military or strategic reason. The scene was depressingly lacking in the normal bustle and movement of a city. There were no streetcars, scarcely any automobiles; a few horse-drawn carts and bicycle-propelled push-carts were the only vehicles moving. Trading took place on street corners or in crudely erected wooden shacks. As the evening came on, the city was completely dark; there was electricity only in our hotel and in a few other buildings spared by the Germans; beyond the circle of light in front of the Polonia made by the only two street lamps in the city, it was perilous to venture unarmed. And because of the destruction of familiar landmarks, it was dangerously easy to lose one's way.

Inside the hotel was physical comfort—light, food and, usually, heat and running water. Outside were ragged men and women and children—hunger, illness and cold. The next morning, and every morning thereafter for months, we saw lines of people forming before the faucets on the main boulevard filling their pails with water for drinking, cooking and washing. It was a grim and weary procession. But the most terrible sight of all was that of the one-legged children.

They were those whose legs or arms were carried away by bombs, or whose gangrened limbs were amputated in mercy. The war left these frail and heartbreaking victims everywhere in Europe. In Warsaw we counted them in sickening numbers. They had found a new occupation, unknown before the war—they hobbled, on crutches made of such sticks as they could find, to open the doors of the few automobiles, and silently held out their hands.

And yet Warsaw was slowly rising from its ashes. It seemed incredible that this capital, destroyed so viciously and systematically, could ever be rebuilt. There had been much opposition, at the first, to re-establishing Warsaw as the national capital, because of the extent of the devastation. But the incurable optimism of the Polish spirit and the desire to retain Warsaw as a symbol of political unity finally overbore the pessimists. Regardless of the political errors and misdeeds of the Polish Government, one must acknowledge that the reconstruction already accomplished, in the face of most discouraging conditions, is a tribute to its vision, courage and relentless perseverance.

However, it was not of Poland's material reconstruction that I was thinking as this first day in Warsaw came to an end. I was thinking of her dream that all her children would now be free. I was thinking, too, of the assurances which President Roosevelt and others had given to the Polish people—that we stood for a strong, free and independent Poland—and of our inability, because of the rigid control of the nation by the Russian and Polish Communists, to fulfill our promises.

CHAPTER TWO

Studying the Background

BEFORE I proceed to the narrative of my experiences in Poland, let me review the circumstances which had brought me to Warsaw, and set forth the recent history of Poland as revealed to me before my arrival there.

In July of 1944, after nearly thirty years' experience in the diplomatic service of the United States, I was serving as Ambassador to Colombia, at Bogotá. On July 17 I received a telegram from the Department of State offering me, on behalf of President Roosevelt, the post of Ambassador to the Polish Government, which was then in exile in London. I was enjoined to keep the appointment secret until the announcement was made from the White House.

My appointment was announced on September 20, when President Roosevelt sent to the Senate the nominations of envoys to Belgium, the Netherlands, Norway and Yugoslavia, in addition to my own. All of these governments were then in London, in exile from their native lands, from which they had been driven by the Nazi invasion. Up to this date the United States had maintained an embassy in London accredited to all the governments in exile there. Anthony J. Drexel Biddle, my predecessor in Warsaw, and Rudolph E. Schoenfeld, later Minister to Rumania, had acted as Ambassador and chargé d'affaires, respectively. In the outcome I never went to London to take up my official duties there.

These simultaneous appointments were made, as I later learned, with the psychological purpose of giving hope to the peoples of those oppressed nations that democratic governments were soon to be reestablished. Coming shortly after the successful invasion of Normandy in June, they presaged the early liberation of those countries, then under Nazi occupation. Also, the Nazis were effectively warned that the day of reckoning was close at hand.

Diplomatic amenities did not permit my departure from Bogotá for some weeks, so that my wife and I did not reach Washington until October 22. Early in August, only two weeks after I had received President Roosevelt's offer (which I had at once accepted), the news had come to Bogotá that the underground forces of Poland had launched into open insurrection against the Nazi forces occupying Warsaw.

In Bogotá, details concerning the insurrection were meager, the news being limited to what was permitted to be announced over a radio under war censorship.

If I had been told, at that moment, that Soviet intrigue had encouraged this revolt deliberately, and would then make sure that it was quelled by Germany, with the sole intent of imposing a Soviet-controlled government upon Poland when the time was ripe, I would have thought it utter fantasy.

I did not know then what I know now.

Russian imperialism? There had been, it is true, within the American colony in Bogotá, some adverse criticism of the allegedly imperialistic aims of Great Britain and of the Soviet Union in the war. But in the interest of Allied unity I had always urged my compatriots to desist from such complaints. Among my South American colleagues in the diplomatic corps I listened to much more violent criticism of Soviet expansionist aims. One ambassador in particular urged me not to believe in Soviet protestations of friendship for the United States. He prophesied that some day we would have a sad awakening. He emphasized the danger of Communism to the whole American continent. But I found myself unable to view the future with such fears. I had had no intimations from my own government that Russia was an ally whose motives were to be suspect. And if I, who had access to certain official documents in Colombia, felt that Soviet aims toward Poland were disinterested and were not to interfere with the creation of a free and independent Poland, how much more natural was it that the people of the United States, without such documentary knowledge, should feel that our Soviet ally was blameless! After all, even some of the highest members of the United States Government appeared to believe in the inviolability of the word of Marshal Stalin.

Moreover, I had formed a close friendship with Mr. Rezanov, the Soviet Minister in Bogotá, an agreeable man with an inscrutable expression, who, although inquisitive regarding the activities of the American Embassy, never gave me information of value as to Soviet interests in Colombia. The Soviet foreign service is unusually well informed, and perhaps he had learned of my impending appointment. Whether he was or was not aware of my future plans, Mr. Rezanov continually spoke to me of the unreasonable attitude of the Poles on the question of the Polish-Russian frontier and on the composition of the government to be set up in Poland when the war was over.

I would have liked to ask the Polish Minister in Bogotá, Mr. Chalupczynski, a friendly career diplomat, for all the confidential information he possessed regarding his country's difficulties with the Soviet Union; but I feared that to do so might divulge to him the secret of my forthcoming mission. Being ignorant at that time of the tragic future which was being prepared for the Polish people by the Soviet Union, I did not fully sympathize with the strong criticism which Mr. Chalupczynski used in private conversation to describe Soviet policy. Once my appointment was announced, late in September, he and I had many long talks about the situation. The insurrection had been maintained, at that date, for more than seven weeks; and still no aid to the Poles had been extended by the Russian forces, close to Warsaw though they were. The Polish Minister bitterly declared that this failure to give aid was intentional. At that time I thought that he had been partly carried away by his emotions and that there must be some important military reason, unknown to us, for the Red Army's failure to move in force upon the Germans in Warsaw.

It was not until I reached Washington, on October 22, three weeks

OUR ARRIVAL AT WARSAW

Extreme left, Foreign Minister Rzymowski *(back to camera)*; Radziwill; Olszewski; Massie, of British Embassy; Lane; and Elbrick.

THE SOVIET AMBASSADOR TO POLAND

Lebedev *(center)* greets us at airport.

THE HOTEL POLONIA
We had cramped quarters here.

WARSAW'S CENTRAL RAILROAD STATION
Our hotel windows looked down on the ruin wrought by the Nazis.

after the collapse of the Warsaw insurrection, that the correctness of Mr. Chalupczynski's information was impressed on me.

I regret that I had no opportunity to learn Secretary Hull's views on Poland when I reached Washington. He had already left the Department for reasons of health, and in November he resigned as Secretary of State. And I was not able to see President Roosevelt until November 20.

The Acting Secretary of State, Edward R. Stettinius, Jr., was so occupied in the formulation of the Dumbarton Oaks plan, the precursor of the United Nations Organization, that I was unable to discuss the Polish question with him until still later.

One of my first calls was made on Charles E. Bohlen and Elbridge Durbrow who were then, respectively, Chief and Assistant Chief of the Division of Eastern European Affairs, under whose jurisdiction lay our relations with the Polish Government in London.

Bohlen, long a recognized authority on Eastern European affairs, was soon to be appointed a liaison officer between the White House and the State Department. He had acted as interpreter for President Roosevelt at the Tehran Conference. He was soon to act in the same capacity at the Crimea Conference, and later as interpreter and adviser of Secretaries of State Stettinius, Byrnes and Marshall in the conferences with high Soviet Government officials at Washington, San Francisco, Potsdam, London and Moscow in 1945; in Paris and New York in 1946; and in Moscow in 1947.

Durbrow, who was shortly to replace Bohlen as Chief of the Division on the latter's promotion, was at that time in charge of the Polish desk in the Department. He had previously been assigned to Moscow and Warsaw and, like Bohlen, was exceedingly well informed on Polish-Soviet relations and Soviet over-all foreign policy.

Bohlen and Durbrow gave me on that day a summary of the Polish situation, emphasizing its uncertain character as a result of the Soviet Government's demands on the Polish Government in London regarding the Polish-Russian frontier. Throughout the eight months of my stay in Washington I had the inestimable benefit of almost daily consultation with these two men.

One of the urgent questions to settle was the selection of a staff. Nathaniel P. Davis, then Chief of the Division of Foreign Service Personnel, was fully alive to the necessity of choosing the highest type of officers and clerks, those who could stand wartime conditions in London, including V-2 bomb raids, and the postwar conditions of ruin and desolation which presumably we would later find in Warsaw. Davis had promptly complied with my initial request from Bogotá that Miss Iona A. McNulty, who was my private secretary there, should be transferred in a similar capacity to the Embassy near the Polish Government in London.

He had also chosen Edmund J. Dorsz, who had previously served in the consulate general in Poland, to be Secretary of Embassy. Dorsz was of inestimable assistance to me in attending to the various administrative matters which were especially complex in this case, for we were uncertain at the outset as to the length of time we were to remain in London; later we were uncertain as to whether we would reach either London or Warsaw; and finally we were to leave for Warsaw without knowing what we were to find in the way of lodging, foodstuffs, communication, office equipment and transportation. On arrival in Warsaw, Dorsz also took charge of all consular activities, including the protection of claimants to American citizenship who had been jailed for political reasons.

Later I was fortunate enough to obtain the assignment as Counselor of Embassy of Gerald Keith, whose fairmindedness, independence of judgment and loyalty had made a deep impression on me during my tenure in Colombia. He had served with me as First Secretary in Bogotá and had later been in charge of the Colombian desk in the State Department, where he had been of the utmost help in enabling me to carry out my instructions.

Thomas P. Dillon, who had had experience in the Soviet Union in Moscow and Vladivostok, was in time assigned as Third Secretary. His knowledge of the Russian language and of the Soviet technique of government proved valuable qualities in Russian-dominated Poland.

Two rooms in the old State Department building were put at the disposal of Dorsz, Miss McNulty and me and we plunged right into a study of the official correspondence relating to Poland. At that time I expected that our departure for London would take place within a month; I never dreamed that more than eight months would elapse before we left Washington, and that then we would go, not to London, but to Warsaw. Those eight months saw me at my desk almost every day, and each day brought from Moscow or from London some fresh item of intelligence whose bearing upon the future of Poland must be carefully weighed.

With this staff as a nucleus we made studies of outstanding political and economic questions affecting Poland. We followed the daily exchanges of telegrams between the Department and the Soviet-controlled countries (as a guide to what we might later expect in Poland), and conferred with the Treasury, War, Justice, Navy, Agriculture and Commerce Departments, as well as with various war agencies, such as the Foreign Economic Administration, on matters in which these branches of the government were interested in Poland.

I also had many conversations with Mr. Jan Ciechanowski, the Polish Ambassador in Washington, whom I had known since 1919, when, as a member of the Polish delegation to the Peace Conference in Paris, he had made several trips to Warsaw to acquaint his government about developments. Later I had known him when he was Counselor of the Legation in London in 1921 and 1922; and then again when he was Minister to the United States from 1925 to 1929. I had always considered Jan Ciechanowski a valued colleague and a keen student of political affairs. In his two assignments in Washington he had made many friends in the United States and was consequently a good judge of conditions and trends in this country.

At the time of my arrival in Washington in October Ciechanowski was evidently pessimistic over the possibility of his country's attaining full independence and sovereignty. As the months passed, and as he witnessed the series of events which were to lead to the liquidation of Polish democracy, his pessimism displayed itself in unconcealed bitterness.

He had represented in the United States the government which had fought Nazism from the outbreak of the war on September 1, 1939, and whose underground representatives in Poland had never ceased their courageous resistance, in the face of gravest danger, against the German occupation forces. Ciechanowski had signed, on behalf of our ally, Poland, the declaration of the United Nations on January 1, 1942, embodying the Atlantic Charter, including the provision:

This is a principle of the Atlantic Charter—the right of all peoples to choose the form of government under which they will live—the restoration of sovereign rights and self-government to those peoples who have been forcibly deprived of them by the aggressor nations.

Ciechanowski resented the fact that we had, for the sake of maintaining friendly relations with Stalin, capitulated to Russian demands at Tehran respecting Poland without consulting the Polish Government then recognized by the United States. Yet we continued to recognize that government as representative of the Polish people.

Perhaps it is true, as has been stated, that Stalin or his emissaries had intimated the Soviet Government's intention to make a separate peace with Germany unless the United States and Great Britain acceded to his requests in Eastern Europe. True or false, Ciechanowski's bitterness was very understandable.

I knew, then, only as the American public did, of the general developments between the Soviet Union and Germany which assured Hitler that he could attack Poland without interference from Stalin; the invasion of Poland on September 17, 1939, by Soviet troops from the east; the agreement between Molotov and Ribbentrop of September 28, 1939, proclaiming that the Polish state no longer existed and fixing the Russian-German frontier generally along the so-called Curzon Line. This line was a tentative armistice line proposed in 1920 under the titular guidance of Lord Curzon, then British Secretary of State for Foreign Affairs, in an effort to prevent further Polish-Soviet hostilities.* It had not been accepted either by the Poles or the Russians. Following the unsuccessful attempt of the Soviet armies to capture Warsaw in 1920, the Treaty of Riga was signed in March 1921. It moved the frontier eastward from the Curzon Line a distance of over one hundred miles in some areas, and added some seventy thousand square miles to Polish territory. Strictly speaking, however, the Curzon Line was never the Russo-Polish frontier. But undoubtedly it served as the basis for the Molotov-Ribbentrop Line, an appellation naturally distasteful today to the Soviet and Polish governments. The euphemism of the "Curzon Line" was therefore generally employed in the negotiations leading up to the Yalta decision.

I had known, in common with the American public, of the flight of the government of Poland to Rumania, then to France, and eventually to London; and of the determination of the government to carry on the struggle of existence from abroad. We knew that when the Nazis attacked the Soviet Union on June 22, 1941, the framework of Polish-Soviet relations had undergone a fundamental change: the establishment of diplomatic relations between the Soviet Government and the Polish Government-in-Exile in London on July 30, 1941. These relations had until then been nonexistent as a result of the attempted destruction of Polish sovereignty by Germany and the U.S.S.R. in September 1939 which had been vigorously denounced by

---

* Based on a provisional line fixed for administration purposes by the Paris Peace Conference on December 8, 1919, it extended from the Polish-Lithuanian frontier along the Niemen River to Grodno, through Brest-Litovsk, and thence along the Bug River to the former Russian-Austrian boundary, or northern frontier of eastern Galicia, which had not yet been formally incorporated into the Polish state.

When Lord Curzon, in a note dated July 11, 1920, to the Soviet Government, described the proposed armistice line between the Poles and the Russians, he unilaterally extended the line of December 8, 1919, to the Czechoslovak frontier, running to the east of Przemysl and to the west of Lwów.

the United States Secretary of State on October 2, 1939. Mr. Hull had said:

Poland is now the victim of force used as an instrument of national policy. . . . Mere seizure of territory, however, does not extinguish the legal existence of a government. The United States therefore continues to regard the Government of Poland in existence in accordance with the provisions of the Constitution of Poland.

I had known that in December 1941 General Sikorski, Premier of the Polish Government in London, met with Marshal Stalin in Moscow. But I had not known what I afterward learned from official Polish sources, that Stalin made as a condition to the improvement of relations between the two countries the establishment of the Polish-Soviet frontier approximately on the Curzon Line; that Sikorski, on the other hand, claimed he had no authority to renounce the Polish frontier as delineated by the Treaty of Riga of 1921, and refused to discuss it. Nor had I known that, at the time of Sikorski's visit, the "Union of Polish Patriots," one of whose leaders was Wanda Wasilewska, a well-known militant Communist of Polish origin, was being organized by the Soviet Government on Russian territory. This was later to develop, with the addition of other elements, into the Polish Committee of National Liberation, and then into the provisional Polish Government in Lublin.

On April 12, 1943, the announcement had been made by the German radio that a mass grave of some ten thousand Polish officers had been discovered at Katyn, near Smolensk. The Germans alleged that these officers had been executed by the Soviet authorities in 1940, when Smolensk was under Russian control. (The official publication of the Soviet Army, the *Red Star,* itself published a statement on September 17, 1940—the first anniversary of the Soviet invasion of Poland—fixing the number of Polish officers captured by the Red Army as being about ten thousand. It did not state what had become of them.) Two days later the Polish Government requested an investigation of the German charge by the International Red Cross.

Both President Roosevelt and Prime Minister Churchill made personal efforts to avert a break between the Soviet and Polish governments. But the Soviet Government was obdurate. It charged the Polish Government as having acted in collusion with Hitler by supporting the Nazi allegation that the Soviet Government had murdered the missing Polish officers. It claimed that the Poles had played into the Nazi Government's hands by having invited the International Red Cross to investigate the Nazi allegations. And on April 26 the Soviet Government had severed diplomatic relations with the Polish Government in London. This step was to have a momentous impact on the Polish nation.

The Polish Minister in Bogotá had told me with great earnestness that, after the resumption of diplomatic relations on July 30, 1941, the Polish Government had made repeated but unsuccessful endeavors to ascertain from the Soviet Government the whereabouts of some eight thousand Polish officers known to have been captured by the Red Army in 1939. Later I learned from official documents, based on information which we received from General Sikorski in 1942, that the Soviet Government replied that every available Polish prisoner of war in the Soviet Union had already been released. The United States Ambassador in Moscow, Admiral Standley, who had been instructed by the Department of State to make inquiries regarding the missing Poles, reported that the Soviet authorities had no information regarding the whereabouts of these missing Polish officers. The British Ambassador was given the same negative answer by the Soviet Government. Despite these denials, the Moscow radio, absolutely under the control of the Soviet Government, made the following broadcast on April 18, 1943, which was published in the *New York Times* the next day:

There were, in fact, some former Polish prisoners in 1941 in the area west of Smolensk. After the withdrawal of Soviet troops from Smolensk, they fell, like so many Soviet citizens, into the hands of German Fascist executioners.

It is significant that, in the light of several statements of the Soviet authorities to the United States Embassy at Moscow disclaiming knowledge of the whereabouts of missing Polish officers, less than one week after the Nazi announcement the official Moscow radio should broadcast that Polish prisoners had fallen into German hands in the area west of Smolensk in 1941.

The identity of the perpetrators of the outrageous massacre of Katyn, contrary to all laws of war and of humanity, has never been definitely established. Perhaps it never will be. But I was to obtain evidence in Poland from Poles whose veracity I had no reason to distrust, which leads me to question seriously the sincerity of the outburst of Soviet indignation over the Polish Government's approach to the International Red Cross. I learned in Poland that when the Soviet Army invaded Poland in 1939 many Polish officers were disarmed by the Russians at the point of machine guns and transported in freight cars to the east, while others, in cavalry regiments, were made to proceed east with their horses. I spoke to Poles who claimed to have escaped from these forced convoys and who expressed their apprehension that all comrade officers who had returned had been executed, probably at Katyn.

A basic tenet of Soviet policy is the eradication of all truly nationalistic elements in areas under Soviet control. This explains the forcible deportation to Siberia of hundreds of thousands of Poles after the occupation of eastern Poland in September 1939. The same policy has been responsible for the liquidation, physical or political, of nationalist elements in Hungary, Bulgaria, Austria and Yugoslavia. It is the policy behind the trial and execution of that great Yugoslav patriot, General Draja Mihailovitch, the branding as traitors of the Knezevitch brothers who, from my actual knowledge of events when I was Minister to Yugoslavia, played an important part in the *coup d'état* of March 25, 1941, which overthrew the Hitler-appeasing government of Prince Paul, Tsvetkovitch and Tsintsar-Markovitch.

Obviously the Nazis, guilty of the most barbarous crimes against humanity, would not have hesitated to murder ten thousand Polish officers, had it served their purpose. They had had no compunction in massacring over three million Polish Jews in the asphyxiation chambers of Oswiecim and Majdanek. But if the Soviet authorities were innocent of the Katyn outrage, why did they not, before April 1943, disclose the whereabouts and welfare of over eight thousand Polish officers who were known to have fallen into Soviet hands in 1939?

After I reached Washington I learned that the United States and British governments had made yet another attempt to break the Soviet-Polish impasse. On August 11, 1943, the American and British ambassadors met in Moscow with Stalin and Molotov and appealed for the resumption of Soviet-Polish relations, making three concrete proposals which were designed to establish a constructive basis therefor:

1. The evacuation of Polish refugees from Russia to the Middle East.
2. The supplying of relief to Polish refugees in Russia by Soviet rather than by Polish organizations.
3. The granting of permission to the Poles in Russia to apply for Russian or Polish citizenship if they so chose.

The Soviet Government on September 27, 1943, rejected these proposals, charging Polish relief and other officials in Russia with espionage activities. It pointed out that the United States and British proposals virtually coincided with the Polish Government's "pretentions," referring "in demagogic fashion to the necessity for liberating and evacuating unfortunate Polish citizens from the Soviet Union. A statement of this type is lacking in any foundation whatever and cannot be considered in any other way than as an insulting attack against the Soviet Union, to which the Soviet Government does not consider it necessary to react."

Despite this diplomatic snub, the United States Government made still another attempt to heal the Soviet-Polish breach. Pursuant to a request of the Polish Government, the United States and British governments agreed to act as intermediaries. On January 19, 1944, the

Secretary of State expressed the hope that, regardless of the merits of the case, the Soviet Government would give most favorable consideration to the Polish efforts to discuss outstanding questions. Mr. Hull stated that the refusal of the Soviet Government, or any hesitancy which it might show in this regard, would adversely affect the cause of general international co-operation. On the other hand, the Secretary continued, far-reaching beneficial effects on world public opinion would be brought about by a solution of Polish-Soviet differences; the restoration of unity in the ranks of the United Nations would be of very considerable advantage to the war effort. The United States Government therefore offered to extend its good offices in arranging for the initiation of discussions between the two governments at loggerheads.

Secretary Hull's advances were, however, again rejected. But this time the Soviet reply, dated January 24, 1944, was couched in more courteous language, at least toward the United States. Molotov berated the Polish Government in London for not disavowing those participating in the "hostile slanderous campaign of the Hitlerites regarding the 'murders in Katyn.' " He charged that the Polish Government was turning to the United States and Great Britain for mediation, not to reach agreement with the Soviet Government, but to deepen the conflict and involve the Allies. Molotov expressed the opinion that the exclusion of all "pro-Fascist imperialist elements and the inclusion in the Polish Government of democratic elements" would create a favorable ground for the re-establishment of relations.

Undoubtedly this was an unfriendly reference to Stanislaw Mikolajczyk, Premier of the Government-in-Exile. Mikolajczyk, one of the leaders of the Peasant Party, had a tremendous following among the Polish people as a patriot and agrarian leader. He had succeeded to the Premiership on the untimely death of General Sikorski in an airplane accident at Gibraltar on July 4, 1943. Because of Mikolajczyk's widespread popularity in Poland, the Russian and Polish Communists aimed from the start at his political extinction.

But the fate of Mikolajczyk and all other non-Communist Polish

CELEBRATION OF POLISH CONSTITUTION DAY, MAY 3, 1919

GENERAL PILSUDSKI ARRIVES AT THE CITADEL

WHO DID THIS TO POLAND'S CHILDREN?

Nazi vengeance, for the Warsaw insurrection in 1944, abetted by Soviet acquiescence, crippled hundreds of children.

political leaders was soon to be linked with the question of Poland's frontiers, which was to be one of the principal matters discussed at the Tehran Conference.

Here I must abruptly interrupt myself. Instead of proceeding with the narrative of diplomatic developments, I must at this point chronicle what I learned in Washington in October and November 1944, and later, of the insurrection which had broken out in Warsaw on August 1 and, due to the Soviet tactics, had been crushed on October 3. These tactics were of a character so revelatory of Soviet ruthlessness that they throw a sinister light not only on Tehran, which had come before, but also on Yalta, which was to come after the revolt.

CHAPTER THREE

The Incredible Crime

FIVE years of suffering inflicted upon the Polish people since their country was overrun in September 1939 had not broken the courage of the Poles. A secret force of two hundred thousand, of whom forty thousand were in Warsaw, had been organized and was impatiently awaiting orders to attack the Germans in open warfare. General Bór-Komorowski was national commander of this Home Army, with Colonel Monter in command of the Warsaw forces. General Bór was in constant communication by radio with the Polish Government-in-Exile in London.

By July of 1944 the Germans were falling back before the Russian advance in Poland. On July 22 the Soviet-sponsored "Committee of National Liberation" was set up in Lublin calling itself, with the approval of Moscow, the true governmental authority over Poland.

In the week following, the Russians had pressed within ten miles of Warsaw. Warsaw, a city whose population before the war numbered 1,200,000—more than that of Pittsburgh, Cleveland or San Francisco—is divided by the Vistula River, which runs through it diagonally from southeast to northwest. By the end of that week the Russians were only seven miles away, at the fringes of Praga, a part of the city east of the Vistula. The sound of the Russian cannonading could be heard. Russian planes passed over the city every day, from bases only twenty minutes distant. Praga was held by little more than a single German division.

General Bór and his staff were confident that the Russians would begin their attack upon the city almost immediately.

He had never been able, however, to establish communications with

Marshal Rokossovsky, the Russian commander. Radio messages went unanswered.

On July 29, at 8:15 P.M., his radio picked up a broadcast from Moscow, a broadcast in the Polish language. According to General Bór, in his published account of the uprising,* the broadcast was a direct appeal to Poles inside German-occupied Poland to rise to arms immediately; and was signed by Mr. Molotov, the Soviet Commissar for Foreign Affairs, and E. Osóbka-Morawski, of the Moscow-dominated "Committee of National Liberation" in Lublin. It said:

> Poles, the time of liberation is at hand! Poles, to arms! Make every Polish home a stronghold in the fight against the invader! There is not a moment to lose!

A few days later our State Department received word from an official source that the broadcast was signed by the Union of Polish Patriots, of which Osóbka-Morawski was a leader, and which was almost identical in membership with the Committee of National Liberation. The Soviet Government has never admitted responsibility for this incitation to arms. But whether Mr. Molotov's name was or was not appended to it, the message obviously had the authority of the Soviet Government, for the simple reason that it could not have been put on the Moscow radio without such approval.

On the following day, July 30, London monitored a similar appeal, broadcast by the Moscow radio. This was addressed not only to all the people of Poland but specifically to the inhabitants of Warsaw, and urged them to assist the Red Army to cross the Vistula and enter Warsaw.

This appeal was almost immediately given greater authenticity in the eyes of General Bór. He had been longing for help from the Russian Army, but he had despaired of getting it, as long as the diplomatic breach continued between Moscow and his government in Lon-

---

* "The Unconquerables," by Lieutenant-General T. Bór-Komorowski, *The Reader's Digest*, February 1946.

don. Suddenly, on July 31, he learned, by way of the British radio, that Premier Mikolajczyk had arrived in Moscow. He called this "the best of news." He assumed from it that conversations between Stalin and Mikolajczyk would lead to immediate contact between the Polish Home Army and the Red Army against their common enemy.

General Bór had deferred action for months, knowing that even if his forty thousand men succeeded in wresting the city from the Germans, they had food and arms to hold it for not more than seven days at the utmost, if help from outside did not come. But the radio appeal to the people to arise was so unequivocal, the Russian Army so close that its entrance into Warsaw was surely only a matter of hours, and the news that Stalin was conferring with Mikolajczyk so heartening, that Bór immediately held a conference with Vice-Premier Jankowski, who also was in Warsaw. He pointed out that if the Red Army did not enter Warsaw within a week after the Home Army had struck the first blow, the insurrection would certainly fail; but the Vice-Premier agreed that all signs pointed to the wisdom of an immediate attack. General Bór, in his narrative of these events, permits himself a naïve reflection in discussing the Moscow broadcast that called the citizens of Warsaw to arms. He says:

> . . . There could be no purpose in inciting the people to an action which, if unsupported, would surely spell their slaughter, with no gain to the Russian advance.

Perhaps General Bór was naïve. But who could believe that there were men so cold-blooded as to contrive a trap by which two hundred fifty thousand men, women and children would perish?

General Bór could not conceive of such duplicity. He ordered the Home Army to attack at once. Zero hour was at 5:00 on the afternoon of August 1, 1944.

General Bór would have been even more heartened if he had known—as the United States Government was later informed by the Polish Government in London—that on July 31 Mr. Molotov himself admitted to the Polish Premier that Russian troops were within ten kilometers of Warsaw; and still more confident of speedy victory if he had known that Stalin was then assuring Mikolajczyk that the Red Army would enter Warsaw on August 6, a mere matter of five days.

But General Bór did not hear this then from Mikolajczyk or anyone else. The Moscow radio had fallen strangely silent. Mikolajczyk was not permitted to use it.

General Bór's unconquerable Poles, emerging from the underground, fought on almost without weapons, or food, against the overwhelming superiority of the Nazi artillery, tanks, planes and man power.

During the first twenty-four hours the Home Army captured from the Germans all the important buildings in the central sector of the city—the main post office, the gasworks, the waterworks and the central railway station, together with the electric plant, the city's only source of electric light and power, on which depended the patriots' ability to produce their limited supply of munitions and to preserve their radio contact with the outside world. By the second day (August 2) the Home Army held two-thirds of Warsaw, including the western suburb of Wola, through which any troops for the reinforcement of the Nazi forces east of the Vistula must pass.

The Russian artillery fire could be heard on the other side of the Vistula, closer than before.

But no word came from the Soviet High Command. On the Moscow radio there was no mention of the insurrection.

On August 3 German bombers with fighter escort attacked Bór's positions in Warsaw, the first time the capital had been bombed since 1939.

Russian Army air fields were close by. For ten days Soviet planes had been attacking German positions in Warsaw almost every night.

Now they suddenly stopped coming.

On August 4 Premier Mikolajczyk discovered that the discussion of aid to General Bór was far from being Marshal Stalin's only reason for inviting him to Moscow. He was told by Stalin that if he did not immediately come to some sort of satisfactory "arrangement" with the so-called Polish Committee of National Liberation, of Lublin, Stalin would back that committee as the real governing body of Poland and deal only with them.

Mikolajczyk's heart must have sunk as he listened to this ultimatum. He must have known that it meant the end of the Polish Government-in-Exile in London, as then constituted. But he was given no alternative. He agreed to consult with the Lublin leaders, Stalin's puppets. Stalin nodded. He would telegraph them, he said, and ask them to come to Moscow in the next day or two.

They arrived the very next day, August 5, by plane. The celerity with which they arrived leads to the suspicion that they had had their luggage already packed, in readiness, and that the whole business had been planned with this end in mind.

There were three of them. One was Boleslaw Bierut, now President of Poland. He was a Pole who had been known as a Communist since 1933. It is reliably reported that after two years in Moscow he had been made head, in 1936, of the Polish section of the Foreign Department of the NKVD, and that in 1939-1941 he had aided his Russian masters in shipping thousands of Poles to Siberian prison camps. In 1943 he was chosen by Moscow to be leader of the Polish Workers (or Communist) Party, newly invented by the Soviet Government, and was sent into Poland to await the next step.

The second delegate was Edward Osóbka-Morawski, chairman of the similarly Soviet-created "Committee of National Liberation," nominally a Socialist. His name had been signed to the radio appeal of July 29, broadcast to the Polish people.

The third was Marshal Rola-Zymierski, still another Pole acting under orders from Moscow, as a member of that committee.

As these three dignitaries stepped from the plane, they were given a conspicuously official reception. They were welcomed by Andrei Vishinsky, Vice-Commissar for Foreign Affairs, and a group of other high Soviet officials. A guard of honor was provided for them. The *"Internationale"* and the Polish national anthem were played.

The Moscow press described this reception, but made no mention of the reason for their visit—the meeting with Mikolajczyk. The press of Moscow had not even been permitted to announce Mikolajczyk's presence in the city.

The conferences continued for five days. At their conclusion Mikolajczyk returned to London to place Stalin's proposals before his government. They were a heavy blow. First, his government must agree to its own virtual extinction: it must reconstitute itself as a compromise between the London and the Lublin regimes, and admit the "National Committee of Liberation" to fifty per cent of the cabinet posts. Secondly, it must agree that the eastern frontier approximate the "Curzon Line."

Shortly before the conferences were concluded, Mikolajczyk, on August 9, received renewed assurances from Stalin that military aid to General Bór's forces in Warsaw would be given. He departed for London without knowing that no help had been given, or would be given.

Mikolajczyk had hardly left Moscow when Molotov, on August 11, made a curiously self-contradictory statement to Ambassador Harriman. He assured Harriman that the Soviets would make every effort to assist the Polish insurrectionists and to drop a Red Army officer into Warsaw by parachute, to establish a liaison. But he added that the insurrection had started prematurely; that it would be too costly for the Red Army to make a frontal attack; and that it would take time to outflank the city.

The foreign press gave little prominence to the radio appeal, which had been monitored by the British Broadcasting Corporation, broadcast from Moscow twelve days before, calling on the Poles to strike.

The fortune of the fighting in Warsaw, which had been so successfully waged during the first seven days of August, began to turn against General Bór's Home Army on the eighth, by the sheer weight of the Nazi mechanized power. But, although they were being slowly driven back, the Poles still fought on in the hope that help from Russia must surely come soon.

It was not necessary for any of the three delegates from Lublin to point out to Stalin, after Mikolajczyk's departure, that if promises to help General Bór and his forces were carried out, and the Nazis were driven from Poland, the London government would be acclaimed by the people as the real saviors of Poland, and it would then be difficult indeed to set up a government in Poland controlled by the Soviet Union. It is plain that the destruction of the Polish Home Army had been the premeditated purpose of the Soviet political strategists from the first.

As he reached London, Mikolajczyk sent a message to Stalin on August 13, renewing his pleas for assistance to the beleaguered fighters in Warsaw. He urged that the Red Army bombard the Nazi airdromes in Warsaw, the Nazi armored tanks and trucks; he pleaded for Soviet fighter planes to operate against the Luftwaffe; for more supplies to be dropped; and he urged on Stalin the political effect of an entry into Warsaw by the Red Army as liberators, rather than to delay until much of Warsaw's population were massacred.

Before Stalin replied to him, an answer came from another source with brutal bluntness. This was a statement by the official Soviet news agency, Tass, broadcast by the official Moscow radio on August 14. It made it clear that the Soviet position had already been decided on: not only would it be inadvisable, from the Soviet point of view, to give help, but it was also high time that the blame for a useless sacrifice of blood be placed on the Polish Government in London. The broadcast, heard both in London and by General Bór in Warsaw, said:

Information from Polish sources on the rising which began in Warsaw on August 1 by order of the Polish émigrés in London has recently appeared in various newspapers abroad. The Polish press and radio of the émigré Government in London have asserted that the Warsaw insurrectionists were in contact with the Soviet High Command and that this command has sent them no help. This announcement is either a misunderstanding or a libel against the Soviet High Command.

Tass is in possession of information which shows that the Polish circles in London responsible for the Warsaw rising made no attempt to coördinate this action with the Soviet High Command. In these circumstances, the only people responsible for the results of the events in Warsaw are the Polish émigré circles in London.

"The effect of this announcement, in Warsaw, was stupefaction," says General Bór.

Stalin did not answer Mikolajczyk's telegram until August 16. He then said that, as he had promised, he had ordered dropping by parachute of "extensive" supplies, and of a liaison officer who, unfortunately, had been killed in the fall. He added that after a re-examination of the whole position he had concluded that the insurrection in Warsaw was merely a reckless adventure, undertaken by the Poles without consulting him. Calumnies in the Polish press, he asserted, had made it clear to Soviet authorities that they had been deluded about the motives for the rising. Stalin concluded by stating that he had abandoned any idea of giving assistance and would not assume responsibility for what was occurring.

From then on, for more than forty days and nights, the Home Army fought on, with only such scanty supplies as were dropped to them by intrepid British and Polish airmen who made the long flight from their bases in Italy. No aid whatever came from the Russians until an entire month had passed. Then, in mid-September, a small amount of food and munitions was dropped, but, as parachutes were not used, the weapons were damaged beyond use. Still, the moral effect was great. "Soldiers and people were uplifted," says General Bór, "with the certainty that the Russians would come at any hour now." They did not, however, approach closer than near-by Praga.

On August 14, the same day as the Tass broadcast repudiating Soviet responsibility for the uprising, Ambassador Harriman requested permission of the Soviet Government for a flight of American four-engine bombers with fighter escort to undertake a shuttle operation from England on the morning of August 15, weather and operational conditions permitting. We outlined our plan that part of the force should drop arms for the Polish resistance forces in the Warsaw area, that the balance should attack the airfields in the vicinity and then proceed to the shuttle bases in the Soviet Union. Our authorities pointed out that British bombers from Italy had recently dropped a small quantity of supplies on Warsaw by night, but that the length of the trip from Italy to Warsaw and return rendered this type of operation most difficult and ineffective. The Anglo-American command had therefore reached the decision that the most effective operation would be a daylight shuttle mission of American bombers to the Soviet bases.

The Soviet Government's attitude was clearly set forth in Vishinsky's reply of August 15:

The Soviet Government could not go along with this proposal; the "demonstration" in which the Warsaw population had been drawn was a purely "adventurist" affair; the Soviet Government could not lend its hand to it; and, as Stalin had notified Churchill on August 5, one could not imagine how a few Polish detachments of the so-called National Army, possessing neither artillery, aviation nor tanks, could take Warsaw at a time when the Germans had assigned four tank divisions for the city's defense.

On August 17 President Roosevelt personally took a hand. He authorized Ambassador Harriman to request the Soviet Government to reconsider its attitude and co-operate with the British and American governments in furnishing assistance to the Polish underground forces. The President made it clear that the United States forces intended in any case, in so far as militarily feasible, to continue to give aid. We saw no grounds for departing from our consistent policy of lending all possible aid to any forces of the United Nations who were engaged in fighting our common enemy.

Harriman made it clear to Molotov at this time that public opinion in the United States and in the American air forces would be greatly affected if we should be obliged to undertake the Warsaw missions without the protection of fighter planes, especially as the security of fighter planes could be made available if the Soviet Government permitted our missions to land in the Soviet Union. The Soviet Government was asked to explain why, in view of Stalin's promise on August 9 to Mikolajczyk to aid the Polish insurrection, the position had changed some time between August 9 and 14.

Molotov replied that during the latter period it had become clear that the Warsaw insurrection was a "purely adventuristic, light-minded affair which was causing many sacrifices and that the Soviet support of it would only lead to increasing sacrifices." When asked whether the Soviet Government had any information, not yet made public, which had caused it to change its position, Molotov again evasively referred to the "adventuristic character of the uprising" and to attempts which had been made to take advantage of it for purposes hostile to the Soviet Union.

Molotov told Harriman and the British Ambassador, Sir Archibald Clark-Kerr, on August 17, that the Soviet decision to abandon the Poles in Warsaw was based on the criticisms launched by press and radio against Russia, by Poles who warned the world to put no trust in Soviet intentions toward Poland.

Harriman asked whether it was true that toward the end of July the Soviet radio had exhorted the Poles to rise up and fight for liberation. Molotov remained evasive and noncommittal.

Despite the pleas of the United States Government, the Soviet Government continued to decline to give permission to American or British aircraft which had dropped arms in the region of Warsaw to land on the territory of the U.S.S.R. The Soviet Government again gave as its excuse that it did not wish to associate itself directly or indirectly with the Warsaw "adventure."

As a result of the Soviet attitude, Ambassador Harriman expressed his personal opinion in a telegram to the State Department, dated August 19:

When the American public understands fully the facts, there will be serious repercussions in the public opinion in the United States towards the Soviet Union and even in its confidence and hopes for the success of post-war collaboration.

This expression of opinion was brought vividly to my mind on a cloudy Sunday morning in October 1945. We had heard from various sources that in September 1944 an American army plane had crashed in the Paderewski Park on the other side of the Vistula from the main part of Warsaw, having been shot down either by Nazi fighter planes or by antiaircraft defense. Accordingly, Lieutenant Colonel Edward J. York, our Embassy's Military Attaché for Air, and I, accompanied by some American newspaper correspondents, visited the park and found fragments of a plane scattered over an extended area near the lake. We placed a wreath on the wooden monument which had been erected by the Warsaw people to the memory of the dead fliers. The fragments of the plane were so badly damaged that they did not serve to identify the nationality or the manufacture.

We were told by some of the spectators who had been attracted by the ceremony at the monument that another plane had fallen in the Praga section of Warsaw, about two miles away from Paderewski Park, sometime after September 13, 1944, the date of the entry of Soviet troops into Praga. A young boy agreed to accompany us and show us the spot. Colonel York had no difficulty in identifying as of United States manufacture the remnants of a plane in a field almost in the center of Praga.

York had distinguished himself as the pilot of one of the planes in General Doolittle's squadron which had bombed Tokyo. He had later been interned by the Russians. He spoke Polish and Russian fluently.

On questioning inhabitants of near-by houses, he learned that the plane had crashed in flames on September 15, 1944; Russian soldiers had removed from the remains of the American aviators their "dog tags" and all identifying documents. Our blood boiled as we heard of this treatment of our fliers who had been deprived of the assistance of fighter escort because Stalin desired the Warsaw insurrection to fail.

Under date of August 20, 1944, President Roosevelt and Prime

Minister Churchill addressed a joint appeal to Marshal Stalin, stating that they were thinking of world opinion if the anti-Nazis in Warsaw were in effect abandoned. They expressed the hope that all three nations should do their utmost to save as many of the patriots in Warsaw as possible; that the Soviet authorities would immediately drop supplies and munitions to the patriotic Poles, or would at least assist our planes in aiding them. The extreme importance of the time element was stressed.

Finally permission was received for one shuttle flight, which took place on September 18, 1944. Unfortunately the Poles were unable to reach most of the "drops." Permission was also received for a second flight which for operational reasons did not take place.

Because of lack of supplies and of food the heroic insurrection finally came to an end on October 3, 1944.

Soviet opposition had prevented the United States from extending any effective assistance to the Warsaw insurrectionists forming part of the army of one of the United Nations. Who knows how many American lives were lost as a result of the brutal policy of liquidating the Polish underground movement?

The Red Army waited at the gates of Warsaw from September until the middle of January—a full four months—before entering the city. In this period the Nazis completed the demolition of Warsaw. The Nazi commander of Warsaw had virtually fulfilled his promise not to leave a stone standing.

But in two essential respects the cold-blooded, premeditated crime against Poland, conceived by the Soviet Government with the aid of its puppets, had succeeded:

(1) The Polish Government in London had been discredited;

(2) The Polish Home Army had been broken, so that no leadership remained there to dispute the authority of the Lublin gang.

The incredible betrayal was complete. What did it matter to its perpetrators if a great city had been laid waste and two hundred fifty thousand of its people slaughtered? Had not their objectives been attained?

When I reached Washington from Colombia, late in October 1944, the Warsaw insurrection had already been quenched, General Bór was a prisoner of the Germans, and the Red Army was still crouched outside the gates of Warsaw, contentedly watching while the Nazis destroyed the patriot organization whose ruin was so fervently desired by the Soviet Government. I read, at the State Department, the messages our government had sent to Moscow in our attempt to aid the fighting Poles while there was still time. I read the evasive Soviet replies. I noted the final outcome. And, with a sense of deep discouragement, I occupied my days in Washington by continuing my study of my government's recorded efforts to obtain from the Soviet Union guarantees which would insure justice to Poland, and to all liberated peoples, after the war. The record disclosed little that could lighten the prospect. It was obvious that the British and American appeasement of Stalin had begun at Tehran.

CHAPTER FOUR

Between Tehran and Yalta

THE discussions at the conference at Tehran in December 1943 among Roosevelt, Churchill and Stalin remained an official secret at the time of my stay in Washington. Even within the Department of State the truth of what happened at this momentous conference was probably not known, except perhaps to two or three. Some key officials, indeed, who had the responsibility of making important recommendations on matters dealing with the United Nations Organization, in conversations with me shortly after President Roosevelt's death in April 1945, deplored the fact that no records of the Tehran meeting were available even to them. Perhaps none had been made. But far-reaching decisions had been made, and Poland was one of the nations principally affected.

Neither the White House nor the State Department disclosed to me what had taken place at Tehran with respect to Poland. Ambassador Ciechanowski, however, told me, while I was in Washington, that Mr. Churchill had attempted, very soon after the conversations at Tehran, to induce the Polish Government-in-Exile to agree to the concessions which he advocated.

On January 22, 1944, shortly after Churchill's return to London from Tehran, he endeavored to persuade Premier Mikolajczyk and Foreign Minister Tadeusz Romer to agree to the following five points:*

1. The Polish Government to agree to accept the so-called Curzon Line (prolonged through eastern Galicia) as a basis for negotiations with the Soviet Government.

* From: *Defeat in Victory,* copyright, 1947, by Jan Ciechanowski, reprinted by permission of Doubleday & Company, Inc., p. 269.

2. The final settlement of the eastern frontier to be linked with the grant to Poland of East Prussia, Danzig and Upper Silesia to the Oder River.

3. All Poles left on the Soviet side of Poland's eastern frontier would be given the right to return to Poland.

4. All the German population within Poland's new boundaries to be removed from Poland.

5. The solutions as enumerated above would receive the approval and guarantee of the three principal United Nations.

Churchill offered, in the event of the acceptance of these five points by the Polish Government, to approach Stalin and to endeavor to obtain an amelioration of Polish-Soviet relations. As point No. 5 obligated the three nations which had just participated in the Tehran Conference to guarantee the first four points, it is clear that Churchill would not have committed the United States and U.S.S.R. to a course which did not previously have their approval. And, as these points were later publicly agreed on at the Yalta and Potsdam conferences by the United States of America, the United Kingdom and the U.S.S.R., it is logical to conclude that the framework had been constructed at Tehran for the final disposition of the question of Polish frontiers.

Mikolajczyk refused to accept Churchill's proposal. First of all, he had no constitutional authority to do so. Secondly, acceptance would entail submission to Soviet demands without possibility of revision and would conceivably encourage further encroachments on Polish territory.

According to Ambassador Ciechanowski,* he had, under instructions from his government, endeavored in Washington to see President Roosevelt to ascertain:

1. Whether the United States Government considered it advisable to enter upon the final settlement of territorial problems in Europe.

---

* *Ibid.*, p. 270.

LAST STRONGHOLD OF THE UNDERGROUND ARMY
The Nazis bombed the Warsaw insurrectionists daily from low altitudes and, after the surrender, systematically destroyed almost the entire city.

HERE FELL SOME OF WARSAW'S PATRIOTS
In 1945 guards of honor protected these Polish shrines; a year later the insurrection was officially ignored.

PRESIDENT ROOSEVELT RECEIVES PREMIER MIKOLAJCZYK AT THE
WHITE HOUSE IN JUNE, 1944

2. Whether the United States Government was prepared in principle to participate in bringing about such settlements and to guarantee them.

3. Whether the United States Government regarded it possible to lend its support to Churchill's plan and to its realization.

Ciechanowski reports that he was unable to see President Roosevelt, but that on January 27, 1944, he asked Secretary Hull to give him replies to the three questions. The former Polish Ambassador states that Assistant Secretary Dunn, on February 2, handed to him a memorandum from the White House containing the President's reply to the questions asked. Ciechanowski adds that he was taken aback in reading the memorandum to note that the President had for the first time reversed his attitude of nonrecognition of territorial settlements in time of war by adding that such principles did not exclude attempts to bring about "amicable settlements between countries." But the President likewise indicated that it would not be possible for the United States to guarantee Polish independence as suggested by Mr. Churchill.*

Direct evidence as to the Tehran decision regarding Poland is now afforded by former Secretary of States James F. Byrnes, in his book *Speaking Frankly* (published in October 1947).** Mr. Byrnes quotes President Roosevelt as saying at Yalta that "he still held the view he had expressed at Tehran that it would be desirable to adjust the southern end of the [Curzon] line so that the city of Lwów and at least a portion of the oil fields should be inside Polish territory." Mr. Churchill, Mr. Byrnes continues, pointed out that (after the Tehran Conference and before Yalta) he "had supported the Curzon Line in Parliament including the Soviet Union's retention of Lwów."

On June 7, 1944, Mikolajczyk, who had arrived from London on the very eve of the invasion of Normandy, was received at the White House by the President. Mr. Roosevelt was in high spirits, greeted

---

* *Ibid.*, p. 272
** *Speaking Frankly*, by James F. Byrnes (Harper & Brothers), p. 29. Copyright, 1947, by Donald S. Russell, Trustee of the James F. Byrnes Foundation.

the Premier as an old friend, and expressed his confidence that "Poland would again arise strong and independent." He chatted jovially about his meetings with Stalin and Churchill at Tehran; said that he understood Stalin much better than Churchill did; but, when Mikolajczyk reminded him that the Soviet Government had made, as a condition of understanding with the Polish Government, demands irreconcilable with the idea of Poland's independence and sovereignty, the President replied that he was aware of this fact. He pointed out, however, that the Soviet Union had five times the population of Poland and "could swallow up Poland if she could not reach an understanding on her terms." And he added the cryptic sentence, "When a thing becomes unavoidable, one should adapt oneself to it." The interview in the morning was followed by a formal dinner that night at the White House, in Mikolajczyk's honor, and the dinner by a two-hour conversation in the President's study, devoted largely to discussion of the strength and the plans of Poland's underground army, for which Mr. Roosevelt expressed glowing admiration. He volunteered the suggestion that he might make a personal request of Stalin to receive Mikolajczyk and talk over the Polish situation "in a human way, as man to man." The Premier and Ciechanowski, who was present at all these meetings, left the White House "definitely under his spell."

But five days later Mr. Roosevelt told Mikolajczyk and Ciechanowski that he was still undecided whether to send any message to Stalin. He again referred to the fact that this was his "political" year. And at their final conversation, on June 14, he reminded the Premier that "you cannot risk war with Russia. What alternative remains? Only to reach an agreement."*

In the presidential campaign of 1944 both the Republican and Democratic parties considered that the votes of Americans of Polish descent might well be a deciding factor, especially in the key political states of New York, Pennsylvania, Illinois, Indiana, Ohio and Michigan.

---

*Ciechanowski, *op. cit.*, pp. 291-309.

The Polish-American Congress, under the presidency of Mr. Charles Rozmarek, of Chicago, was founded in Buffalo in May 1944. It represented Americans of Polish descent, numbering about six million. At this Buffalo meeting of the Congress a memorial to President Roosevelt on the Polish question was approved and a committee was chosen to present it. But the request for an interview with the President, although presented to him in May, was not granted until five months later.

On October 8 of that year, on the occasion of the celebration of Pulaski Day in New York City, Governor Dewey, then the Republican candidate for the presidency, was scheduled to speak at the celebration. His speech was interpreted by members of the Polish-American Congress as a strong stand in favor of a free and independent Poland.

A day or two before Governor Dewey's speech, but after Mr. Dewey's participation in the ceremonies had been announced, the members of the Memorial Committee were invited to come to the White House on October 11. They were received by President Roosevelt at the White House on that date. Mr. Rozmarek, who acted as spokesman for the delegation, expressed their doubts and fears, as loyal supporters of the President, that great American directives such as the principles of the Atlantic Charter and the Declaration of the Four Freedoms were being abandoned and sacrificed.

Mr. Rozmarek's concluding words were:

In view of the attitude of Soviet Russia to the Polish Government, we ask for your assurance, Mr. President, that you will insist that neither an alien nor a puppet system of government shall be imposed upon Poland nor that any part of her population will ever be disposed of or transferred against the really freely expressed will of the Polish people.

Our Polish War Relief is anxious to contribute its share to the relief of the Polish nation without delay. The urgency of Poland's need is great. However, as Americans, we consider that our aid and assistance, whether it is given through UNRRA or by ourselves, must be distributed to the people of Poland under the American flag and under American supervision, which, in the present circumstances, can alone prevent American gifts from becoming instruments of expansionist political pressure.*

The President's meeting with this Polish-American delegation was considered unusually significant at the time. The President confined himself to generalities that "Poland must be reconstituted as a great nation," and he concluded his remarks by saying, "It is very important that the new Poland be one of the bulwarks of the structure upon which we hope to build a permanent peace."

An interesting feature of the interview was that a large map of Poland, with the prewar boundaries as laid down by the Treaty of Riga in 1921, had been placed, before the delegation entered, in the room in which the President received his visitors. As is evident from photographs taken of the scene, the Curzon Line is not emphasized on this map. Whether or not Mr. Roosevelt was aware of the implication, the Polish-American community interpreted the reproduction of the map as indicating the President's approval of the restoration of Polish territory east of the Curzon Line. And yet, as a matter of fact, in the light of Mr. Byrnes's subsequent disclosures, Mr. Roosevelt had already agreed at Tehran to the sacrifice of a great area east of the Curzon Line to the Soviet Union.

Mr. Roosevelt's silence on specific points did not go unnoticed. On October 12, "Mr. John A. Giminski, president of the Pulaski Republican League of New York State, stated that President Roosevelt, 'with his usual artful dodging,' had failed to 'satisfy any of the demands' made to him by a group of Polish-Americans who called at the White House on Wednesday.

" 'He said nothing about the legal Polish Government in London, nothing about boundaries,' Mr. Giminski said."**

An interview which Mr. Rozmarek had with President Roosevelt on October 28, 1944, in Chicago in the President's private car was immediately capitalized for political purposes. The Foreign Language

---

* *New York Times,* October 12, 1944, p. 8, cols. 1 and 2.
** *Ibid.,* October 13, 1944, p. 15, col. 2.

Division of the Democratic National Committee on that date quoted Mr. Rozmarek as follows:

Poland as the test case of the validity of the Atlantic Charter must be reconstituted after this war undiminished in area, strong and truly independent.

During the visit of the Polish-American Congress delegation to the White House on October 11 and during my conversation with the President on October 28 in Chicago he assured me that he will carry out the pledges of the Democratic Party with regard to our foreign policy and that he will see to it that Poland is treated justly at the peace conferences.

Because I am convinced of his sincerity I shall vote for him on November 7 for President of the United States of America.*

Mr. Rozmarek's endorsement of the President's position was made known through the Polish language press to Polish-American groups throughout the country, who largely supported the Democratic ticket on the basis of the President's assurances to Rozmarek.

Mr. Rozmarek informed me, in September 1947, that his meeting with the President on Mr. Roosevelt's train in the Illinois Central Station at Chicago, at 5:30 P.M. on October 28, 1944, was initiated by the President and not by him. According to Mr. Rozmarek, the President assured him there that the plank which the Democratic convention had adopted in its platform to uphold the principles of the Atlantic Charter and the Four Freedoms would under no circumstances be abandoned by him, and Mr. Roosevelt made it clear that these principles included the integrity of Poland.

President Roosevelt, however, Mr. Rozmarek reported to me, warned him in this conversation, as he had cautioned the Polish-American group in the White House on October 11, that "Stalin had fooled him twice and might possibly fool him again."

Later Mr. Rozmarek wrote to me:

* *Ibid.,* October 29, 1944, p. 32, col. 6.

President Roosevelt in his talk with me expressed distrust of Stalin, having been fooled by him, as he stated, on a number of occasions. He plainly indicated that he was fearful that Stalin might again collaborate with Hitler as he did in the initial stages of the war and the president wanted at all costs to prevent such an alliance. He kept on repeating to me: "Let us win the war with Germany first." The president let it be understood that once Hitler was defeated, he would know how to handle Stalin.

A few days after Mr. Roosevelt's re-election Mr. Rozmarek wrote to him, on November 14, reminding him in these words of his pre-election promises:

Americans of Polish stock [who have] voted for you . . . firmly believe that . . . you will not allow our trusted ally, Poland, to be deprived of one half of her ancient lands, nor do they believe that you will allow a foreign-sponsored puppet government to be forced upon Poland against the will of her people. Freedom is a god-given right, and the thirteen million inhabitants of the centuries-old Polish lands to the east, which are now being coveted by a powerful neighbor, never renounced their right to be free.

Mr. Rozmarek expressed the opinion that had the Yalta Conference been held before the presidential elections of 1944, Mr. Roosevelt would not have been re-elected, because of the votes of Americans linked by blood to those nations which had been "sold down the river."

When President Roosevelt gave these assurances to Polish-American voters, did he not recall that less than a year before he had, at the Tehran Conference, agreed to Stalin's plan for a Soviet-Polish frontier along the Curzon Line, which lopped off seventy thousand square miles of Polish territory, without consulting the Polish people or its constitutional government?

The ostensible policy of the United States with respect to Poland was enunciated in a letter addressed to Premier Mikolajczyk by President Roosevelt under date of November 17, 1944. The contents of this letter, which had been drafted in the Department of State and had accordingly been approved by the Acting Secretary, had been fully discussed at conferences in which I took part. The principal question at issue was the most efficacious means of approaching Stalin to obtain, if possible, an amelioration in favor of Poland of the Soviet-Polish frontier, including the city of Lwów and the near-by oil fields. If Mr. Roosevelt should approach Stalin directly by telegram, there was the probability that Stalin would give an emphatic negative answer, thus definitely closing the door on the matter and putting the President in the unenviable position of having his request refused. If, on the other hand, Harriman should be authorized to discuss the situation with Stalin, it would be possible through personal contact to explain far more thoroughly than telegraphic communication permitted why the United States Government considered it wise, for reasons of public opinion, for Stalin to make at least this concession in favor of Poland. The latter procedure had the further advantage of enabling Harriman, on passing through London en route to Moscow, to inquire of the Polish Government whether it would have any objection to Harriman's broaching to Stalin the question of Lwów and the oil fields. No approach to Stalin was made, for the Polish Government considered that approval of such a move on its part could be considered a virtual recognition of the Curzon Line as the Polish eastern frontier and on this point the government was adamant.

President Roosevelt's letter of November 17 to Mikolajczyk, while general in tone, strongly stated his position on the paramount question of Polish independence.

My dear Mr. Prime Minister:

I have had constantly to mind the problem you are facing in your endeavors to bring about an equitable and permanent solution of the Polish-Soviet difficulties and particularly the questions which you raised in your message of October 26. I have asked Ambassador Harriman, who will bring you this letter, to discuss with you the question of Lwów.

While I would have preferred to postpone the entire question of this Government's attitude until the general postwar settlement in Europe, I fully realize your urgent desire to receive some indication of the position of the United States Government with the least possible delay. Therefore, I am giving you below in broad outline the general position of this Government in the hope that it may be of some assistance to you in your difficult task.

1. The United States Government stands unequivocally for a strong, free, and independent Polish state with the untrammeled right of the Polish people to order their internal existence as they see fit.

2. In regard to the future frontiers of Poland, if mutual agreement on this subject including the proposed compensation for Poland from Germany is reached between the Polish, Soviet, and British governments, this Government would offer no objection. In so far as the United States guarantee of any specific frontiers is concerned I am sure you will understand that this Government, in accordance with its traditional policy, cannot give a guarantee for any specific frontiers. As you know, the United States Government is working for the establishment of a world security organization through which the United States together with the other member states will assume responsibility for general security which, of course, includes the inviolability of agreed frontiers.

3. If the Polish Government and people desire in connection with the new frontiers of the Polish state to bring about the transfer to and from territory of Poland of national minorities, the United States Government will raise no objection and as far as practicable will facilitate such transfer.

4. The United States Government is prepared, subject to legislative authority, to assist in so far as practicable in the postwar economic reconstruction of the Polish State.

Very sincerely yours,

(Signed) FRANKLIN D. ROOSEVELT.

I had requested an appointment with President Roosevelt as soon as I arrived in Washington from Colombia. I was told at the White House that because of his absorption in the presidential campaign he would probably not be able to see me until after the election. I was subsequently given an appointment to be received by President Roosevelt on November 20, 1944, at 11:00 A.M. Arriving a few minutes before the hour, I found Ambassadors Stanley Hornbeck and Lithgow Osborne, recently appointed, respectively, to the Netherlands and to Norway, also waiting to see the President. As the three of us awaited our turns in the large anteroom, Major General Edward M. Watson, the President's military aide, requested us to limit each of our interviews to a maximum of five minutes, due to the President's unusually heavy schedule.

At eleven o'clock promptly General Watson ushered me into the President's oval study. Mr. Roosevelt was sitting at his desk, which was covered with a collection of souvenirs—miniature vessels, ship's bells, and so forth. I had not seen the President since June of 1942 when I accompanied Dr. Alfonso López, then President-elect of Colombia, on an official trip to Washington, where Dr. López was the guest of the President at the White House. I was very much concerned over the change in the President's outward appearance. Although as cordial and informal in manner as usual, his face had a grayish pallor, and when I held a match to his cigarette I noticed that his hand was trembling very perceptibly.

I started the conversation by thanking the President for having named me Ambassador to Poland and expressed my congratulations on his successful campaign for the Presidency. As he nodded his appreciation, I informed the President that Acting Secretary Stettinius had agreed to the advisability of my remaining in Washington on a week-to-week basis pending developments in the Polish situation as a result of the refusal of the Polish Government in London to accept Stalin's proposal to fix the Soviet-Polish frontier approximately along the Curzon Line, even though Mikolajczyk recommended it. My usefulness in Warsaw after its forthcoming liberation would be greatly jeopardized if, in the meantime, I should take up my duties in London where an obdurate group would not heed the advice of its premier and might possibly cause the government's fall.

The President said that this procedure suggested for me would be entirely agreeable to him. He said that Mikolajczyk, with whom he had had several long conversations in June of that year, had impressed him more favorably than had any of the statesmen from the countries to be liberated who had visited him; that he was a man of practical common sense and a patriotic Pole.

I remarked that I intended, when presenting my letters of credence to President Raczkiewicz in London, to include in my remarks an excerpt from the President's letter to Mikolajczyk of November 17, 1944, in which the President had emphatically referred to our standing for a free and independent Poland. The President indicated with a nod that he approved my making such a statement.

I said that in my opinion it was very important that we insist with the Soviet Government that the independence of Poland be maintained, and I added that if we were not going to be strong at a time when we had the largest Army, Navy and Air Forces in the world and at a time when the President had just received another mandate from the American people, I did not see when we ever would be strong.

The President asked rather sharply and with a note of sarcasm, "Do you want me to go to war with Russia?"

I replied that there was no thought on my part that we would have to go to war, but that if we would take a strong line and not deviate from it, I felt confident we would accomplish our objectives. I observed, however, that the Soviet view of an independent Poland was quite different from our conception.

The President stated that he had entire confidence in Stalin's word and he felt sure that he would not go back on it. (I, of course, was not aware at that time of the quite contrary opinion attributed by Mr. Charles Rozmarek to the President, in their conversation at Chicago less than a month before.)

I said that I regretted I could not agree with him, as Stalin's previous actions had shown him not to be dependable. I had in mind Stalin's treacherous attack on Poland in September 1939, regardless of the existence of the Polish-Soviet nonaggression pact of 1932 mutually binding on the two nations until December 3, 1945; the Soviet exhortation to the Poles in Warsaw to revolt against the Nazi occupation forces in July 1944, and their subsequent abandonment by a professed ally and friend; the obvious attempts to set up a Communist-manipulated group as the government of Poland regardless of the wishes of the people; and the forcible incorporation into the U.S.S.R. of the Baltic States of Estonia, Latvia and Lithuania where I had served as American Minister in 1936 and 1937.

Mr. Roosevelt said that he thought Stalin's idea of having a *cordon sanitaire,* in the shape of a Poland under Russian influence, as a bulwark to protect the Soviet Union against further aggression was understandable; Stalin himself had pointed out to the President that after World War I the Allies had formed a *cordon sanitaire* to the east to protect them from the threat of Bolshevism and now he claimed a corresponding right to protect himself from the west.

The President suggested that perhaps the simplest way to arrange the eastern boundary of Poland would be to hold a plebiscite in ten or fifteen years. I expressed doubt whether such a project would be practicable as it would mean that the whole government of eastern Poland would be in suspense for that period and that therefore the nature of the government of Poland would likewise be dependent on the settlement. Such procedure would merely keep open the Polish question for an indefinite period.

The President did not press the matter further. He closed the interview by asking me to give his best regards to Premier Mikolajczyk and to President Beneš of Czechoslovakia, both of whom were then in London.

That was my last meeting with President Roosevelt.

During my talk with the President I did not inquire what agreements were made at the Tehran Conference of December 1943, for at the time I did not know that any understanding had been reached among him, Churchill and Stalin on the matter of Poland's frontiers. Nor did the President volunteer any information on this subject.

Although the Polish Government had been given an unmistakable hint on January 22, 1944, by Mr. Churchill, that the Big Three had agreed at Tehran on an approximation of the Curzon Line as the permanent Soviet-Polish frontier, it was not until October 1944 that the hint emerged as a definite statement of fact. This was when Molotov informed Mikolajczyk at Moscow, in the presence of Churchill, Eden and Harriman, that the Big Three had made that agreement, and invited the three listeners to deny his statement if it were untrue. The three, it is reported, sat silent.

Surely the substance of these conversations, taking place in October as they did, must have been reported to Mr. Roosevelt by Ambassador Harriman many days before my conversation with the President on November 20, and even before Mr. Rozmarek's conversation with him on October 28. A special means of communication had been established between the White House and our Embassy in Moscow, through the use of the United States Navy facilities, thus rendering it possible for the President—or Harry Hopkins—to telegraph directly to Harriman without having recourse to the Department of State—the channel normally used by a President of the United States when desiring to communicate with any American ambassador abroad. Thus the Department of State often was unaware of messages exchanged between the White House and the Embassy at Moscow.

Premier Mikolajczyk, on returning to London from this conference in Moscow, urged, for the sake of securing harmony with the Soviet Union, that the four political parties constituting his government should accept Stalin's proposal for the Polish eastern frontier, *i.e.,* the Curzon Line and its continuation south through eastern Galicia.

The members of Mikolajczyk's Peasant Party alone accepted their leader's advice. The other three parties—Socialist, Democratic and Christian Labor (Catholic)—refused to support the Premier.

Accordingly, on November 24, Mikolajczyk resigned.

President Raczkiewicz thereupon entrusted the formation of a cabinet to Jan Kwapinski, Deputy Prime Minister and member of the Socialist Party. Kwapinski failed, due to the opposition of the Peasant Party.

The representatives of the press in the United States, sensing the importance of the dissension among the London Poles over the Soviet-Polish frontier, inquired of the Department of State what our position would be in the face of this Polish Government crisis. The official statement of November 25 begged the question. It was that the "guarantee of the Polish frontier by this Government was not and could not have been an issue (between Poland and the Soviet Union) since this Government's traditional policy of not guaranteeing specific frontiers in Europe is well known."

After Kwapinski had failed in his effort to form a cabinet, the task was entrusted to Tomas Arciszewski, a member of the Socialist Party whose policy had been identified with hostility toward the Soviet Union. Arciszewski had served as Minister to Estonia, and during the war had been an influential leader of the left-wing element of the Polish underground and had left Poland for London in the summer of 1944. Arciszewski succeeded in forming a cabinet on November 30, 1944, but without the participation of Mikolajczyk or of the Peasant Party.

To the Soviet Government, which was evidently intending at all costs to establish a Communist Government within Poland and to liquidate the existence of the Polish Government-in-Exile, the accession of Arciszewski was a godsend. First of all, Arciszewski's anti-Soviet attitude was a convenient target to attack. Secondly, the persistent refusal of Arciszewski and his collaborators to compromise with the Soviet Government would more quickly bring on the crisis which now appeared inevitable. Thirdly, the elimination from the London Government of the Peasant Party, representing over sixty per cent of the Polish electorate, would render far easier the Soviet political domination of Poland.

The chances of a free expression of the people's will in Poland were not aided by the famous address of Prime Minister Winston Churchill before the House of Commons on December 15, 1944, on the "grim, bare bones of the Polish problem." In this speech Churchill chided the Polish Government for not having followed his advice in October to accept the Curzon Line and its prolongation to the southward as Poland's eastern frontier with Russia. Churchill again urged the Polish Government to accept this line and stated that in compensation, "the Poles are free, so far as Russia and Great Britain are concerned, to extend their territory at the expense of Germany." Churchill referred, of course, to the proposal which had been agreed on at Tehran and which had been put forward as a finality at the October 1944 conference in Moscow among Churchill, Stalin and Mikolajczyk. This was later construed by the Soviet and Polish governments that Poland should receive East Prussia, with the exception of the city of Königsberg, as well as the territory west of the former Polish-German frontier as far as the Oder and the western Neisse rivers.

The American press immediately made inquiries whether the United States Government approved of Churchill's policy toward Poland. Finally, on December 18, Secretary of State Stettinius felt obliged to make a statement. It virtually repeated Mr. Roosevelt's letter of November 17 to Mikolajczyk and may be summarized as follows:

1. The United States Government stands unequivocally for a strong, free and independent Polish state.

2. The United States Government will not raise any objection to the delineation of Poland's frontiers before the ending of hostilities, if a mutual agreement is reached by the United Nations directly concerned.

3. If as a result of such an agreement the Polish Government and people should favor the transfer of national groups, the United States Government will assist Poland, so far as practicable, in such transfers.

4. Subject to legislative authority, the United States Government will assist Poland and other United Nations in repairing the devastation of war.

Although this statement of Mr. Stettinius echoed Mr. Roosevelt's expression of policy in favor of the independence of Poland, it did nothing to remove certain grave doubts in my mind.

First, it afforded no assurance that the United States would back up its position in favor of Poland's independence by diplomatic or other means, in opposition to the Soviet Government. Quite to the contrary, one was given to infer that, if the Soviet Government forced the Polish Government to accept the frontiers which had been proposed by Stalin, the United States Government would entertain no objection. In fact, our offer to assist in the transfer of national groups indicated more than tacit acquiescence.

Following my talk with the President on November 20, Mr. Stettinius, who had been Acting Secretary of State since Mr. Hull's serious illness in October 1944, instructed me on November 22 to defer my departure for London pending developments on the Polish question. I had not had any extended talks with him, as he was evidently very much preoccupied with the administration of the Department and was unable to devote much time to the complexities of the Polish problem.

A few days later he was appointed Secretary of State. The feeling in the Department of State at the time was that President Roosevelt, on the advice of Mr. Harry Hopkins, had appointed Mr. Stettinius during this critical period of our international relations so that the President and Mr. Hopkins might have complete personal control over our foreign policy, especially as relating to the Soviet Union.

I had endeavored on several occasions to obtain an interview with Mr. Hopkins so as to be as well informed as possible on our attitude toward the Polish situation, but for various reasons advanced by the White House I was never able to get an appointment.

Lacking the opportunity to discuss in person the complexities of the problem with Messrs. Stettinius and Hopkins, I made recommendations to the Secretary in writing. Having become apprehensive, after the action of the British Government in backing Marshal Tito, that the same political fate as had befallen General Draja Mihailovitch and his patriotic body of Serbs might later crush the democratic elements in Poland, I addressed a memorandum to him on December 20, 1944.

In my memorandum I pointed out that Mr. Churchill's speech of December 15 confirmed these fears. It indicated, I observed, a complete reversal of British policy regarding the integrity of the Polish frontier of August 1939, as set forth in a speech by Mr. Eden on July 30, 1941.

I reminded Mr. Stettinius that President Roosevelt in his letter to Prime Minister Mikolajczyk of November 17, 1944, had strongly stated our position, insisting on the independence of Poland. I expressed the opinion that the practical value of our declarations would, however, depend on the interpretation of what is meant by "independence." If it was to mean that a minority, under Russian influence, was to be the nominal government of Poland, we would almost certainly have a repetition of the situation which then prevailed in Yugoslavia—namely, a Communist dictatorship under Marshal Tito. We would be responsible, I added, if we acquiesced in Soviet and British plans, for setting a pattern in Europe which could lead only to the destruction of our prestige and possibly to war.

Knowing that negotiations were then going on among Roosevelt, Churchill and Stalin for a forthcoming meeting of the Big Three, I ended my memorandum:

For the foregoing reasons I urge that at the next meeting of the leaders of the United States, Great Britain and the Soviet Union we insist on the right of the Polish people to choose their own government without molestation from any external force, and that such a government be permitted to govern the country as it sees fit. With the greatest army, navy and air forces in history at our disposal, and in the light of the great material assistance we are giving to Great Britain and the Soviet Union, our views on this all-important matter should be given by the other parties the consideration which they deserve. There is no threat implied in this statement regarding our present military force, but it does emphasize that the basic American policy for which we have been fighting should not be disregarded by our Allies.

Undoubtedly emboldened by the British Government's indicated policy of support of Stalin's proposal for Polish frontiers, as shown by Churchill's attitude in the Moscow conversation in October, the

Soviet Government was now openly taking steps to transform the Polish Committee of National Liberation in Lublin into the Provisional Government of Poland. This trend was considered so far-reaching by President Roosevelt that under date of December 16 he sent a personal message to Marshal Stalin to this effect:

While fully appreciating the desirability from Marshal Stalin's point of view of having a clarification of Polish authority before the Soviet armies moved further into Poland, he hoped that Stalin would refrain, because of the great political implications involved, from recognizing the Lublin Committee as the government of Poland before their forthcoming meeting. He hoped that this meeting would take place immediately after his forthcoming inauguration on January 20, 1945. He believed it to be of the highest importance that, pending the meeting and thorough discussion of this troublesome question, no action should be taken on any side that would render discussions more difficult. He asked that, pending his meeting with Stalin and Churchill, the Soviet Government deal with the Lublin Committee in its then present form.

Marshal Stalin's reply, received December 27, was substantially as follows:

Subsequent to Mr. Mikolajczyk's visit to Moscow in October 1944, the Soviet Government had come into possession of evidence convincing it that Mr. Mikolajczyk's negotiations with the Lublin representatives in Moscow had served as a summons for sabotage by his adherents in the rear of the Soviet Army in Poland. These acts of sabotage had included the killing of Soviet soldiers and officers. The recent coming to power of Arciszewski's government had made the situation even worse and created a gulf between Poland and the Government-in-Exile. Meanwhile, the Lublin Committee had made serious progress in strengthening the Polish state, expanding the Polish Army and implementing a number of important governmental measures, particularly agrarian reforms, all leading to a consolidation of democratic power in Poland. The committee's authority among the wide masses in Poland and in wide circles abroad had been enhanced. The question of Soviet relations with Poland involved close friendly contact daily with the power which had been established by the Polish people on its own soil, which had grown strong, and which had its own army fighting with the Red Army against the Germans.

In view of the above considerations, if the Lublin Committee transformed itself into a Provisional Government, then the Soviet Government would not have any serious ground for postponing recognition. The problem of Poland was inseparable from the problem of the security of the Soviet Union. The Red Army successes in Poland would depend greatly on the maintenance of a peaceful and trustworthy rear in Poland. The Lublin Committee recognized this fact, while the émigré government, on the other hand, was creating civil war in the rear of the Red Army. As a first step the allied countries should agree on an immediate exchange of diplomatic representatives with the Lublin Committee, with a view to its subsequent recognition as the legal government of Poland.

President Roosevelt replied on December 29 to Marshal Stalin's message which, he said, disturbed and deeply disappointed him. He continued, in substance:

No serious inconvenience would have been caused to the Soviet Government and to its armies if the purely juridical act of recognition would be postponed for the short period of the month remaining before Stalin and he were to meet. There was no suggestion in his request that the Soviet Government should curtail its practical relations with the Lublin Committee nor was there any thought that it should deal with or accept the London government as then constituted. He had urged the delay in recognition because of the extremely unfortunate effect on world opinion and on enemy morale if the Soviet Government should formally recognize one government in Poland while the majority of the other United Nations, including the United States and Great Britain, continued to recognize and maintain diplomatic relations with the Polish Government in London.

There was no prospect of the United States Government transferring its recognition from the government in London to the Lublin Committee as then constituted. There had been no evidence to justify the conclusion that the Lublin Committee represented the people of Poland. Only a small fraction of Polish territory west of the Curzon

Line had been liberated. Consequently, the people of Poland had had no opportunity to express themselves in regard to the Lublin Committee. If, subsequent to Poland's liberation, a provisional government with popular support were established, the attitude of the United States Government would of course be governed by the decision of the Polish people.

With regard to Mr. Mikolajczyk, he found it most difficult to believe that the latter had any knowledge of any terrorist instructions. In fact, Mikolajczyk was the only Polish leader in sight who seemed to offer the possibility of a genuine solution of the Polish question.

He was more than ever convinced that when Marshal Stalin, Mr. Churchill and he met together they could reach a solution of the problem. He therefore still hoped that Marshal Stalin would hold in abeyance until then the formal recognition of the Lublin Government as the government of Poland. From a military angle he could not see any objection to the delay of a month.

On December 31, 1944, the Lublin Committee announced itself as the Provisional Government of Poland.

Instantly, in order to leave no doubt as to our attitude toward the Lublin Committee, Secretary of State Stettinius stated to the press on January 1, 1945:

"This government continues to maintain formal diplomatic relations with the Polish Government-in-Exile in London."

The British, although barely on speaking terms with its members after Mr. Churchill's speech of December 15 excoriating the policy of the Polish Government-in-Exile, likewise continued a formal relationship with that government.

Ignoring the earnest plea for a delay which the President of the United States had addressed to Marshal Stalin, the Soviet Government announced on January 5, 1945, that it had recognized the Lublin Government as the Provisional Government of Poland. Stalin's message of December 27, 1944, with its hypocritical references to the authority of the Lublin Committee, which continued to be a Soviet automaton, clearly indicated his intention to face the United States with a *fait accompli* at the forthcoming conference. His deliberate rejection of the request of the Government of the United States, which as an ally had so effectively contributed to supplying the Red Armies with arms, munitions, equipment and food supplies, indicated how lightly the Soviet Government regarded Mr. Roosevelt's serious exposition of our position. It showed that the Soviet Government intended to go ahead with its policy of expansion, regardless of the effect on Soviet-United States relations.

The Polish situation had brought the diplomatic conflict to a head.

When the news that Stalin had recognized the Lublin Government came to me on January 5, I wondered what we could do, in the face of Soviet military control of Poland, to mitigate this defiance of our stand in the interests of the people of Poland.

CHAPTER FIVE

Yalta—Deathblow to Poland's Hopes

FROM this time on, the Polish situation developed rapidly. On January 17, 1945, Marshal Stalin announced that Warsaw had been liberated by the Red Armies. Since September 13, 1944, they had been in possession of the eastern bank of the Vistula across the river from the capital. Stalin understandably did not state in his announcement that, had the Soviet Government extended the promised assistance to the insurrection which had terminated on October 3, the "liberation" of Warsaw would have surely been greatly accelerated. And, as a result of their refusal to aid the rebellion, the Red Army marched into a city of rubble. For three months the Nazis had systematically destroyed the city, leaving a mass of ruins to terrify those inhabitants who were later able to return from Nazi concentration camps.

Politically the taking of Warsaw on January 17 was opportune for Stalin's policy. Mr. Roosevelt was to be inaugurated for his fourth term as President of the United States on January 20. He would leave immediately thereafter for his conference with Stalin and Churchill at Yalta in the Crimea. For reasons of military security the location of the meeting place was carefully kept secret and even many of us in the Department of State had no knowledge of the exact place chosen. Stalin's hand in supporting the Lublin Committee as the Provisional Government of Poland would be greatly strengthened by the fact that, under the protection of the Red Army, this group had already commenced to function in the capital of Poland as an organized administration. On the other hand, members of the London Government were at loggerheads among themselves on the question of compromising on the frontier. Furthermore, they were outside of Poland and could exert little political influence.

On the eve of the President's departure for Yalta, I had talks with high officials in the State Department on the Polish situation. The fact that they did not disclose to me what our stand would be at Yalta, except in a general way to insist on a "strong, free and independent Poland," filled me with misgivings. I could not help being apprehensive. Furthermore, I was disturbed by President Roosevelt's exaggerated confidence in the power of his charm to persuade diplomatic and political adversaries to his point of view. He seemed to feel that this charm was particularly effective on Stalin. Close advisers of Mr. Roosevelt confided to me that this overconfidence had been noticeable at Tehran. Yet Roosevelt had been unable there to gain the principal decisions over Stalin.

His intimate staff had strongly recommended that the meeting should be near enough to the United States to entail the minimum of fatigue to the President. But Stalin was obdurate in refusing to be out of direct physical communication with the Soviet Union, ascribing his attitude to the necessity of directing his military campaign. The trip to the Crimea, by way of Egypt, was indeed a heavy physical strain on the President's impaired health. No doubt it hastened his death, less than three months later. But here again Stalin had his own way.

We were still at war and undoubtedly there were reasons of military strategy which might force us to make concessions to the Soviet Union at the expense of Poland for the sake of shortening the conflict and saving American lives. After all, Poland was but one of many questions to be discussed at the Conference. It was understandable that the issue of one nation—such as Poland—could not be considered paramount to the general Allied aim of overwhelmingly defeating the enemy in Europe and in the Pacific. In the circumstances would the United States be in a position to fulfill its promises, so often and eloquently enunciated, for "a strong, free and independent Poland"?

Nevertheless, Mr. Byrnes, in his account* of the discussions at Yalta, states:

Not only Poland's boundaries but Poland itself was one of the most serious issues of the entire conference. More time was spent on this subject than on any other.

Mr. Byrnes attributes to Stalin the following amazing statement at Yalta:

For the Russian people, the question of Poland is not only a question of honor but also a question of security. Throughout history, Poland has been the corridor through which the enemy has passed into Russia. Twice in the last thirty years our enemies, the Germans, have passed through this corridor. It is in Russia's interest that Poland should be strong and powerful, in a position to shut the door of this corridor by her own force. . . .

This was an astounding statement indeed, when it is remembered that it was the Soviet Union itself, when it signed the 1939 pact with Germany, which opened the corridor door! If it was allowed to pass without comment from Mr. Churchill or Mr. Roosevelt, as it seems to have been, their silence is hardly to be wondered at, considering the spirit of appeasement prevailing at that conference.

Perhaps the officials in the Department of State with whom I spoke did not themselves know what our line of policy was to be at Yalta. It would be, in the last analysis, the decisions of Mr. Roosevelt, and of his intimate advisers who were accompanying him to Yalta, such as Mr. Hopkins and Mr. Byrnes, then Director of the Office of War Mobilization and Reconversion, which would determine to what extent we would oppose Soviet policy for expansion at the expense of Poland and other European nations. In fact, the Department of State was not kept advised of the progress of the Crimea Conference. It is true that Secretary Stettinius and some of his principal advisers,

---

* *Speaking Frankly,* by James F. Byrnes, (Harper and Brothers), p. 31. Copyright, 1947, by Donald S. Russell, Trustee of the James F. Byrnes Foundation.

such as H. Freeman Matthews and Charles E. Bohlen, were at Yalta. Yet the first word regarding the Conference which reached the State Department in Washington was the report by Jonathan Daniels, Administrative Assistant to the President, given out for release on February 12, 1945, at 4:30 P.M., Eastern War Time. A copy was immediately brought to me at my desk in the State Department. As I glanced over it, I could not believe my eyes. To me, almost every line spoke of a surrender to Stalin!

That portion of the Yalta agreement relating to Poland read as follows:

A new situation has been created in Poland as a result of her complete liberation by the Red Army. This calls for the establishment of a Polish provisional government which can be more broadly based than was possible before the recent liberation of western Poland. The provisional government which is now functioning in Poland should therefore be reorganized on a broader democratic basis with the inclusion of democratic leaders from Poland itself and from Poles abroad. This new government should then be called the Polish Provisional Government of National Unity.

M. Molotov, Mr. Harriman and Sir A. Clark-Kerr are authorized as a commission to consult in the first instance in Moscow with members of the present provisional government and with other Polish democratic leaders from within Poland and from abroad, with a view to the reorganization of the present government along the above lines. This Polish Provisional Government of National Unity shall be pledged to the holding of free and unfettered elections as soon as possible on the basis of universal suffrage and secret ballot. In these elections all democratic and anti-Nazi parties shall have the right to take part and to put forward candidates.

When a Polish Provisional Government of National Unity has been properly formed in conformity with the above, the government of the U.S.S.R., which now maintains diplomatic relations with the present provisional government of Poland, and the government of the United Kingdom and the government of the U.S.A., will establish diplomatic relations with the new Polish Provisional Government of National Unity, and will exchange ambassadors by whose reports the respective governments will be kept informed about the situation in Poland.

The three heads of government consider that the Eastern frontier of Poland should follow the Curzon line with digressions from it in some regions of five to eight kilometres in favour of Poland. They recognize that Poland must receive substantial accessions of territory in the North and West. They feel that the opinion of the new Polish Provisional Government of National Unity should be sought in due course on the extent of these accessions and that the final delimitation on the western frontier of Poland should therefore await the peace conference.

Signed: WINSTON S. CHURCHILL
FRANKLIN D. ROOSEVELT
J. STALIN

My disappointment had a four-fold basis:

First, the terms of the decision were of so general a nature that they would be susceptible of varying interpretations. Developments were to demonstrate that the interpretation of the United States and British governments as to what constituted "free and unfettered elections" was very different from the officially expressed opinion of the Soviet Government and of the Polish Provisional Government of National Unity.

Second, no provision was made for the supervision of the elections by the three Allies. It was merely provided that the ambassadors to be appointed would inform their respective governments about the situation in Poland. And how could elections be free as long as Red Army forces and the NKVD remained to enforce the will of the Kremlin?

Third, the United States Government had openly and irrevocably surrendered to the Soviet and British thesis that the Polish-Soviet frontier should follow the Curzon Line. This would deprive Poland of enormously rich timberlands, oil fields and the cherished city of Lwów, which not even in the partitions of Poland in the eighteenth century had ever been incorporated into the Russian Empire. True, Poland was to obtain some compensation in the north and west at the expense of Germany, but in addition to a net loss of twenty-seven thousand square miles, the population of Poland was to be diminished from thirty-five million to twenty-three million.

Fourth, no provision was made for the safe return to Poland of the Polish Army abroad. It had rendered tremendous assistance to the Allied cause and, at Monte Cassino especially, had covered itself with glory.

On February 13, after the announcement of the Yalta decision, the Acting Secretary of State, Joseph C. Grew, informed the press that I would remain in the Department of State "for the present in further consultation pending developments." This meant that neither I nor the staff which had been assembled to assist me would go to London.

It was hoped, of course, that an agreement could be reached among the three powers without delay, to permit a truly democratic government to be set up within Poland. Diplomatic relations could then be established on the basis of the Yalta decision, and our staff could proceed to Poland to assume our duties.

But the hostility of the Soviet Government to the London exile group still prevailed: at Yalta, as I was later told, Stalin had bitterly assailed Mikolajczyk and had opposed his being consulted on the composition of the new government. Mr. Roosevelt, however, had taken a strong stand in favor of the former Polish Premier. On his suggestion and as a compromise, the Moscow Commission was set up. It was to start functioning immediately after the Yalta Conference and was to choose those Polish leaders who, in addition to the Provisional Government in Warsaw, were to be invited for consultation in Moscow regarding the composition of the Provisional Government of National Unity.

Mr. Roosevelt returned to Washington from the Crimea Conference, mortally fatigued by his journey, on the last day of February. On March 1 he addressed a joint session of Congress to report on the decisions reached at Yalta. He began, informally, with an apology for remaining seated while he spoke.

. . . I know you will realize it makes it a lot easier for me in not having to carry about ten pounds of steel around on the bottom of my legs and also because of the fact that I have just completed a 14,000-mile trip.

He asserted that:

I am returning from this trip . . . refreshed and inspired. I was well the entire time.

But members of Congress noted that he was grayer, thinner and looked considerably more aged than when he had last appeared before them, two years earlier.

In regard to the decisions relating to Poland, the President said:

One outstanding example of joint action by the three major Allied powers was the solution reached on Poland. The whole Polish question was a potential source of trouble in post-war Europe, as it had been some time before, and we came to the conference determined to find a common ground for its solution, and we did.

Our objective was to help create a strong, independent and prosperous nation. That's the thing we must always remember, those words agreed to by Russia, by Britain and by me, the objective of making Poland a strong, independent and prosperous nation, with a government ultimately to be selected by the Polish people themselves.

To achieve that objective it is necessary to provide for the formation of a new government, much more representative than had been possible while Poland was enslaved. Accordingly, steps were taken at Yalta to reorganize the existing provisional government in Poland on a broader democratic basis, so as to include democratic leaders now in Poland and those abroad. This new reorganized government will be recognized by all of us as the temporary government of Poland.

However, the new Polish provisional government of national unity will be pledged to hold a free election as soon as possible on the basis of universal suffrage and a secret ballot.

Throughout history Poland has been the corridor through which attacks on Russia have been made. Twice in this generation Germany has struck Russia through this corridor. To insure European security and world peace a strong and independent Poland is necessary to prevent that from happening again.*

The decision with respect to the boundaries of Poland was quite a compromise. I didn't agree with all of it by any means, but we could go as far as Britain wanted in certain areas, go as far as Russia wanted in certain areas and we could go as far as I wanted in certain areas. It was a compromise. The decision was a compromise under which the Poles will receive compensation in territory in the north and west in exchange for what they lose by the Curzon Line in the east.

The limits of the western border will be permanently fixed in the final peace conference. We know roughly that it will include in the new strong Poland quite a large slice of what is now called Germany. And it was agreed also that the new Poland will have a large and long coastline and many a new harbor. Also that East Prussia, most of it, will go to Poland and the corner of it will go to Russia. Also . . . I think Danzig would be a lot better if it were Polish.

It is well known that the people east of the Curzon Line are predominantly White Russian and Ukrainian. They are not Polish, to a very great majority. And the people west of the line are predominantly Polish, except in that part of East Prussia and East Germany which will go to new Poland. As far back as 1919 the representatives of the Allies agreed that the Curzon Line represented a fair boundary between the two peoples. You must also remember there was no Poland, there had not been any Polish Government, before 1919, for a great many generations.

I am convinced that this agreement on Poland, under the circumstances, is the most hopeful agreement possible for a free, independent and prosperous Polish state.**

By President Roosevelt's own admission, the Yalta agreement with respect to Poland was a compromise. To put it more brutally, it was a capitulation on the part of the United States and Great Britain to the views of the Soviet Union on the frontiers of Poland and on the composition of the Polish Provisional Government of National Unity.

---

* Comparison of this statement with the remarks credited to Stalin by Mr. Byrnes (see p. 79) shows a remarkable similarity of wording used by Mr. Roosevelt and Marshal Stalin in discussing the necessity of maintaining a strong Poland.

** *New York Times,* March 2, 1945, p. 12.

Yet at the time the report as a whole was acclaimed by Members of Congress of both parties as an outstanding achievement. The American people hailed it as a definite milestone along the highway of international peace.

The newsreel pictures of the participants in the Yalta Conference clearly showed the physical and mental exhaustion under which President Roosevelt was laboring. I was shocked by the extent to which he had aged since I had last seen him in the previous November: he was more haggard, less characteristically vibrant. Patently he could have been no match for the wily, tough Stalin in a battle of wits which required sustained physical and moral strength to achieve victory.

"At the Yalta Conference the physically disabled President of the United States was outwitted, outmaneuvered and outfoxed by Stalin," asserts Charles Rozmarek, President of the Polish-American Congress, in a recent letter to me. Immediately after the announcement on February 12, 1945, of the Yalta decisions, Mr. Rozmarek had stated publicly:

It is with sorrow, dismay and protest that we greet the decision of the Big Three to give all land east of the so-called Curzon Line to Russia in direct contradiction to all sacred pledges of the Atlantic Charter. This tragic revelation is a staggering blow to the cause of freedom.

The docile submission to Russia's demand for all the lands, seized during the partitions of Poland as Germany's collaborator and even Lwów, which, prior to the war, was never at any time under Russian rule even illegally, is a distortion of our war aims. It means re-affirmation of the Molotov-Ribbentrop Line of 1939 which gave one half of Poland and all of Lithuania, Latvia and Estonia to Russia.

When the Germans were at the gates of Moscow and Stalin was making frantic pleas for help, Stalin renounced his claims to all the territories he had seized as Germany's partner. As soon as Russia, thanks to American lend-lease aid, began pushing the Germans back, Stalin re-affirmed the Molotov-Ribbentrop Boundary Line and abruptly broke off relations with the London Polish government which he had always recognized as the only legitimate government of Poland.

It is also shocking to learn that the members of the Stalin hand-picked Lublin government, composed of professional communists, who are working for the incorporation of Poland into the Soviet Union, are to continue in power in a newly-reorganized government in violation of the constitution of Poland. The imposition of a government "without the freely expressed wishes of the people concerned" would mean the end of freedom and the beginning of serfdom for the people of Poland.

As for the Poles not subservient to the Kremlin, they had no hesitation in terming the Yalta decision the betrayal of Poland. To them it was the negation of their hopes for independence and for the restoration of the territory which their enemies had confiscated in 1939 in the face of nonaggression treaties. But this time it was not the enemies but the allies of Poland, comembers in the United Nations, who gave the *coup de grâce* to the aspirations of the Polish people for a restoration of their liberty and democracy.

Some weeks later, after the meetings of the Moscow Commission to be described in the next chapter had ended in a stalemate, I gave Secretary Stettinius a memorandum dated April 5, 1945, recommending that the public be told about the deterioration of Soviet-American relations principally as a result of the Polish question. The pertinent portions follow:

Recent developments indicate that the Soviet Government does *not* intend to fulfill its obligations with respect to Poland under the Yalta communiqué prior to April 25, 1945 (the date set for the opening of the San Francisco Conference). If action, in accordance with the Crimean understandings, is greatly delayed, it will have only an academic value: the passage of time will enable the Soviet authorities to organize Poland through the NKVD—both politically and administratively—in such a manner as to render the term "free and unfettered elections," should they ever be held, a farce. Any Polish government, therefore, which may emerge will be no more representative of the Polish people as a whole than are the present Warsaw (formerly Lublin) or Arciszewski (London) governments.

According to the terms of the Yalta communiqué, the American

Ambassador (as well as the British) is obligated to report to his government "about the situation in Poland." It is implicit that facilities shall be rendered to the American and British ambassadors to enable them to make their reports. It is doubtful, however, whether the Soviet Government or any Polish Government (which did not sign the communiqué) would admit any obligation on this point. Furthermore, the difficulties which we have had in obtaining information in Bulgaria, Rumania and Yugoslavia and in taking legitimate steps to protect American interests in those countries indicate that the Soviet Government will likewise obstruct us in Poland in carrying out our dual obligation (a) under the Yalta communiqué to report "about the situation in Poland," and (b) under international law, to protect our national interest. The recent last-hour action of the Soviet Government which prevented the diplomatic corps accredited near the Czechoslovak Government in London from accompanying the Government to Prague is illustrative of this phase of present Soviet policy.

The initial function of the American Embassy in Poland will be primarily to report to the Department on political and economic conditions, as well as on the condition of American citizens and property in Poland. Unless the attitude of the Soviet Government should undergo a radical change for the better prior to the arrival of the Embassy in Poland, it would seem inevitable, on the basis of present information, that we shall be obstructed in our endeavors to accomplish fully what the Department would normally expect of a mission in reporting and in protecting American interests. . . .

Appeasement or apparent appeasement can be as dangerous to United States interests in 1945 as it actually was in 1940 and 1941.

Sooner or later the facts regarding the Soviet actions in Poland, as well as elsewhere, and the deterioration of Soviet-American relations will become more fully known to the American public. The question arises as to when it would be advisable in our national interest to place publicly the responsibility for the difficulties in the settlement of the Polish problem squarely on the Soviet Government, where it belongs. Such a public statement should refer to the efforts on our part at Yalta and elsewhere to effect the closest possible working agreement with the Soviet Government. It should indicate how greatly we regret having been brought to the conclusion, by the recent actions and attitude of that Government, that it is not equally concerned in the importance of effectively carrying out the terms of the Crimea agreement. Consideration should be given to the advisability of specifically referring to the breakdown of the Moscow conversations and the evident intention of the Soviet Government and the puppet regime now set up in Warsaw to prevent democratic Poles from outside of Poland taking part in the formation of a representative Polish Government.

Secretary Stettinius was to make an address in New York City before a meeting of the Council of Foreign Relations on the following day. My memorandum apparently did not come to his attention before he left Washington for New York; or, if it did, had no effect on the tone of his speech, which was optimistic over the Moscow negotiations to a degree that I felt entirely unwarranted.

From March to June, I examined the incoming reports of the discussions going on in Moscow as to the formation of Poland's Provisional Government. These came to my desk in the State Department with promptness; and each one strengthened me in my conviction that the United States had already gone so far on the road to appeasement that it would be virtually impossible to check the Soviet machinations in Poland, even with the strongest rebuke.

CHAPTER SIX

The Moscow Commission

BUT prior to March and immediately after the Yalta Conference, I had been engrossed in studying the dispatches from Ambassador Harriman to the State Department regarding the deliberations of the Moscow Commission.

In accordance with the agreement reached at Yalta, the Moscow Commission, composed of Mr. Molotov and Ambassadors Harriman and Clark-Kerr, first met on February 24, 1945. Durbrow, because of his wide knowledge of the intricacies of the Polish situation, was sent to Moscow to assist Harriman; and Lieutenant Tonesk was assigned temporarily to the Embassy at Moscow so that his services as interpreter would be available.

In addition to the mutual desire to establish diplomatic relations between the United States and Great Britain, on the one hand, and the proposed Polish Provisional Government of National Unity, on the other, it was considered essential that Poland should be represented at the first meeting of the United Nations Organization, scheduled to be opened at San Francisco on April 25, 1945. It was accordingly the hope of the United States Government that the Provisional Government of National Unity would be constituted prior to that date.

But from the start the Moscow Commission struck snags.

At its first meeting, on February 24, Mr. Molotov insisted, contrary to the clear wording of the Yalta decision, that the Warsaw Provisional Government should be consulted in the first instance as to the Polish leaders from Poland and London to be invited to Moscow for consultation in connection with the formation of the proposed new government.

Compliance with Molotov's proposal would have given the Warsaw group (which was Communist-controlled) virtual veto power over any names that might be submitted by the British or United States representatives. Thus, it would be possible for the Communists to prevent any outstanding non-Communists from taking part in the discussions.

Ambassador Harriman, replying, made it clear that the United States would have no objection to members of the Warsaw Provisional Government coming to Moscow ahead of the others, provided that invitations were sent simultaneously to an agreed list of other Polish democratic leaders. A telegram was thereupon sent, inviting the Provisional Government to Moscow, stating the commission desired to meet with representatives of the Warsaw Government as well as with Bishop Sapieha, Messrs. Wincenty Witos and Zygmunt Zulawski and Professors Bujak and Kutrzeba from within Poland, and Messrs. Mikolajczyk, Grabski and Romer from London.* It was pointed out in this telegram that these men invited from within Poland and from abroad were being summoned for consultation and not necessarily as representatives of the new government. The observations of the Warsaw Government on the foregoing points were invited.

The Warsaw Government's reply indicated that it did not have a correct understanding of the Yalta decision. First of all, the Polish Provisional regime stated that it would be necessary that those persons taking part in the consultations should represent the will of the people and should define the principles on which the decisions of the Crimea Conference were based. This was undoubtedly an allusion to Mr. Mikolajczyk who, like so many Poles as well as Americans who were hopeful of Polish independence, may have evidenced a lack of enthusiasm, to put it mildly, regarding the vague wording of the Yalta agreement.

---

* Mr. Grabski was a venerable member of the Polish Democratic Party, who had served as Minister of Education in the prewar Polish Government. Professor Kutrzeba was an eminent historian, living in Kraków. Of the eight names suggested by Clark-Kerr and Harriman, Molotov agreed only to those of Grabski and Kutrzeba.

The government in its telegram, after stating that it had no knowledge regarding the whereabouts of Mr. Wincenty Witos, the famed leader of the Peasant Party, made an unfriendly insinuation about him. Although Witos had been known for over thirty years as the spokesman of the Peasant movement, as a supporter of democratic ideals and as a bitter anti-Nazi during the German occupation, the Warsaw group stated that if Witos were in Poland he was in fact concealing himself, following the liberation of the country, whereas during the German occupation his whereabouts were known to everyone. The government drew the conclusion that his participation in the consultations was therefore impossible.

It developed that Witos, although eventually invited to take part in the consultations, was unable to do so because of his health, which was precarious.

Witos, a true champion of democracy, died in Kraków eight months after this, in October 1945. I was privileged to talk with him for more than an hour a few weeks before his death, at which time he unburdened himself of his views regarding the character and policies of the Warsaw group. In 1919 Witos had been considered by the Pilsudski group a revolutionary firebrand because of his liberal and progressive views, his desire for agrarian reform, and his antipathy toward Polish feudalism. In 1945, however, since he was strongly against Communism, the Warsaw group opposed him and his principles. When I interviewed him in a Kraków hospital on October 8, 1945, his piercing eyes still held their fire, although his lined face showed the weariness of age. His bristling mustache and his refusal ever to wear a necktie were physical characteristics which were as widely known as his unassailable intellectual integrity. He decried to me the vicious methods of the police state into which Poland had been transformed through the power usurped by a Communistic minority which did not have the support of the people. From what was to be his deathbed, he begged me to use my influence to persuade the United States Government to give no financial assistance to the Polish Provisional Government unless and until freedom of speech were restored and free elections held; otherwise, Mr. Witos argued, the Polish people would feel that the United States had acquiesced in the terrorist system which had been imposed on the people of Poland against their will.

At the second meeting, on February 27, Mr. Molotov suggested that as neither the British nor the United States governments had adequate information about the present situation in Poland they might send someone to observe conditions there and report. Sir Archibald Clark-Kerr hailed this as a constructive suggestion and said he was prepared to recommend it to his government—on condition, however, that such a step would not entail official recognition of the Warsaw regime. Ambassador Harriman expressed agreement with the British Ambassador's view, but suggested that it would be advisable to await the talks with the Warsaw group before taking such steps. Molotov then said he would withdraw the suggestion, but the British and American ambassadors asked that it merely be held in abeyance.

Another stumbling block became apparent at the third meeting, on March 1, when no agreement could be reached on the names of persons to be invited to Moscow, outside of the Warsaw Government. Mr. Harriman and Sir Archibald Clark-Kerr submitted over twenty names of Polish democratic leaders from Poland and abroad. Molotov claimed, however, that with the exception of Mr. Mikolajczyk he did not have sufficient information about these persons. Furthermore, he expressed the opinion that the Warsaw Government would not approve of the participation of Mikolajczyk, on the ground that he had opposed the Crimean decision as well as the transfer of Lwów to the Soviet Union. Because of the inability to agree on the invitations to be extended, the commission telegraphed the members of the Warsaw Provisional Government on March 1, requesting them to defer their visit to Moscow for the present.

At the fourth meeting, held on March 5, Molotov proposed that, in addition to the three members of the Warsaw Government—President Boleslaw Bierut, Prime Minister Osóbka-Morawski, and Marshal

Rola-Zymierski—a delegate to be selected by the government should be invited. Besides these four, he suggested that the following should be summoned from London for the consultations: Mr. Grabski; and General Zeligowski, who had, under Pilsudski's orders, captured the city of Wilna from Lithuania in 1920. Molotov also proposed that Professor Kutrzeba be summoned from within Poland. He objected to inviting Mr. Mikolajczyk until the matter could be discussed jointly with the Warsaw Provisional Government.

The United States and British ambassadors pointed out to Mr. Molotov that if his proposal were adopted, in effect giving the Warsaw Government four representatives out of seven, a prejudice against the commission would immediately be created in the United States and Great Britain and would make it impossible to achieve the aims of the commission.

There followed exchanges of lengthy notes between the British and United States governments on the one hand, and the Soviet Government on the other. Although Molotov himself had suggested that the United States and British governments should send observers to Poland, he sent an *aide-mémoire* to Harriman and Clark-Kerr on March 22 in which it was stated that the Soviet Government had learned "with amazement" the intention of the United States Government to send British and American observers to Poland! The communication stated that this proposal could "sting the national pride of the Poles to the quick," especially as this subject had not been mentioned in the Crimean decision! It was suggested to the United States Government that the best means to explore this question would be by communicating directly with the Polish Provisional Government.

The fifth and sixth meetings, held on March 23 and April 2 respectively, indicated that there was no likelihood of agreement on the persons to be invited for consultation. Molotov stated at the sixth and last meeting that the insistence of the British and American representatives that Mikolajczyk be called for consultation would not permit the commission to make further progress. The Soviet attitude was clearly illustrative of the desire to prevent outstanding non-Communist leaders from being included in the conversations leading to the formation of a new government.

The impasse in reaching an agreement regarding the composition of the proposed Polish Provisional Government of National Unity was having a profound effect on the United Nations Conference, the date of whose first meeting was so rapidly approaching. The Acting Secretary of State, Mr. Grew, had told the press on March 5 that "while Poland is a member of the United Nations, an invitation to the San Francisco Conference is not being extended at this time to either the London Polish Government or the Provisional Government now functioning in Poland." Mr. Grew expressed the hope that the new Polish Provisional Government of National Unity would be formed in time for it to send representatives to the United Nations Conference. On March 9 the Soviet Ambassador in Washington submitted a communication to the Department of State suggesting that representatives of the Polish Provisional Government functioning in Warsaw should be invited to the San Francisco Conference. On the other hand, on March 11 the Polish Government in London protested against its exclusion from the San Francisco Conference despite the fact that it was a member of the United Nations and was recognized as such by the United States. On March 14 the Polish Ambassador in Washington, Mr. J. Ciechanowski, called on Secretary Stettinius and, in my presence, protested orally against the Polish Government's exclusion. Mr. Stettinius pointed out to him that the intention still was to invite the government which was to be formed in accordance with the procedure agreed on at Yalta. This view was again conveyed to the Polish Ambassador in Washington in a note dated March 22.

The Department of State apparently still hoped that Molotov would not persist in his obstructionist attitude, for on March 31 Secretary Stettinius authorized the following statement to be attributed to the Department of State:

It is the hope of this government that the formation of the new Provisional Government of National Unity in conformity with decisions of the Crimea Conference would be completed in time to send a delegation to the San Francisco Conference. In view of the current consultations respecting the formation of this new government, reorganized on broader democratic basis with the inclusion of democratic leaders from Poland itself and of Poles abroad in accordance with the Crimea agreement, the United States Government does not agree to the extension of an invitation to the present Provisional Government now functioning in Warsaw.

As Molotov still firmly opposed the extension of an invitation to Mikolajczyk and insisted that the opinion of the Warsaw Government should be the guiding influence in selecting persons to be invited, it was obvious that the commission was at a breaking point. President Roosevelt had as recently as April 1 sent a strong message to Stalin, pointing out the necessity of reaching an agreement in accordance with the understanding reached at the Crimea Conference.

The contents of that message are summarized by former Secretary James F. Byrnes in his book *Speaking Frankly* in this manner:

The President opened his message by stating he could not conceal "the concern with which I view the development of events" since Yalta. He expressed his regret at "the lack of progress made in the carrying out, which the world expects, of the political decisions which we reached at Yalta, particularly those relating to the Polish question," and added that he could not understand the "apparent indifferent attitude" of the Soviet Union. The President said he felt the situation arose from the Soviet interpretation of the Yalta agreement as meaning that the new Provisional Government should be little more than a continuation of the present Warsaw government. The President emphasized that he could not reconcile that position either with the agreement or with the discussions preceding the agreement. He said he must make it plain to the Marshal that "any such solution which would result in a thinly disguised continuation of the present government would be entirely unacceptable, and would cause our people to regard the Yalta agreement as a failure." If the right of the commission to select the Poles to be invited to Moscow for consultation were either limited or shared with the Warsaw government, he went on, the foundation of the Yalta agreement would be destroyed.

President Roosevelt said that he would not bar or veto any candidate proposed by Molotov for the consultation, and that our Ambassador should be accorded the same confidence. He told Stalin that there should be a maximum of political tranquility in Poland and that we should use our influence to see that dissident groups ceased measures and countermeasures against each other. He also urged that, in view of our responsibilities, representatives of the American and British members of the commission be permitted to visit Poland, reminding Stalin that Molotov himself had suggested this at an early meeting and subsequently withdrew the suggestion.

The President pointed out "how important it is, for the successful development of our program of international collaboration," to settle the Polish question. Otherwise, he warned, "all the difficulties and dangers to Allied unity" they had considered at Yalta "will face us in an even more acute form."*

Because of the stalemate which had been reached, Ambassador Harriman was instructed to return to the United States immediately for consultation. He left Moscow on April 17 and arrived in Washington in time to engage in the talks which took place among the foreign ministers of the three powers prior to the opening of the San Francisco Conference.

While the Moscow Commission was in session, a sinister development took place, clearly indicating the intention of the Soviet Government to nullify the political influence of any non-Communist leaders of prominence; and even to employ treachery when necessary.

On March 3, 1945, Colonel Pimienov of the Soviet Army in Poland had extended an invitation to Jan Jankowski, Vice-Premier of the London Government, who had remained in Warsaw throughout the years of its occupation by the Nazis, and to other Polish political leaders to meet with General Ivanov, Commander of the Soviet First White Russian Army, in Pruszków, near Warsaw. The letter gave the writer's absolute guarantee on his "word of honour that from the moment of your arrival amongst us I shall be responsible for everything

---

* Byrnes, *op. cit.*, pp. 54-55.

THE MAP THAT DID NOT TELL THE WHOLE TRUTH

A delegation of American citizens of Polish descent who were received at the White House by Franklin Delano Roosevelt during the 1944 campaign for his re-election inferred from the map behind his desk that he would insist on the territorial integrity of Poland. What they were not told was that he had secretly agreed at Tehran, almost a year before, to Stalin's demand that 70,000 square miles of Polish territory be ceded to Soviet Russia. (At extreme right of photograph is Charles Rozmarek, chairman of the delegation.)

THE YALTA CONFEREES

Front row, left to right: Churchill; Roosevelt; and Stalin. *Rear row, l. to r.*: Eden; Stettinius; Molotov; and Harriman.

THREE MEMBERS OF THE POLISH POLITBURO

Left to right: Hilary Minc, Minister of Industry; Jakób Berman, Undersecretary of State of the Council of Ministers; and Wladislaw Gomulka, Secretary General of the Polish Workers (Communist) Party.

that happens to you and that your personal safety is completely assured."*

The Polish Government in London, now headed by Arciszewski, reported to the United States Government that Colonel Pimienov had inquired of Jankowski and other political leaders in Poland whether they would be prepared to proceed to Moscow, on the invitation of the Polish Government in Warsaw (*i.e.,* the Lublin group) to participate in a conference and whether they would be willing to issue beforehand a statement clarifying the attitude of the various political parties. These leaders had replied that they would gladly go to Moscow if invited by the tripartite commission then meeting there, but could not commit themselves on the political situation before conferring with Mr. Mikolajczyk.

A few days later a representative of the Lublin group in London had suggested to a representative of the Government-in-Exile that an agreement be reached directly between the London and Lublin regimes and added that the Soviet Government was opposed to the participation of the United States and Great Britain in Polish affairs. If this correctly expressed the view of the Soviet Government, the statement was indeed extraordinary, coming only a few weeks after the Yalta agreement on Poland among the three principal powers.

According to a later official press release by the Polish Government in London, Jankowski had confirmed, before leaving for his conversation with Ivanov on March 27, that Pimienov's letter was authentic and that the invitation had been extended on behalf of Colonel General Ivanov. Jankowski was accompanied at this meeting by General Leopold Okulicki, who had succeeded General Bór-Komorowski as commander in chief of the Home Army, and by Kazimiesz Puzak, an outstanding member of the Polish Socialist Party and chairman of the Council of National Unity which had been functioning throughout the occupation as the underground parliament of Poland.

On March 28 other important political personages met with Gen-

---

* *The Dark Side of the Moon* (1947), p. 293, by permission of Charles Scribner's Sons and Curtis Brown Ltd.

eral Ivanov at his invitation, including three ministers of the London Government, representatives of the Peasant, Christian Labor and Democratic parties, and an interpreter. In addition to the assurances of personal safety from Colonel Pimienov, they had received, so the London Government stated afterward, a definite promise that on March 29 twelve of these representatives, in addition to the three already named, would be given the use of an airplane to fly to London for consultation with the Polish Government-in-Exile and with Polish political circles there.

When the leaders did not return from their meetings with the Soviet general, the Polish Government in London asked the United States and British governments to make representations in Moscow with a view to effecting their immediate release. Such representations were palpably justified, as the names of several of the men who had disappeared had been proposed by the United States and British ambassadors in Moscow as suitable persons to be invited to Moscow for consultation.

Ambassador Harriman thereupon inquired on April 9 of Mr. Vishinsky, Vice-Commissar for Foreign Affairs, regarding the reports which had come to the attention of the United States Government that fifteen Polish political leaders had disappeared from Warsaw and were negotiating with the Soviet Government about the broadening of the Warsaw Government. Vishinsky scoffed at the rumors and said there was no truth in them. Another diplomat who also made inquiries of Vishinsky about the fate of the fifteen missing leaders reported that he had never seen Vishinsky so ill at ease as when he denied the truth of the report.

President Franklin Delano Roosevelt died on April 12. Vice-President Harry Truman was that evening sworn in as Mr. Roosevelt's successor.

I first heard the news about 6:30 P.M. at my hotel, shortly after my return from the State Department. I immediately went back to the Department and called on my old friend George T. Summerlin, the

Chief of Protocol, and offered my services should he require them. Summerlin told me that he had no news as yet about the arrangements for the diplomatic corps attending the funeral. Should the White House require the attendance of State Department officials, he would let me know.

Late that afternoon I had attended a formal ceremony in the State Department: the signature of the Atlantic Charter by the representatives of Saudi Arabia and Syria and Lebanon. After the ceremony, the officials who had participated and the members of the State Department who had been invited foregathered at the Blair-Lee House across Pennsylvania Avenue from the old State Department. Secretary Stettinius, who was present at both functions, gave no sign that he was aware of Mr. Roosevelt's passing.

The next morning at the State Department Mr. Roosevelt's death was reflected in a hushed atmosphere, but it was natural that, especially in the Eastern European Division, there was speculation whether the accession of Mr. Truman would alter in any way the very firm policy which Mr. Roosevelt had initiated in his last personal telegrams to Stalin on the Polish question. Mr. Roosevelt, so one of his close advisers later told me, had finally understood that Stalin did not intend to comply with the Yalta commitments, in Poland or any other satellite countries. His confidence in the integrity of Stalin's words, as expressed to me on November 20, 1944, had apparently been sadly shaken as a result of Soviet unilateral policy immediately before and after Yalta.

I had met President Truman twice—once at an informal dinner in 1942, where he showed a keen interest in international affairs, and again on November 16, 1944, when I called on him in the Senate Office Building soon after his election as Vice-President. On that occasion I had expected to be leaving for London shortly. He had shown himself in favor of a vigorous foreign policy and strongly opposed to isolationism.

At the very moment when the Soviet Government was blocking

the efforts of the Moscow commission to set up a Provisional Government of National Unity and was detaining leading Poles who were possible candidates for inclusion in the new government, it was taking positive steps to emphasize that the Lublin group was to be the permanent government in Poland.

On April 16, 1945, immediately before Molotov's departure for the San Francisco Conference, the Soviet Foreign Office informed the United States Embassy in Moscow that a Soviet-Polish treaty of mutual assistance was under preparation, similar to those which the Soviet Government had concluded with Yugoslavia and Czechoslovakia. The Department of State, under date of April 17, straightway instructed the Embassy to tell the Soviet Government that the United States Government was very much disturbed over the authority then functioning in Poland. The Department requested, therefore, that this action be deferred until the United States Government had an opportunity to present its views to Mr. Molotov, who was due to arrive before long in Washington. A note in this sense was sent to the Soviet Foreign Office on April 18.

(According to Mr. Byrnes,* April 17 was also the date on which a telegram was sent. It had been drafted by the British Foreign Office and our State Department, after Mr. Roosevelt and Mr. Churchill had agreed to send a joint reply to a message from Stalin dated April 7. Stalin had charged that the United States and Great Britain were responsible for the deadlock over those who were to be invited to take part in the Moscow discussions. He agreed conditionally to the invitation of Mikolajczyk. The joint reply to Stalin was not ready for Mr. Roosevelt's signature before his death, but was sent by Mr. Truman and Mr. Churchill. They denied Stalin's charge and asserted their belief that he was attempting to revert to the position he had originally taken at the beginning of the Yalta Conference—that if any persons were to be added to the Lublin Government he must make certain that they did not affect the Soviet Union's control of it.)

---

* *Op. cit.*, pp. 56, 60 and 61.

On April 21 a reply came from the Soviet Government to the effect that the pact was a natural reflection of the aspirations and vital interests of the Polish and Soviet peoples; that it should not arouse any concern, since it would strengthen friendly relations between Poland and the Soviet Union. These considerations, and the fact that the Soviet Government had already informed the Polish Provisional Government of its agreement to the conclusion of a treaty of friendship and mutual assistance, would not permit the postponement of the signature of the treaty. The note ended with the hypocritical observation that undoubtedly the conclusion of the treaty would have great importance for the future strengthening of the United Nations.

This pact, signed on that date in Moscow, a few hours after the United States Embassy got the note, came into force immediately and was to continue for twenty years. It provided for mutual military and other assistance against Germany until final victory; mutual respect for independence and sovereignty; adoption of measures to remove any threat of repetition of aggression by Germany or any state united with Germany; assistance to be given to the other in the event that either party became involved in hostilities with an aggressive Germany or some state united with Germany; no armistice or peace treaty to be concluded with a Hitlerite government without mutual consent; no participation in any coalition directed against the other contracting party; and postwar collaboration to develop and consolidate economic and cultural ties and restoration of economy.

As in the case of the recognition of the Lublin regime as the Polish Provisional Government shortly before the Yalta meeting, the Soviet Government had again confronted the United States with a *fait accompli* on the eve of an important international conference.

On April 16, the day before Harriman's departure for Washington, he was received by Marshal Stalin. The Generalissimo suggested, in view of the stalemate which had been reached in the labors of the Moscow Commission, that the same formula be used in setting up the new Polish government as had been employed in forming the Yugoslav Government. In other words, four-fifths of the members of the Provisional Government of National Unity would be nominees of the Lublin group and would presumably therefore be Communists or Communist-controlled, while the remaining one-fifth of the portfolios in the cabinet would be given to non-Communist elements, which, according to conservative estimate, represented ninety per cent of the electorate. (When Subašic and Sutej, nominees of the London Yugoslav Government-in-Exile for the coalition government set up as a result of the Yalta Conference, had been removed from it, this same procedure had given Tito and his Communists complete control of the country, regardless of the will of the people.)

Harriman pointed out to Stalin that the Polish and Yugoslav situations were not comparable. He expressed the hope, however, that as Molotov was proceeding to the United States to attend the San Francisco Conference, an opportunity would be afforded the foreign ministers of the three Yalta Powers to reach an understanding on the Polish question.

Any hope of obtaining a satisfactory settlement during Molotov's stay in the United States was soon dissipated. He had arrived in Washington on April 22 and seen President Truman briefly. He had had an extended conference with Secretary of State Stettinius and Foreign Secretary Eden at which Undersecretary Grew, Ambassadors Harriman and Clark-Kerr were present, as well as Mr. Gromyko, the Soviet Ambassador to the United States.

At these conferences Molotov was advised that we could not accept the Yugoslav formula as applied to Poland. He had brought up this proposal, repeating Stalin's suggestion that the proportions used in Yugoslavia be used as a yardstick in selecting the Polish Government. The United States representatives said that the acceptance of such a formula would be counter to the Yalta agreement and that we could not approve the formation of a government which would not be representative of all democratic elements. The disappointment of the United States Government was expressed over the failure of the Soviet

Government to carry out its consultations with Polish leaders other than those who were now members of the Warsaw regime.

It was made very clear to Mr. Molotov that the United States and the other members of the United Nations were prepared to proceed with the plans for world organization, no matter what difficulties or differences might arise over the Polish or any other question.

He was told plainly that the failure of the three principal Allies which had borne the brunt of the war to reach a just settlement of the Polish question would cast most serious doubt on the unity of purpose regarding postwar collaboration. He was reminded of Mr. Roosevelt's message of April 1 to Stalin in which the President in forthright language stated that no policy of the United States, whether foreign or domestic, can succeed unless it enjoys public confidence and support. It was bluntly pointed out to Mr. Molotov that, while the United States had completely lived up to the conditions of the Yalta declaration on Poland, the Soviet Union had failed to do so. President Truman and Prime Minister Churchill had in fact on April 18 sent similar messages to Stalin outlining the last position which we would be willing to accept on the Polish question.

The Soviet Government, although recognizing the impasse which confronted the Moscow Commission, continued to insist throughout the month of April, both through diplomatic channels and through the press, that the Warsaw provisional regime should be invited to San Francisco. The Department of State repeated the reply already given to the Polish Government in London. According to the Department's note to the Soviet Embassy, "the view of the United States Government remains that an invitation to the conference at San Francisco should be extended only to a new Provisional Government of National Unity formed in accordance with the Crimea agreement."

As the discussions between Ambassador Harriman and Marshal Stalin proceeded, I had the privilege of examining Mr. Harriman's reports on them as they came into the State Department from day to day.

At the San Francisco Conference Molotov exploded a diplomatic bombshell. With none of the evasiveness which had marked Vishinsky's disclaimer of information as to the fate of the fifteen Polish leaders who had vanished, Molotov announced to Secretary Stettinius and Foreign Secretary Eden at a dinner on May 3 that sixteen—not fifteen—Polish leaders had been arrested, on the charge that they had engaged in "diversionary activities" in the rear of the Red Army when it was driving the Nazi forces from Poland.

The Soviet press agency, Tass, confirmed this statement on May 5, and added that the accused had maintained illegal radio stations in the rear of the Soviet Army. An investigation was being held in Moscow, the announcement said, which would determine whether the group would be turned over to the Soviet courts.

This statement brought to a head the negotiations among the Yalta Powers. The conversations looking to the formation of the Polish Provisional Government of National Unity, as envisaged by the Yalta decision, were suspended. The attitude of the United States Government was tersely set forth in Stettinius' statement made in San Francisco on May 5, 1945:

For the last month we have been asking the Soviet Government about the report that a number of prominent Polish democratic leaders in Poland had met for discussion with Soviet authorities during the latter part of March. Mr. Molotov has now officially informed Mr. Eden and myself that these leaders were arrested on the charge of "diversionist activities against the Red Army."

We told Mr. Molotov of our great concern on learning, after such a long delay, of this disturbing development which has a direct bearing on the working out of the Polish problem. The Crimea agreement on Poland provided for consultations with representatives of the Warsaw Provisional Government and with Polish democratic political leaders from within Poland and from abroad. We have asked Mr. Molotov for a complete list of the names of these Polish political leaders who have been arrested and a full explanation of this action. Further discussion must await a reply.*

_____
* *New York Times*, May 6, 1945.

From the adamant refusal of the Soviet Government to agree to any Polish leaders, other than the Soviet-controlled Warsaw regime, being invited by the Moscow Commission for consultations, it was clear that it did not desire the establishment of a truly representative government in Poland. And it was shown by the arrest of the sixteen Polish leaders that the Soviet Government would resort to any means necessary to break opposition to the government which it had already imposed on the Polish people. That these arrests should have been made while the Moscow Commission was endeavoring to fulfill its functions as prescribed by the Yalta decision was in itself a cynical disregard of the obligations implicit in that agreement.

Secretary Stettinius, in his speech on April 6 in New York, had stated that the United States Government was doing all in its power to bring about the establishment of the Polish Provisional Government of National Unity envisaged in the Crimean agreement. He expressed disappointment in the delay in carrying out the Crimean decision on Poland, but added that nothing had happened to shake his belief that it would be carried out.

When I heard Mr. Stettinius make this public statement I was greatly surprised and chagrined, because I knew of no development reported by Ambassador Harriman which would give rise to such hopefulness. Had not Molotov indicated that, due to our insistence on the outstanding Polish leader Mikolajczyk being invited for consultation, the Moscow Commission could make no further progress?

Since at San Francisco, too, the press reflected the apparent optimism of the United States delegation regarding the conversations then taking place among Stettinius, Molotov and Eden, I decided to put my views before Acting Secretary Grew. This I did in a memorandum dated May 4, before I knew of Molotov's statement of May 3 about the arrests of the sixteen Polish leaders. The pertinent portion of my memorandum follows:

Since April there have taken place the abortive conversations in Washington with Molotov and Eden, the further telegraphic ex-

changes between President Truman, Mr. Churchill and Marshal
Stalin, and the present conversations at San Francisco between the
three Foreign Secretaries.

The San Francisco conversations have been characterized, both
officially and in the press, as presenting a more hopeful picture of the
Polish question because of the reported willingness of Marshal Stalin
to permit Mikolajczyk and perhaps Grabski or Stanczyk to proceed to
Moscow in accordance with the terms of the Yalta agreement. The
record does not, however, justify optimism. No American or British
observers of the Moscow commission have been permitted to enter
Poland to investigate conditions; 15 Polish underground leaders, under assurances of their personal safety, left for a conference with Soviet authorities on March 29 and have not been heard from since; in
other "liberated" countries in which Soviet military forces have control, our representatves are confronted with the greatest obstacles in
obtaining information. Even should Mikolajczyk proceed to Moscow,
what assurance can we have that he will be allowed to participate in
the formation of a free, democratic and independent government or
that he will not disappear in the same manner as the 15 underground
leaders? In my opinion Stalin, sensing that President Truman intends to adopt a strong stand with respect to Poland, is now endeavoring to temporize by offering, as a concession, a principle already
agreed upon at Yalta.*

I view with grave apprehension any public manifestation of hopefulness on our part. Not only is such an attitude an encouragement to
the Soviet Government to persist in its present policy to prevent the
formation of a truly democratic and independent government but it
gives to the American people an erroneous impression of the present
state of relations between Great Britain and ourselves, on the one
hand, and the Soviet Union, on the other.

There is only one satisfactory solution: to stand firm on our final
position as communicated in President Truman's message of April 18
and in Mr. Churchill's telegram of April 28 to Marshal Stalin. Any
deviation or compromise on our part will be interpreted as weakness
by the Soviet Government and will merely serve to encourage it to
make further demands or conditions. It would, furthermore, be disastrous to the prestige and interests of the United States.

---

* This clause should have read: "the acceptance of a principle already agreed upon at
Yalta."—A.B.L.

I recall your telling me on April 25 at Blair House that the Department would maintain a strong position with respect to Poland. Since my convictions conform so fully to such a stand, I feel the present moment appropriate for me to state that it is only on the basis of the maintenance of this position that I could conscientiously continue in my present position.

Mr. Grew read this memorandum in my presence and said, "I agree one hundred per cent with your views."

CHAPTER SEVEN

Reluctant Departure

THE Polish problem was only one of many at that period which were affecting our relations with the Soviet Union and giving our government great concern. The Yalta agreement had already, although barely four months old, been violated by the Soviet Government in six countries—Austria, Bulgaria, Hungary, Rumania, Yugoslavia and Czechoslovakia—as well as in Poland. (It had been violated in Albania, too, but as we did not then have a representative in that country there was as yet no official record in the Department of State.)

In Austria the Soviet Government had permitted Dr. Karl Renner to form a provisional government despite our having expressed the hope that no action would be taken until the Allies had been able to consult with one another in accordance with the Yalta decision. The Soviet official excuse, as conveyed to the American Embassy in Moscow by Vice-Commissar Vishinsky on May 3, 1945, was that the Soviet forces operating on Austrian territory required the organization of an administration composed of local persons. Completely ignoring the terms of the Yalta decision, Vishinsky stated that it was exactly this type of organization which had been created by the formation of the Provisional Austrian Government through the agreement of the leaders of all of the democratic "non-Fascist" Austrian parties.

In Bulgaria Communist pressure had been behind an endeavor to hold elections on the basis of a single election list which would give the Communists representation out of all proportion to their actual voting strength. When the United States Government brought this to the attention of the Soviet Government and suggested that a tripartite Allied committee be constituted in Bulgaria to insure that all democratic groups would have full freedom to present their platforms and lists of candidates to the attention of the voters, the Soviet Government questioned the motives of the United States and said that the Soviet public would be dumfounded if there were foreign interference in Bulgarian elections!

Contrary to the spirit of the Yalta decision, the Soviet Government had also intervened directly in the internal affairs of Hungary. On March 13, 1945, Marshal Voroshilov informed the Prime Minister that he "could not accept any responsibility for what might happen if the land reform bill were not acted upon within ten days."

In Rumania Vishinsky had demanded that King Mihai should dismiss the Radescu Government, and on March 1 Vishinsky named Groza as the Soviet choice for Prime Minister. The King was forced on March 6 to accept the Groza Government when Vishinsky said that failure to do so would be considered by his government as a hostile act. Although the Yalta decision had been signed only three weeks before this development, the Soviet representatives in Rumania had not consulted with their American colleagues or kept them informed. When Ambassador Harriman, in Moscow, reminded the Soviet Government of common Allied responsibilities in Rumania and our desire for an exchange of views on the situation, the Soviet Government merely replied that the Radescu Government was unrepresentative, Fascist, and incapable of maintaining order. Finally, on March 14, the United States formally invoked the Crimean declaration and proposed tripartite consultation on the political situation in Rumania. But our proposal was bluntly rejected by the Soviet Government on March 17 on the ground that order had been restored and that no steps were necessary.

In Yugoslavia, in March 1945, the agreement between Tito and Subašic, who was soon to be eliminated from the government, was implemented by the appointment of a regency council. The formation of an enlarged legislative body as recommended by the Crimea Conference had not yet taken place, but Communist-dominated governments had been set up in the six federal states and in each case no semblance of democratic procedure had been followed.

In addition to these cases indicating its intention to disregard the provisions of the Yalta decision, the Soviet Government had taken other action in these satellite states directly at variance with the interests of the United States:

In Bulgaria the representative of the United States was not permitted to participate actively in the work of the Bulgarian Allied Control Commission.

Although the Czechoslovak Government informed the Soviet Government on February 9, 1945, of its plan to bring to Czechoslovakia Allied diplomats accredited to the Czechoslovak Government-in-Exile in London, the Soviet Government refused to give permits for them to pass over Rumanian territory then under Soviet military control. In consequence, members of the United States Embassy staff were not able to arrive in Prague until May 29, 1945.

In Hungary the Soviet authorities failed to inform the United States representative to the Allied Control Commission about various measures taken, even though some directly affected American property interests. Besides, the plant of the Tungsram, in which American citizens had a substantial interest, was dismantled and removed to the Soviet Union despite American protests.

In Rumania the Soviet Government removed to the Soviet Union the petroleum field equipment of American oil companies and refused to permit representatives of American-owned companies to enter the country.

It was so evident from these developments that the Soviet Government did not intend to live up to its commitments under the Yalta decision that, under date of June 1, 1945, I submitted a memorandum at the request of the Department of State, giving my recommendations as to what our next steps should be in our relations with Poland.

I suggested that my resignation as Ambassador—which had been submitted as a matter of customary procedure when the new President, Mr. Truman, took office—should be accepted and that the other members of my staff then in Washington should be assigned to other duties. I also recommended that Mr. Schoenfeld, as chargé d'affaires ad interim with the rank of minister, be retained in London, thus enabling our government to continue to communicate officially with at least one group of representative Poles.

I set forth to the Department that if these principles regarding the American Embassy to Poland be carried out before the next Big Three meeting, which was to be held in Potsdam in July and August 1945, it would serve to emphasize to the American public that, as a result of the unilateral actions of the Soviet authorities, this government was deeply disappointed and pessimistic over the situation in Poland. I maintained that the suggested action, if taken immediately, would indicate that the United States Government had no intention of appeasing the Soviet Government further, and that we definitely refused to whitewash the Soviet-controlled regime in Warsaw as a democratic government. I felt that such action would be a source of satisfaction to the other United Nations which looked to the United States for leadership in democracy. I recommended also that we seriously consider the advisability of giving publicity to the situation in all Soviet-controlled countries, of which Poland was an important example.

Suddenly and secretly, in the last days of May, Harry Hopkins and Bohlen left for Moscow in the hope of persuading Stalin to modify his intransigent attitude on the formation of the Provisional Government of National Unity.

Hopkins had visited Stalin first in 1941 immediately after the Nazi attack on the Soviet Union. He had been instrumental then in arranging for the granting of Lend-Lease assistance to the Soviet Government at an hour when Russia was dangerously pressed. This had won him Stalin's confidence. Probably he would have a better chance than anyone to influence Stalin toward a more reasonable point of view.

I was, however, filled with misgivings over the Hopkins mission. I feared that, with a view to achieving unity among the Yalta Powers, a compromise would be reached which would result in the Warsaw Government remaining as the authority in power in Poland. Then, as had been the rule in other satellite states, I feared that the really democratic elements would be eliminated from the government. Furthermore, I feared, since so much time had already been lost since the Yalta agreement, that surely the Warsaw Government had, through the aid of the Soviet secret police, been able to build up its own political organization to the detriment of all opposing parties.

In fact, the Communist-controlled Polish Socialist Party (PPS) and Peasant Party (SL) had already been established in Poland following the "liberation" of the country by the Soviet forces.

Parties with these identical names had existed in Poland for years. Zygmunt Zulawski, a courageous democrat and a famed orator, was the leader of the genuine Polish Socialist Party (founded in 1892) which, although representing ninety per cent of the Socialists in the country, was not permitted to operate as an independent political organization. Witos, the leader of the genuine Peasant Party, which had been in existence for fifty years, was, after his death, to be succeeded by Mikolajczyk. The original and non-Communist branch of the party changed its name in the summer of 1945 to Polish Peasant Party (PSL), not only to avoid confusion but also to emphasize that it was Polish and not foreign in character. A Communist-controlled Democratic Party had also been set up. Subsequently a schism would take place in the Christian Labor Party, generally known as the Catholic party, dividing it into a Communist and a non-Communist branch.

Thus, in June 1945, there were five recognized parties: Polish Workers, Polish Socialist, Democratic, Peasant, and Christian Labor. The establishment of the Polish Peasant Party was to raise the total to six.

Regardless of the failure of the Moscow Commission to arrange for the setting up of a Provisional Government of National Unity, the framework of a government was being organized. The executive branch, headed by E. Osóbka-Morawski as Prime Minister, had stemmed from the early Lublin days. In addition, a legislative branch, known as the National Council of the Homeland, had been formed under the presidency of Boleslaw Bierut. Abbreviated as KRN, it was appointed by the Lublin Government and not elected by the people. It had one or two representatives in the smallest villages, a larger number as the size of the towns increased, and even more important representation in the capital of each of the twenty-eight states, and, finally, the Presidium, or presiding board, the controlling body of the KRN in Warsaw. This latter was headed by Bierut and was composed of six other members.

The functions of the National Council were primarily to legislate and, as the delegates were appointed by the government in power, it was to be expected that they would follow the government line. No matter what the proportion of other parties in representing the electorate, the government minority group was always able to exercise control. The KRN was in substance a provisional legislative body acting until such time as elections could be held to the Sejm, or parliament.

But there was one group in Poland about which nothing was officially said. It was generally known, however, that this group, which corresponded to the Politburo in the Soviet Union, acted under the direction of the Kremlin and was the controlling force in Poland. Its members were all of the Polish Workers Party: Jakób Berman, who was later to be Undersecretary of State for the Council of Ministers; Hilary Minc, later to be Minister of Industry; Colonel Roman Zambrowski, a liaison officer between the Russian Secret Police and the Polish Ministry of Security; Wladyslaw Gomulka, Secretary General of the Polish Workers Party; Jerzy Borejsza, Director of the government-controlled Printing Co-operative, known as the Czytelnik; and General Marian Spychalski, who corresponded to a political commissar in the Red Army.

When word came to me of Hopkins' departure for Moscow, I immediately sought an interview with the Acting Secretary of State, Joseph C. Grew, a close friend under whom I had had the privilege of serving in Bern in 1922, and in Washington in 1924 and 1925 when he was first appointed Undersecretary of State. I mentioned to him on June 1 my view that we should not make any compromise with the Soviet Government on the Polish question, for I felt that any deviation from the strong position we recently had assumed would merely serve to encourage Stalin to make further demands on us. I asked Grew, therefore, if he would arrange for me to see President Truman as soon as possible.

Grew, who expressed cordial agreement with my views, said he felt sure the United States would not weaken in that position. He had strongly advocated the maintenance of active control of strategic air and naval bases, appreciating that the most fatal thing for the United States would be to place any confidence in the sincerity of the men in the Kremlin. I knew he had advocated a stiffening of our policy toward the Soviet Union all along the line. When he volunteered to accompany me to the interview with the President, which was fixed for June 4, at 12:20 P.M., I was delighted, for I felt sure he would give me his moral support. He did.

At a meeting with the President on April 25, when he had received at Blair House all the American ambassadors and ministers who then happened to be in Washington, our conversation on the Polish question had of course been of the briefest nature.

On June 4, as I walked from the State Department to the Executive Offices with Mr. Grew, I said I intended to make my remarks to the President as brief as possible so as better to emphasize my point: the necessity of our not compromising on the principles to which we had agreed at Yalta.

President Truman received us immediately on arrival, was most cordial and appeared keenly interested in the exposition of my point of view.

I outlined to the President, in Mr. Grew's presence, my apprehensions over the possibility of our being able to fulfill our Yalta commitments because of the Soviet obstructionist attitude. As earnestly as was in my power I expressed my feeling that we should under no condition appease the Soviet Government by agreeing to its proposal on the composition of the Polish Government, i.e., adoption of the Yugoslav formula. To do so would be to abandon the Yalta agreement. I also referred to the most unfortunate effect which had been created by the arrest of the sixteen Polish leaders. This, I said, was conclusive evidence of the Soviet Government's intention to disrupt the Yalta commitments to set up a Polish government representative of the people.

I came away from this conference satisfied that the President fully understood the situation and would pursue a course thoroughly in keeping with the American tradition of fulfilling international commitments. I was encouraged, too, by noting that the President, unlike his predecessor when I last saw him, appeared in the best of health, vigorous and determined.

From what I learned later, Hopkins pointed out to Stalin that the effect on the American people, if it became known that the Soviet Government was, through the employment of various tactics, preventing the formation of the type of government for Poland that had been agreed on at Yalta, would be most unfortunate. He also emphasized that once the details of the arrest of the sixteen Polish leaders became known the Soviet Government would be severely criticized.

Apparently Hopkins was able to impress on Stalin the seriousness of the situation. It is my understanding that Stalin told Hopkins the Polish leaders would be dealt with leniently, the only serious charge against them being that they were in possession of clandestine radio transmitters which might be used to the detriment of the Red Army. Nevertheless, Stalin did not promise to release them! But he did agree to send invitations to various political leaders in Poland and in London, including Mikolajczyk.

Because of Stalin's acquiescence, the Moscow Commission was once more in a position to operate and issue invitations. On June 19, the following announcement was made simultaneously in Washington, London and Moscow regarding the Poles to be invited in conformity with the Crimea decision.

The People's Commissar for Foreign Affairs of the U.S.S.R., V. M. Molotov, the British Ambassador, Sir Archibald Clark-Kerr, and the Ambassador of the United States of America, Mr. W. A. Harriman, authorized by the Crimea Conference of the three Allied powers to consult with members of the Provisional Polish Government and with other democratic leaders in Poland and abroad concerning the re-organization of the Provisional Polish Government on a broader democratic basis with the inclusion of democratic leaders from Poland itself and Poles from abroad, and concerning the formation of a Po-lish Provisional Government of National Unity, have agreed that the following persons should be invited for the above-mentioned consul-tations envisaged in the Crimea agreement on Poland:

1. Representatives of the Polish Provisional Government.

According to information received from Warsaw, Boleslaw Bierut, Edward Osóbka-Morawski, Wladyslaw Kowalski and Wladyslaw Gomulka have been appointed representatives of the Polish Pro-visional Government.

2. Democratic leaders from Poland: Wincenty Witos, Zgymunt Zulawski, Stanislaw Kutrzeba, Adam Krzyzanowski and Henryk Kolodjieski.

3. Democratic leaders from abroad: Stanislaw Mikolajczyk, Jan Stanczyk and Julian Zakowski.

All the above-mentioned persons have been invited to arrive in Moscow by June 15.

With the exception of Wincenty Witos, all the persons who were invited accepted.

But on June 19, four days after their arrival, the trial of the sixteen arrested Polish leaders was begun in Moscow. The Moscow press gave great prominence to this trial, which overshadowed the meetings of the various Polish leaders who had been invited by the Moscow commission. The Yalta agreement was brushed aside in favor of physical force.

Despite Stalin's assurances to Hopkins that the principal charge against the accused was the operation of illegal radio transmitters, the following allegations were brought against them by the prosecutor:

1. Organization of subversive activities in the rear of the Red Army.

2. Deceiving the Soviet command regarding the alleged dissolution of the Home Army.

3. Execution of terroristic and diversionary acts in the rear of the Red Army.

4. Maintenance and operation of illegal radio transmitters and concealing supplies of arms.

5. Conducting espionage activities on behalf of the London government.

6. Publication of underground newspapers containing propaganda against the U.S.S.R. and the Red Army.

With the exception of General Okulicki, all the accused confessed to the charges.*

I was to learn that the sixteen had been taken to Moscow by airplane, thinking they were proceeding to London; that the plane had landed in the snow in a field many miles from Moscow, in the wintry weather at the end of March; that they had been taken to the Lubianka prison in Moscow where each had been placed in solitary confinement. During their imprisonment they had been subjected to continual exposure, night and day, to glaring electric light, preventing rest or sleep. Questioned and requestioned under this mental torture for weeks, they finally admitted to the charges and readily confessed them when interrogated publicly by the prosecutor. It was a repetition of the technique employed in the Moscow trials of 1937—a technique now in use in all Soviet-dominated nations.

The holding of this trial during the Moscow conversations must

---

* Three of the sixteen were pronounced innocent and acquitted; another, owing to illness, was not tried; the other twelve were condemned to imprisonments ranging from four months to ten years. All who had not completed their prison terms at the time of the amnesty granted in 1946 were then released. But Stanislaw Mierzwa, who had been deputy secretary-general of Mikolajczyk's Peasant Party, was rearrested in the summer of 1947, tried by a military court in Kraków and sentenced to fifteen years' imprisonment, on the fabricated charge of treasonably giving information to the British and American Ambassadors (Mr. Victor Cavendish-Bentinck and me). Kasimierz Baginski, vice-president of the Council of National Unity, who had been sentenced at the Moscow trials to a year in prison, reportedly escaped from Poland in October 1947.

have given a most uneasy feeling to the non-Communist Polish leaders there. It undoubtedly indicated to them what their fate might be if they should adopt an attitude in opposition to the Communist nucleus composing the government to be constituted. Certainly this judicial farce must have greatly diminished the prospects of the non-Communist group of reaching a satisfactory understanding. And, even more significantly, it indicated Stalin's disregard of American public opinion for, as soon as Hopkins had left Moscow, he had defiantly held the trial while the meetings with the Moscow Commission were on.

Those of us who were eagerly following Polish affairs in the Department of State were not sanguine of any agreement, for we doubted that the elements independent of the Warsaw Government could accept a compromise which would deprive them of a majority control. It was a surprise, therefore, when a telegram from Moscow reached the Department to the effect that on June 21 conversations among the Poles had taken a favorable turn. It had been agreed that the presidency of the National Council of the Homeland should be entrusted to Bierut; that Osóbka-Morawski should be Premier, or President of the Council of Ministers; and that Gomulka and Mikolajczyk should be vice-premiers. The Ministry of Foreign Affairs was to be assigned to Wincenty Rzymowski, president of the Democratic Party; the portfolios of Public Administration, Education, Agriculture and Public Health would be allotted to Mikolajczyk's Peasant Party; the Ministry of National Defense was to be under Marshal Rola-Zymierski, technically a nonparty man; the Socialists would have the portfolios of Justice, Finance and Reconstruction; while the Communists would obtain the strategic ministries of Public Security, Restituted Western Territories, Industry, Propaganda, Navigation and Foreign Trade.

The newly formed government then proceeded to Warsaw where a popular demonstration was accorded Mikolajczyk as the various members drove into the city from the airport. On the other hand, the Lublin group, now the nucleus of the government, was still little known, except as Soviet stooges, and was ignored by the populace.

How could one expect the people to wax enthusiastic over their arrival?

The turn of events in Moscow had not tempered my pessimism. I still stood by the views expressed in my memorandum of June 1. But, when I consulted a friend of old standing in the State Department—one of our foremost experts on the Soviet Union and Poland—he strongly advised me not to relinquish my post, even though he agreed with me that under Soviet control "free and unfettered" elections could not be held in Poland. His argument was: First, that if I did not proceed as the first Ambassador to reconstituted Poland it was quite possible that certain elements in the United States, which were strongly in favor of appeasing Stalin, might succeed in bringing about the appointment of an envoy who would whitewash Communist activities in Poland and would thus further contribute to the Polish betrayal. In this connection he said that it would be most important for our government to have the reports of a professional observer who would transmit the facts and would not be deceived by the appearances which it was customary for Communists to fabricate. Consequently, he argued, it was essential for the Polish people to feel that we were establishing contact with them through one whose friendship for the Polish nation had been known from the past. He said, and I agreed, that we must distinguish between the Polish people and that minority of the Polish Government which had been imposed by Moscow, and which would undoubtedly control the country.

The logic of my friend's presentation of the case convinced me that I would indeed be doing a disservice not only to my own government but to the Polish people if I withdrew from my assignment at that crucial time. Recognition of the Polish Provisional Government of National Unity by the United States and Great Britain was expected momentarily, and my staff and I would be asked to leave for Europe as soon as this legal formality was announced. And so, with serious misgivings, I decided to go whenever the call should come.

In preparation for leaving I made arrangements on June 26 with the War Department to put at the disposal of our staff a C-54 plane to transport us from Washington to Paris as soon as I had definite instructions to proceed to Warsaw. Members of our staff were told (secretly, because of wartime restrictions) to be ready to leave on short notice.

In the meantime word was sent to President Bierut and his collaborators, through Ambassador Harriman, that the United States expected certain normal facilities to be accorded to us on arrival, such as freedom of communication, transportation within the country and the establishment of consular offices in Poland. We also emphasized the importance of permitting American newspaper correspondents to enter Poland freely and to report on conditions without molestation. While the Department of State did not make recognition of the new government conditional on the granting of these facilities, it pointed out that prompt compliance would speed up the establishment of normal diplomatic relations.

Word came from the members of the new Polish Provisional Government of National Unity that they would gladly accede to all our requests. Agreement was reached with the British Government that announcement of recognition by the United States and United Kingdom would be made simultaneously on July 5, 1945.

On July 3, Mr. James F. Byrnes assumed the duties of Secretary of State.

The next day, the Fourth of July, I had an appointment to see the new Secretary at 10:00 A.M. Because of the heavy pressure of business which was thrust on Mr. Byrnes he was able to give me only the briefest of interviews. In fact, he received me together with my friends, Dr. Frank P. Corrigan, Ambassador to Venezuela, and Nelson A. Rockefeller, Assistant Secretary of State. The Secretary was so pressed for time that we remained standing, as did he, during the few seconds we had to wish him well in his important position.

I did inform the Secretary, however, that everything was in order for recognition of the new Polish Government on the following day, and that I expected to leave early the next morning for my new post.

Mr. Byrnes, despite his preoccupation, was friendly and cordial. Nevertheless, I was deeply disappointed that I would not have a chance, before proceeding to take up my duties, to discuss with him one of the thorniest problems confronting the United States.

Mr. Byrnes effected the recognition of the Polish Provisional Government of National Unity on July 5, through a telegram replying to the suggestion of Edward Osóbka-Morawski, President of the Council of Ministers, that diplomatic relations be initiated. Mr. Byrnes added the announcement that President Truman had designated me United States Ambassador.

CHAPTER EIGHT

Potsdam Interlude

AT NOON on July 5 my wife and I, accompanied by the nucleus of the staff of our Embassy to Poland, left Gravelly Point airport, Washington, by the special C-54 plane. Because we believed that very limited accommodations would be available in Warsaw, our group was confined to twelve.* After a brief stop early that evening at Gander, Newfoundland, for refueling, we flew directly to Paris and arrived in time for lunch on July 6.

Immediately upon arrival we telephoned to Ambassador Robert D. Murphy, Political Adviser to General Eisenhower, at Frankfurt, for permission to traverse the Soviet zone en route to Warsaw. Murphy, a valued friend of many years' standing, promised to take up the matter with Marshal Zhukov at once. We also made preliminary arrangements with the United States Army authorities so that three planes would be available to us, once permission was obtained from the Soviet authorities, to convey our staff as well as thirty-four tons of food and office supplies from Paris to Warsaw.

At the suggestion of Ambassador Caffery, Keith, Elbrick and I called at the Quai d'Orsay to obtain the latest available information from the French Foreign Office officials dealing with Poland. We learned that Monsieur Roger Garreau, who had been in Warsaw to arrange for the repatriation of French military personnel liberated from Nazi imprisonment by the Red Army in Poland, would be French Ambassador at Warsaw. We were told that Mr. Jedrychowski, who had until now been in Paris as the representative of the Polish Com-

---

* It consisted of the following, besides my wife and me: Messrs. Keith, Elbrick, Dorsz, Dillon, Jacobs and Major Hresan, and Misses McNulty, Hille, Wallence and Springer.

mittee of National Liberation, had just been app
Navigation and Foreign Trade and was leaving ?
No diplomatic representative of the new Provis
National Unity had yet been appointed in F
French official who had just returned from Warsav,,
received a great ovation on his arrival in Poland from Mu.
he was evidently the most popular personality in the new government.

Later that afternoon we called on Mr. Jedrychowski and his assistant Mr. Bekier, who received us very cordially. They were the first
new government officials whom we had met. They assured us that
they would grant us visas to permit all members of our group to proceed to Warsaw, and would obtain general permission for our first
flight into Poland and for our first automobile convoy, which would
take those supplies too bulky to transport by airplane. I informed
Jedrychowski that we were then awaiting a report from Lieutenant
Tonesk, who should be about to arrive in Warsaw from Moscow, as
to housing conditions. The number of our first group would depend
on this information. It was agreed that Jedrychowski and I would
both approach the Soviet Ambassador in Paris for permission for our
planes and convoy to cross the Soviet military zone in Germany
en route to Poland. In taking leave of these two officials of the new
regime, I emphasized the great interest of the people of the United
States in the welfare of Poland and their consequent desire to see our
mission established.

On July 9 Mr. Caffery took me to call on the Soviet Ambassador,
Mr. Alexander Bogomolov, a tall, heavy-set man, who had formerly
been Ambassador to the Polish Government-in-Exile in London. He
impressed me as scholarly and keenly intelligent, with charm of manner and a sense of humor. The conversation for the most part was
general. Bogomolov asked what our policy was going to be with regard to the new government. I replied that President Truman's statement expressing satisfaction on the establishment of relations spoke
for itself. I added that my aim would be to maintain friendliest relations with Poland, with which the United States was so intimately

because of the large community in the United States of American citizens of Polish descent. Bogomolov advised me to obtain permission to cross Soviet-controlled territory in Germany through Marshal Zhukov.

On July 10 I had my first contact with officers of the Polish Army taking their orders from Warsaw when Colonel Naszkowski and Lieutenant Szczerba of the Polish Military Mission called on me. They wished to make contact, now that official diplomatic relations had been established between Warsaw and Washington, with United States Army headquarters in Frankfurt to arrange for the repatriation to Poland of members of the Polish Army who had been liberated by the United States and who were consequently in the American zone of occupation in Germany. This was my first association with the problem which later was to emerge as a most bitter controversy between the Polish Government and the officers and men of the Polish Army abroad. The latter, under the command of General Anders, had for the most part refused to return to Poland, except under certain conditions, including the retention of their arms and guarantees of their personal safety. But, regardless of pious expressions of hope that the Army would return so that free and unfettered elections could be held, I always seriously doubted the Polish Government's desire for the repatriation of the Polish Army or of Polish displaced persons. Nationalistic and anti-Communist by tradition, the cream of the Polish Army would have constituted a serious element of opposition to the Polish Government.

In this case I communicated their desire to Colonel Anthony J. D. Biddle, my predecessor in Warsaw, then acting as liaison officer between General Eisenhower's headquarters and foreign army groups. Colonel Biddle stated he would be glad to confer with Colonel Naszkowski, but pointed out the difficulties of Naszkowski's having contact with the Polish officers in the American zone because of the open hostility of the latter to the new Warsaw Government, which they regarded as imposed by the Russians and therefore not representative of the people.

In reference to housing our staff in Warsaw, Naszkowski, who had recently returned from there, said that the Hotel Polonia was still in existence, that there were gas and electricity in the city, which however was practically destroyed. He was very optimistic over the food situation, open markets having been established in the city squares. He said that as of that date Warsaw had a population of about three hundred thousand as contrasted with its prewar population of more than one million, and estimated that five hundred thousand people had been killed in Warsaw, excluding those deported or executed outside the city.

Although almost daily in touch by telephone with Ambassador Murphy's office at Frankfurt, we received no satisfactory word from the Soviet authorities for our group to proceed to Poland. Obviously the oral assurance which I had from Jedrychowski would be of no avail in crossing the Soviet military zone. On Murphy's suggestion, therefore, Dorsz and I flew to Frankfurt on July 17 where I called on General Eisenhower, as well as on Lieutenant General J. K. Cannon, commander of the American Air Forces in the European Theater. We received the utmost co-operation from these high Army officers, who assured us that we would receive the transport equipment necessary for our flight and for our automobile convoy. They stressed, however, the absolute necessity of obtaining Soviet acquiescence. In the past there had been unfortunate incidents, including the shooting down of our planes, when clearance had not been formally secured. General Eisenhower promised to do everything possible to facilitate our getting permission from Zhukov.

Frankfurt was the first bombed city I had seen since I had been in Belgrade after its bombardment in 1941. Belgrade, in comparison, had been undamaged. Row on row of houses, especially in the industrial part of the city, had been blown to bits. It was a shell of the Frankfurt I had last visited in 1936, but I was told that it was far less damaged than Berlin, Hamburg or Essen.

During the days that followed while we awaited our clearance, we had numerous talks with Mr. C. H. Matthieson of the Office of Army-

Navy Liquidation Commission and representatives of his organization about our desire to allocate one thousand trucks for the use of the Polish Government from United States Army surplus war material. They indicated their willingness to transfer the material at once, provided a duly authorized representative of the Polish Government would come to Paris, sign the necessary documents and choose the types of automotive vehicles most needed.

Having in mind the necessity of maintaining the morale of our staff, especially during the cold, dark Polish winter months, we approached Major General Sawbridge, Chief of the Office of Special Services, hoping to obtain a weekly series of sixteen-millimeter motion picture films and a continuous supply of books and magazines such as were being furnished to United States Army personnel. General Sawbridge said that motion-picture distributors in general insisted that films in the possession of the Army could be shown only to men in uniform, except in an "isolated spot." The general felt sure that Warsaw could accurately be so designated. Thanks to his assistance, we received regularly for months to come motion pictures and other material which helped to brighten the otherwise dreary evenings of our staff.

On July 25 Murphy telephoned from Berlin that at last Soviet permission for our flight across Germany had been received—"signed, sealed and delivered." As several days' advance notice was necessary, we made arrangements to leave Paris via Berlin on July 30.

During my stay in Paris I had talks daily with Ambassador Caffery or with members of his staff. When I called on the Ambassador on July 27 he told me that he had just returned from a visit to the Potsdam Conference. He said he had been suddenly summoned there in connection with French participation in the decisions, and he told me to my great surprise that President Bierut and other members of the Polish Provisional Government of National Unity were then in Potsdam. Caffery was not aware of the nature of the conversations between the Poles and the Big Three at Potsdam, but he understood that the principal problems discussed were economic and those relating to frontiers. I felt regret that I had not been officially informed of these developments so that I might be prepared on arrival in Warsaw to deal with the government with an accurate understanding of current matters.

We took off from Villacoublay airport on Monday morning, July 30, at 8:30. It was a bright, cool day with a tang of autumn in the air. On the three-hour flight to Berlin, a few miles to the east of Rheims and directly over Bonn where we crossed the Rhine, our three airplanes flew together, the wing tips seeming almost to touch. Although the country in France and Germany seemed rich and well-cultivated, almost all rail and road bridges were down. Arriving at Gatow airport, which was being used under United States Army jurisdiction as the air terminal for the Big Three conference, we were met by Brigadier General Cutler and Colonel Jones, the commanding officer at the field, who took us to luncheon at the officers' mess. Our good friends Donald Heath and Jacob Beam, from Ambassador Murphy's staff, joined us there and soon afterward we had the welcome company of Ambassador Harriman, who had been summoned from Moscow to attend the Potsdam Conference.

During luncheon General Cutler told us that the weather had taken a turn for the worse and, as communication between the Gatow and Warsaw airports was nonexistent, he strongly advised that we spend the night at Babelsberg, where President Truman, Secretary Byrnes and all personnel of the United States delegation were housed, and go on to Warsaw in the morning. I greatly welcomed his advice, for this would give me the opportunity to ascertain from the American delegation the developments of the Conference affecting Poland and would also enable me to meet the principal members of the Polish Government.

After luncheon Keith and I drove into Babelsberg with Averell Harriman, who recounted to us in a general way the purpose of inviting the Polish Government: the question of the holding of elections; the granting of economic assistance; the determination of Polish boundaries; the transfer of population incidental to territorial transfers or wartime displacements; and the participation of Poland in reparations, war crime trials, as well as in international activities, such as relief. Harriman, who had taken such a keen and sympathetic interest in the Polish problem, said to me earnestly, "I feel that I am handing over to you my own child."

On arrival at Babelsberg I called on Assistant Secretary Dunn and H. Freeman Matthews, Director of the Office of European Affairs. Dunn told me he had recommended to Secretary Byrnes that I be summoned to Potsdam so as to acquaint myself with the proceedings affecting Poland, but for some reason Mr. Byrnes did not consider my presence necessary. Dunn showed me the draft resolutions respecting Poland, which left under Polish administration that part of Germany east of the Oder and the western Neisse rivers, as well as that portion of East Prussia south of a line drawn roughly east and west a few miles to the south of Königsberg. The Polish Government was to be required to make a commitment to hold free and unfettered elections as soon as possible, and Allied newspaper correspondents were to be permitted to enter Poland freely and report on conditions before and during elections. These drafted resolutions were subsequently accepted and incorporated in the Potsdam Declaration, which was completed on August 2, but the final text of which did not reach me in Warsaw until many weeks after. For convenience, that part of the text relating to Poland is quoted here:*

The Conference considered questions relating to the Polish Provisional Government and the western boundary of Poland.

A. On the Polish Provisional Government of National Unity they defined their attitude in the following statement:

We have taken note with pleasure of the agreement reached among representative Poles from Poland and abroad which has made possible the formation, in accordance with the decisions reached at the Crimea conference, of a Polish Provisional Government of National Unity recognized by the three Powers. The establishment by the British and United States Governments of diplomatic relations with the Polish Provisional Government has resulted in the withdrawal of their recognition from the former Polish Government in London, which no longer exists.

---

* From *International Declarations* (London: National Peace Council), 1945.

OUR EMBASSY STAFF EN ROUTE TO WARSAW

Left to right: Frederickson; Miss McNulty; Chylinski; Miss Hille; Jenkins; Jacobs; Lane; Elbrick; Mrs. Lane; Keith; Dillon; Miss Yarborough; Dorsz; Gist; and Major Treece.

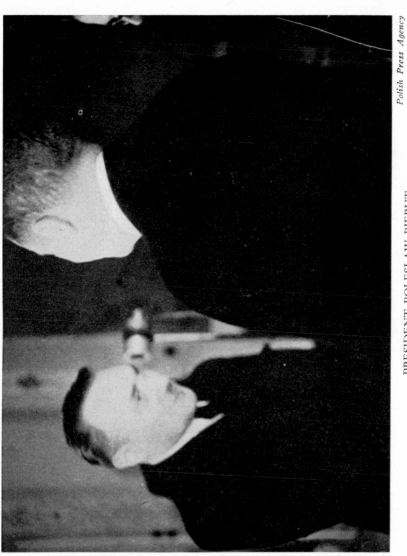

PRESIDENT BOLESLAW BIERUT

His resemblance to Hitler and his evasive glance were widely remarked

Polish Press Agency

The British and United States Governments have taken measures to protect the interest of the Polish Provisional Government, as the recognized Government of the Polish State, in the property belonging to the Polish State located in their territories and under their control, whatever the form of this property may be. They have further taken measures to prevent alienation to third parties of such property. All proper facilities will be given to the Polish Provisional Government for the exercise of the ordinary legal remedies for the recovery of any property belonging to the Polish State which may have been wrongfully alienated.

The three Powers are anxious to assist the Polish Provisional Government in facilitating the return to Poland as soon as practicable of all Poles abroad who wish to go, including members of the Polish armed forces and the merchant marine. They expect that those Poles who return home shall be accorded personal and property rights on the same basis as all Polish citizens.

The three Powers note that the Polish Provisional Government, in accordance with the decisions of the Crimea conference, has agreed to the holding of free and unfettered elections as soon as possible on the basis of universal suffrage and secret ballot, in which all democratic and anti-Nazi parties shall have the right to take part and to put forward candidates, and that representatives of the Allied Press shall enjoy full freedom to report to the world upon developments in Poland before and during the elections.

B. The following agreement was reached on the western frontier of Poland:

In conformity with the agreement on Poland reached at the Crimea conference, the three heads of Government have sought the opinion of the Polish Provisional Government of National Unity in regard to the accession of territory in the north and west which Poland should receive. The President of the National Council of Poland and members of the Polish Provisional Government of National Unity have been received at the conference and have fully presented their views. The three heads of Government reaffirm their opinion that the final delimitation of the western frontier of Poland should await the peace settlement.

The three heads of Government agree that, pending the final determination of Poland's western frontier, the former German territories east of a line running from the Baltic Sea immediately west of Swinemunde, and thence along the Oder River to the confluence of the western Neisse River and along the western Neisse to the Czecho-slovak frontier, including that portion of East Prussia not placed under the administration of the Union of Soviet Socialist Republics in accordance with the understanding reached at this conference and including the area of the former free city of Danzig, shall be under the administration of the Polish State and for such purposes should not be considered as part of the Soviet zone of occupation in Germany.

Keith and Elbrick accompanied me when I called that afternoon on Mr. Zygmunt Modzelewski, Vice-Minister for Foreign Affairs. The Polish delegation was housed in an attractive villa some five miles from our quarters at 10 Domgasse, Babelsberg. This villa was situated in the Soviet zone. We were stopped at several points by Red Army sentries who courteously permitted us to pass, once we had exhibited our credentials. Modzelewski received us with cordiality. He spoke excellent French and appeared to be informed in detail of all matters affecting Polish foreign affairs.

Modzelewski was a keenly intelligent, well-educated official and, although unimpressive in his appearance, seemed to have the qualifications of an able negotiator—knowledge, force, intuition and lack of rigidity.

At this first informal conversation with a member of the Polish Foreign Office I took advantage of the opportunity to express the hope that prompt steps be taken to give us a rate of exchange which would permit our staff to live in Warsaw at a reasonable cost. I said that our first reports from Tonesk had indicated it was virtually impossible to subsist at the rate of twelve zlotys to the dollar. Modzelewski said a rate for the diplomatic corps would be arranged without delay, adding that the government fully appreciated foreign embassies could not live in Poland under present conditions.

I mentioned also my hope that American press correspondents would be allowed to enter Poland at once. I said that there had been many unfavorable reports in the United States about present conditions in Poland. If, as I hoped, those reports were exaggerated or incorrect, it would be to the advantage of the Polish Government to permit foreign correspondents to tell the truth. Modzelewski said that correspondents would be very welcome but that probably there would not be proper facilities for sending messages by radio until the end of August. He indicated, however, that some censorship might be imposed. As the Polish delegation had not as yet adhered to the portion of the Potsdam decision guaranteeing freedom of reporting for Allied correspondents, I made no comment.

Modzelewski agreed with me that it would be highly desirable for Poland to encourage the export of coal, not only to help itself but western Europe as well, especially as postwar Poland was greatly in need of getting fats, meats and oils in exchange.

Modzelewski said the government meant to appoint as Ambassador to the United States either Oskar Lange or one Barcikowski, President of the Polish Supreme Court. Modzelewski asked me what I thought of the possible appointment of Lange, a naturalized American citizen of Polish origin, who had been professor of economics at the University of Chicago. He had called on me in Washington in December 1944, and had then advised me, "as a friend," not to proceed to London. I said to Modzelewski that while I could not speak for my government, my personal opinion was that it would be most inadvisable for Lange to be appointed, because of his American citizenship. Even should he become a naturalized Polish citizen, an unfavorable impression would be created in my country, especially among the Polish-American community, with which Dr. Lange had already engaged in bitter discussions.

Lange had long had the reputation of being a Communist sympathizer. I felt sure that the Polish-Americans in the United States, who were almost universally anti-Communist, would greatly resent the appointment of a man of his reputation.

Later, in Warsaw, after Lange's appointment as Ambassador had been announced, I reported to him the substance of my conversation with Modzelewski, saying that my view was not based on any personal dislike but on my feeling that renunciation of American citizenship in order to serve a foreign country would not be understood in the United States. Lange, who accepted my observation in very good spirit, said that he, too, had been of the opinion that he should not accept the appointment, but he had finally done so largely because of a letter, the original of which he showed me, from Joseph E. Davies, former American Ambassador to the Soviet Union, urging him to do so in the interest of maintaining good relations between the United States and the Soviet Union. It seemed incongruous to me that Davies, well-known in the State Department for his advocacy of a policy of appeasement toward the Soviet Union, could arrive at the conclusion that the appointment of an American citizen as Polish Ambassador to the United States would further our relations with Stalin. Later, however, I learned that Stalin had asked Hopkins in June 1945 whether the United States Government would object to Lange holding a responsible cabinet post in the Polish Government, indicating that Stalin could rely on Lange's loyalty to Communist direction. Thus Davies, deliberately or unconsciously, was following the Kremlin's wishes.

Lange showed me also a copy of a letter from Secretary Byrnes to Davies, which Davies had sent to Lange, expressing Mr. Byrnes's satisfaction that Lange agreed to accept the post. This information deeply disturbed me, for it revealed that some appeasing elements in the State Department had apparently been able to exert their influence over the Secretary in favor of a person representing the Communist influence in Poland.

For the reasons which I had set forth to Lange and to Modzelewski, I recommended, in August 1945, to the Department of State that the Polish Government's request for the *agréments* for Lange be refused. The Department, however, decided differently. Lange was eventually appointed the new Provisional Government's first Ambassador to the United States, as well as Polish representative to the United Nations.

While I was conversing with Modzelewski, Keith and Elbrick were talking with Zebrowski, one of his aides, who spoke excellent English, and who was later one of our chief liaisons at the Foreign Office. He had recently been liberated from a German prison camp by the United States Army and was still clothed in a makeshift American uniform. Although not a Communist like Modzelewski, he afterward told us that his leaning was to the left.

Shortly Modzelewski left the room and returned with President Bierut who greeted us with an air of friendly politeness. Bierut, about five feet seven inches in height, with a small, closely-cropped brown mustache and a weak mouth, did not strike me as a dominating personality. While he spoke to me in Polish, through Modzelewski as interpreter, he kept his eyes averted from me. He spoke easily and gracefully, enunciating his phrases in a low but clear, well-modulated voice. His physical appearance reminded me, as it did others, of Hitler, but there was no indication in his manner that he possessed any of Hitler's vicious attributes.

My conversation with Bierut was general. We exchanged the usual amenities. I explained to him the reason for our stopping at Potsdam and our hope that we would arrive in Warsaw the next day. The President kindly offered, through Modzelewski, to notify Warsaw, over a special Soviet telephone line from Berlin, of our prospective departure.

While I was talking with the President, Mikolajczyk entered the room. It was my first meeting with him and, after President Roosevelt's warm words of praise for him, and the months I had spent in studying the Polish patriot's character in his written words, I was deeply impressed. Light-complexioned, with a broad forehead, of medium height, and stocky, he personified the strength of the Polish peasantry. He struck me as a calm man, a man of intellectual and moral force. The direct gaze of his blue eyes, his slow, deliberate manner of speech, made me feel his tenacity and stability. He spoke in good English, punctuated with a characteristic Polish accent. For reasons of protocol, I directed my conversation principally to President Bierut and could not talk freely with Mikolajczyk. But I was able to say that President Roosevelt had asked me in our last talk in

November 1944, when I thought my destination was to be London, to give him his very best wishes. Mikolajczyk responded simply, but with emotion, "I loved that man."

Our interview with these Polish Government leaders soon came to an end. We returned to Babelsberg where I had a further talk with Dunn. He approved the advice I had given to Modzelewski on the appointment of Lange. While I was talking with Dunn, Joseph E. Davies entered the room. Although not a member of the United States delegation, he had preceded the delegation to Babelsberg and had been, so I was told by a prominent participant, seated at the same table with President Truman and Secretary Byrnes, Ambassador Harriman thus being relegated to the background. Members of our delegation opined to me that the prominent position Davies had taken at the Conference would give the Soviet delegation the idea that the Davies policy of appeasement had prevailed. If so, it would undoubtedly embolden Stalin to insist on compliance with his demands.

I had a comprehensive talk also with Will Clayton, Assistant Secretary of State for Economic Affairs. Mr. Clayton and I discussed, as we had in Washington, some of the ways in which we could offer economic and financial assistance to Poland. I acquainted him with the result of my talks in Paris over the allocation of one thousand trucks to the Polish Government from surplus war material.

Clayton told me that he had been very favorably impressed by Mr. Hilary Minc, Minister of Industry, who had had protracted talks with him and other members of the United States delegation over Poland's economic needs. Minc had a remarkable command of Polish economic statistics and had set forth to them a very clear picture of the sorry economic state in which Poland found itself in consequence of the Nazi destruction and occupation.

Clear, windy weather greeted us the next morning. At 11:20 A.M., Berlin time, we took off in our three planes from Gatow airport on our last lap to Warsaw—a flight of approximately two hours.

CHAPTER NINE

My Work in Poland Begins

AFTER an uneventful flight over the plains of eastern Germany and western Poland we arrived at the Warsaw airport, Okecie.

I had learned from my past experience in the Foreign Service that the first official act of a diplomatic representative on arriving at his post is to seek an interview with the Minister for Foreign Affairs. At this initial meeting the representative presents a copy of his letters of credence. It is also customary for the Ambassador or Minister to give the Foreign Minister a copy of the remarks which he proposes to make on presenting his credentials to the Chief Executive.

Accordingly, on the morning of August 1, the first after our arrival, Lieutenant Tonesk drove my wife, Mr. Keith and me in our jeep to the building which then housed the Foreign Office as well as almost all other Polish Government ministries. It was situated in Praga, the section of Warsaw on the other side of the Vistula, about four miles from the Hotel Polonia. Like most of the buildings on that side of the river it was unharmed, though very scantily furnished. There had been, in the wake of the retreat of the German armies, considerable misappropriation of household effects in buildings no longer occupied by the Nazis.

On the way we went through what had been the central part of the city, where no intact buildings remained. At the main street intersections girls in Polish uniforms directed traffic, assisted by Red Army soldiers. Soviet troops took part with the Poles in patrolling the streets. I asked Tonesk to drive by the Zamoyski, or Blue Palace which had been our legation in 1919 and where my wife and I had lived for about four months. We found it completely destroyed, although the walls were still standing. The Zamek, the medieval palace in which Paderewski's office was situated in 1919, had completely disappeared. The Poniatowski Bridge and the railroad bridges were entirely destroyed; only a temporary wooden bridge and a small pontoon bridge for the use of troops joined Warsaw and Praga. We crossed on the wooden bridge, which had been erected by the Soviet Army after its occupation of Warsaw in January 1945. On one end of the bridge large portraits of Stalin and Molotov greeted passers-by; at the other end were affixed large portraits of the Polish Government triumvirate—President Bierut, Prime Minister Osóbka-Morawski and Marshal Rola-Zymierski. We observed thousands of Soviet troops marching east. Many of them were without uniforms, and these we presumed to be liberated prisoners of war from Germany. The troops were accompanied by horse-drawn German carts filled with the spoils of war—goods of all types, sewing machines, bicycles, bedding, bathtubs and other articles of plumbing.

In addition we noted, as we did on many future occasions, groups of men, women and children being marched eastward to the railroad station at Praga, accompanied by Soviet and Polish armed guards. Evidently they were being deported to the Soviet Union. It was prohibited for anyone to question these people who, from their dejected expressions, were not proceeding on their journey voluntarily.

Praga we found to be very little destroyed, compared with Warsaw. One trolley line was already in operation; and the railroad was running from Praga to the east. The life in the Praga streets was normal; the shops were open and doing business. The Germans had not been in occupation of Praga when the Warsaw insurrection was terminated on October 3, 1944. The Nazis therefore could not carry on the systematic destruction which they had practiced in Warsaw proper as punishment for the rebellion.

When I arrived at Foreign Minister Rzymowski's office, I was immediately ushered into his presence. I presented to him the customary formal note reporting my arrival, as well as a copy of the letter of credence.

At this first official meeting I said that I had discussed with General

Eisenhower at Frankfurt the possibility of our bringing a military detachment to Warsaw from which we would select guards for the Embassy, drivers for our cars, and radio operators. I inquired of the Minister whether there would be any objection to bringing in such a detachment. Mr. Rzymowski replied that the protection of foreign diplomatic missions devolved on the Polish Government and that we would not therefore require any American military detachment for this purpose. I pointed out, however, that because of the abnormal conditions in Warsaw at that time I felt we should overlook no opportunity to insure the safety of the members of the mission as well as the care of our archives. Our concern was inspired by reports which Tonesk had given me of nightly shooting, audible from the Polonia, by undisciplined Red Army soldiers, attacks on pedestrians, and breakings into private dwellings.

In principle Mr. Rzymowski agreed to American military personnel coming in with our first convoy of automobiles which we expected soon under the leadership of Secretary Thomas P. Dillon. This convoy was to travel from Paris to Berlin and thence through the Soviet zone of Germany to the Polish frontier.

I also took up with the Foreign Minister the question of the rate of exchange. I referred to the impossibility of the Embassy staff subsisting at the current rate and voiced the hope that a rate would be established under which we might carry on our activities in Poland as efficiently as possible. Otherwise, no members of the staff could afford to remain. Mr. Rzymowski promised to take this matter up with the Minister of Finance and the other appropriate members of the government at the earliest possible moment.

When I left him, Mr. Wyszynski, the acting Chief of Protocol, invited my wife and me to drive through another part of Warsaw— Saska Kepa—to inspect a section which, it was hoped, would house most of the diplomatic corps. Already the French and Yugoslav ambassadors had installed themselves in that district. Like Praga, it had not been systematically destroyed by the Germans, although it had suffered considerable damage from bombs and shellfire.

Wyszynski intimated that even though I had not yet presented my credentials I should be at the airport that afternoon to meet President Bierut, who was returning from Potsdam. Tonesk drove the British chargé d'affaires, Robin Hankey, and me to the airport in the jeep. There I found the Soviet Ambassador, the Yugoslav Ambassador, a pleasant but rather sickly-looking man, and Prime Minister Osóbka-Morawski. Osóbka-Morawski was pleasant but somewhat reserved in his comments, which were translated to me by Tonesk. A small, unimpressive individual, he had a kindly smile, a nervous manner of speaking and pale-blue eyes which stared at one fitfully from beneath heavy eyebrows.

While waiting at the airport I had the opportunity to meet Dr. Sommerstein, the distinguished President of the Jewish Party. Conversing with him in German, I asked about the plight of the Jews in Poland today. He said that out of the four million Jews in prewar Poland there were only fifty thousand left, but that probably considerable numbers would return from the Soviet Union east of the Curzon Line. I was to have further talks with him and other Polish-Jewish leaders on the tragic condition of their race which had suffered even more terribly than the Gentile Poles during the Nazi occupation.

The President's plane soon arrived on the desolate airfield, a guard of honor was drawn up, and a small military band rendered the Polish national anthem. Although the music was indifferently played, it stirred one. It recalled colorful ceremonies during my previous assignment to Warsaw at which the haunting martial melody was always an essential feature.

President Bierut, whom I had met two days earlier at Babelsberg, near Potsdam, broke traditional protocol and greeted me first and then the other members of the diplomatic corps. The others of his entourage, including Mr. Mikolajczyk, Vice-Premier and Minister of Agriculture, arrived on a second plane.

Mr. Wladislaw Kiernik, Minister of Public Administration, called on me at the Hotel Polonia later that afternoon. Slight and slender, a voluble conversationalist, he impressed me as a man of a quick, keen mind. A member of Witos' Peasant Party, he was one of those selected to hold a portfolio in the Polish Provisional Government of National Unity. Before the war the Ministry of Public Administration, corresponding to the Ministry of the Interior in most European countries, had been a most important and strategic ministry, since the police control was vested in it. During the conversations in Moscow in June 1945, among the various Polish political leaders, Kiernik had been deluded into thinking that as Minister of Public Administration he was to have control of the Security Police. In the new government, however, the Security Police organization had been taken away from that department and placed under the control of the Ministry of Public Security, presided over by one Radkiewicz, a Communist with Soviet Russian indoctrination.

Mr. Kiernik said to me that his ministry was able to accomplish little, as it no longer had any teeth. He said that he had been always a close friend of Wincenty Witos, the head of the Peasant Party, that Witos had been offered one of the vice-presidencies in the National Council of the Homeland, but had not yet decided whether to accept. Kiernik reminded me that that day, August 1, was the first anniversary of the outbreak of the insurrection and that it had been declared a national holiday to honor all the brave Poles who had died in this heroic struggle, even those "foolish ones" who started the insurrection. Kiernik said that the rebellion was a brave gesture but foolish politically, as the Nazis were waiting for just such an excuse to justify their destruction of Warsaw. He made no reference to the Soviet part in the appalling tragedy.

This very day we learned that all telegraphic and radio messages out of Poland, both official and private, must pass through Moscow. We were warned that there would therefore probably be considerable delay in the receipt of our telegrams. But more important than the delay was the fact that our official communications would be at the mercy of our professedly friendly ally to the east. We therefore made haste, through our communications officer, Major Treece, to set up a radio transmitter so as to insure prompt contact with the outside world. No more dispiriting prospect could possibly have confronted us, and at the very outset of our mission.

The next day two prewar employees of the Embassy called on me. Both of these men were down and out, their clothes badly worn and shabby; they looked undernourished and discouraged. I told them I hoped we could employ them but I could not then discuss compensation, owing to our ignorance of the rate of exchange which would be established. They said they had never been in politics in Poland and they hoped we would permit them to work for us. One of them thought that although there were many conditions in Poland today which might be criticized, the status of the peasant would be improved. One of the most adverse situations in the past, he said, had been the great distinction between the landowning and peasant classes. The class war was still going on, but, because of the virtual extinction of the large landowners as a class, the peasant was at last coming into his own. The other applicant said that the members of the German Wehrmacht in Warsaw had been fairly human in comparison with the Gestapo and that the Wehrmacht had been strongly opposed to the destruction of Warsaw, which they felt would serve no purpose except to create perpetual hatred of the Germans.

That day I met for the first time, at a luncheon to which Robin Hankey had kindly invited me, Jakób Berman, the former Undersecretary for Foreign Affairs who had recently been appointed Undersecretary of State of the Council of Ministers. The post was classed in importance as Number Four in the government, only the Premier and the two Vice-Premiers being ranked ahead of Berman. Berman, like Bierut, was a Communist.

The conversation at this luncheon was general. Berman spoke freely and apparently knowingly of all the problems of the government. It was at once apparent to me that he was a man of great power within the government. He held it most important that Polish troops abroad should return to Poland as soon as possible. I asked whether perhaps some of the Polish troops in Italy and elsewhere would be apprehensive about coming home to Poland because of fear that they might be tried on political charges due to their association with General Anders. Anders, the commander in chief of the Polish forces abroad, had remained a persistent upholder of the Polish Government in London and had denounced the Yalta decision as a betrayal of Poland. The Bierut Government heartily disliked him. Berman said that sentences given by the Polish courts for political offenses could not be imposed *in absentia,* and that therefore they could not apply to Polish troops abroad. Nevertheless, General Anders and seventy-five of his senior officers were sentenced in 1946, while absent from Poland, to lose their Polish citizenship.*

Berman I thought a highly intelligent man. Quiet in his demeanor and dignified in his bearing, he was elegant but forceful in speech. His mouth was mobile and sensitive, and his lips carefully phrased every syllable he uttered. His eyes were unnaturally bright, his complexion was swarthy, his nose indicated his Semitic origin. His hands attracted my attention. They were delicate both in shape and gesture. Unlike some obvious Communists, his appearance gave no indication of brutality or coarseness. I was to learn that he was one of the Kremlin's principal agents in Poland—one of the men who directed the puppets. We found this out not only from conversations with Polish Government officials, who in many cases said that they would have to consult Berman before giving us an answer on a specific question, but also from colleagues in the diplomatic corps who called him a keyman who knew how to get things done. On many occasions, when I could not secure action from other government officials, I went to Berman.

At 4:30 P.M. next day, August 4, Prince Krzysztof Radziwill, who had succeeded Mr. Wyszynski as Chief of Protocol in the Foreign Office, arrived at the Polonia Hotel to escort me and members of our

---

* Among other officers deprived of citizenship were General Stanislaw Kopanski, hero of Tobruk; General Antoni Chrusciel, chief of staff to General Bór-Komorowski during the Warsaw insurrection; and General Stanislaw Maczek, who, under General Eisenhower's command, had distinguished himself in the Normandy invasion in June 1944.

staff to the Belvedere Palace, where I was to present my credentials to President Bierut. As we arrived at the courtyard the military band rendered the "Star-Spangled Banner." It was done surprisingly well, considering that the band had never played our national anthem before; in fact that morning the Foreign Office had inquired whether we had a copy of the "Star-Spangled Banner," as they could not find the music among their records.

After the formalities of presenting credentials and the delivery of my speech and Bierut's reply—both of which were couched in cordial language and expressed the hope that most friendly relations would exist between our two governments—the President invited me to accompany him into his study. Foreign Minister Rzymowski, Vice-Foreign Minister Modzelewski and Lieutenant Tonesk were also invited, Tonesk to act as my interpreter.

Though I entertained little hope, because of the obvious Soviet policy to control the Polish Government, that the Provisional Government would co-operate wholeheartedly with the United States, I had no wish to prejudice Polish actions and I intended to show the friendliest attitude of which I was capable. I had, however, definitely made up my mind I would not tolerate a violation of United States rights in Poland or mistreatment of American citizens and at the risk of being considered unfriendly would be prepared in such cases to protest vigorously without necessarily awaiting instructions from Washington.

One of the tenets of our policy toward Poland as expressed by President Roosevelt in his letter of November 17, 1944, to Mikolajczyk was to assist in the economic reconstruction of the Polish state. Accordingly, before I left Washington, I had had several talks with Assistant Secretary Will Clayton and his associates about the economic and financial assistance which the United States Government might be in a position to extend to Poland. On the basis of these conversations I outlined to President Bierut eight points on which the United States might be of help in the reconstruction of Poland.

1. *Extension of Relief through UNRRA.* Although UNRRA was

an international organization, the United States Government hoped, through its seventy-two per-cent participation in the financing of UNRRA, to make a very sizable contribution to the Polish reconstruction. The United States had hoped that UNRRA activities in Poland could have commenced in October 1944, but, due to no fault of the American representatives of UNRRA, these representatives had been unable to obtain visas to enter that part of Poland then under control of the Soviet Army.

Although I did not, for reasons of delicacy, mention it at my first meeting with the President, I had in mind that Mr. John P. Gregg, an American citizen who had formerly served with the American Relief Administration in Poland, had been appointed in October 1944 chief of the UNRRA mission in Poland. Gregg and I had been close friends for over twenty-five years and in Washington we had gone over carefully the questions which would confront UNRRA in Poland. Gregg's chief problem at that time was to obtain permission for himself and for members of his staff to proceed into Poland to ascertain, on the ground, the most acute needs of the country. Besides withholding that permission, the Soviet Government had obstructed most effectively the sending of supplies to Poland through Black Sea ports. Gregg had finally resigned his post in despair.

Over my personal protest, Director General Herbert H. Lehman had appointed as director of the first UNRRA mission to Poland the Soviet member of the UNRRA council, Mr. Menshikov, whose first duty would be the negotiation of an agreement with the Polish Government for the reception and distribution of UNRRA supplies. It was no surprise to me when in August the agreement concluded in Warsaw provided that the Polish Government, and not UNRRA, should have complete jurisdiction over the distribution of UNRRA supplies in Poland.

2. *Possible Financial Credits to Poland.* The United States Government desired to express its sympathy with the very difficult economic and financial situation in which Poland was placed by the war and almost six years of Nazi occupation. It would be prepared to

extend credits through the Export-Import Bank, provided the Polish Government would provide us with the necessary information about its financial situation.

3. *Export of Polish Coal Recommended.* The importance of Poland obtaining foreign exchange through the export of coal was stressed. Our government would be gratified if Poland would give serious consideration to the development of a triangular trade policy. Thus, through the export of Poland's Silesian coal to France and Italy, those countries would be enabled to export products marketable in the United States, and so build up a dollar balance for Poland in New York.

4. *Surplus War Material Offered.* The United States Government regretted that, because of various legal restrictions, we could not for the moment give promise of immediate assistance to Poland on a larger scale. As the hostilities with Germany had ended and as Poland was not waging war against Japan, there was no legal provision which would enable us to give assistance to Poland under the Lend-Lease Act. We did feel that we should alleviate the very acute shortage of automotive transportation without delay. I had been authorized, I told Mr. Bierut, before leaving Washington, to make arrangements for the allocation to Poland of one thousand trucks from our surplus war material in France. In Paris I had made arrangements with our authorities that if the Polish Government would send a representative to France the trucks best suited to Poland's needs would be made available to him there. I reiterated the importance, therefore, of sending a representative to Paris at once with full powers to sign an agreement.

5. *German Reparations for Poland.* Based on the conversations I had had a few days before with our representatives in Potsdam, I informed President Bierut that Mr. Edward Pauley, Special Representative of President Truman, was then in Moscow to discuss with the Soviet Government the question of restitution and reparations from Germany. As I had learned that the Potsdam agreement would provide that Polish reparations would be allocated out of the Soviet

share, I suggested to Mr. Bierut that the Polish Government should send a representative to Moscow and join in the consultations with Mr. Pauley. He made no comment, although he must have known that he, together with Modzelewski and others, were to leave the very next evening for Moscow to conclude a treaty with the Soviet Union on the question of reparations, as well as on other matters. Later I learned that members of the Polish Government had been enjoined by the Soviet Government not to disclose the news of their forthcoming visit to Moscow.

6. *Negotiation of New Trade Treaty.* Under instructions from the Department of State, I made the suggestion that private trade between the United States and Poland should be encouraged in accordance with the provisions of the Treaty of Commerce, Friendship and Consular Rights of 1931. I pointed out that this treaty was still in effect, but that because of the time which had elapsed since its conclusion we proposed that an improved treaty be negotiated to the mutual advantage of both countries. Mr. Bierut acquiesced with my statement, and suggested that I take up with the Ministry of Foreign Affairs the negotiation of a new treaty.

Although I mentioned on several future occasions our desire to improve trade relations through a better treaty, the Polish Government never indicated a serious intention to start negotiations. On the other hand, when on one occasion I invoked the Treaty of 1931 in connection with the protection of American rights in Poland, Foreign Minister Rzymowski informed me baldly that the Treaty of 1931 was no longer applicable because it was so antiquated. On reporting this conversation to the Department of State I was instructed to express the surprise of the United States Government to learn that in the opinion of the Polish Foreign Minister a treaty which was still binding on both signatories was not applicable!

7. *Exchange of Technical Experts.* I proposed to the President that, with a view of making effective our intent to assist in the reconstruction of Poland, the Polish Government should send financial and economic experts to the United States as soon as possible. I had been

authorized to say that if such experts would put themselves in touch with the officials of our government, we would do our utmost to assist, under existing legislation, in the reconstruction of the country. I stated furthermore that it was the purpose of our government to assign to our Embassy an agricultural expert and an industrial engineer, both of whom would be available to the Polish Government to proffer advice on agricultural and industrial problems.

To my regret, however, despite my continual requests of the Department of State for these two experts, an agricultural expert did not arrive in Warsaw for almost a year; and our economic counselor, whose assignment had been promised me in July 1945, did not arrive until June 1946. The industrial engineer was never sent.

One of our greatest problems in Warsaw was to obtain adequate personnel for our Embassy from the Department of State. It was not till November 1946, when I personally explained in Washington to the highest ranking members of the Department the inadequacy of our personnel, that I was ultimately able to alleviate our administration problems. Starting off with an embassy of thirteen, we grew in one year to a staff of two hundred and yet could not take care of the tens of thousands of passport and visa applications satisfactorily.

8. *Assistance from the American Red Cross.* In addition to the relief assistance which we hoped to extend through our participation in UNRRA, the American Red Cross was ready to send representatives to Poland at the earliest possible moment, primarily to arrange for the dispatch of children's clothing from the United States. Like UNRRA, it had been endeavoring to enter Poland since October 1944, but for various reasons which were the fault neither of the United States nor of the Polish Government, permission had not been granted. For example, Dr. J. H. Bauer, a specialist in public health, lent to the American Red Cross by the Rockefeller Foundation, and his assistant Mr. Grady, had been waiting in Paris for visas for Poland since early July. The President promised that he would have instructions issued at once for granting of visas to Dr. Bauer and to Mr. Grady.

Although the American Red Cross had allocated one million dollars in October 1944 for Polish relief, its representatives had from that date until September 1945 been unable to secure permission to enter Polish territory. Until the establishment of the Polish Government of National Unity in June 1945, the responsibility for the refusal of visas rested on the Soviet authorities in Poland. On the basis of Soviet policy elsewhere the Soviet authorities evidently considered that our Red Cross representatives were proceeding to Poland primarily as United States Government spies and, hence, were undesirable in that they might learn prematurely the real feeling of the Polish people toward the Communist-controlled Lublin regime.

These delays and obstructions to the shipping of supplies for Poland continued until on May 22 the American Red Cross notified the Soviet Government that it would be necessary to withdraw its million-dollar allocation for Polish relief unless clearances were immediately given. However, on the insistence of Mr. Hopkins, who arrived in Moscow early in June, this ultimatum was not carried out.

Despite President Bierut's promise, the Polish Embassy in Paris did not receive authority to issue visas to Bauer and Grady.

Nevertheless, a month after this, when I was returning in September by way of Paris from a short trip to London, I invited them, on the strength of Mr. Bierut's assurance to me, to accompany me to Poland. This was to run the risk of their deportation, because they still had no Polish visas. Once in Poland they were permitted to circulate freely and were able to prepare their report on Polish needs for American Red Cross aid.

After Bauer and Grady had arrived in Poland, an official of the Polish Foreign Office advised the Embassy that three telegrams were sent to Paris authorizing visas for the American Red Cross officials, the first two via Moscow, the last by wireless via London. The first two telegrams were never received by the Embassy in Paris, the third arrived subsequent to Bauer's and Grady's departure. Obviously the Soviet Government had countermanded Bierut's instructions.

While I was discussing the foregoing eight points, Mr. Modzelewski looked pointedly at his wrist watch. There were still several matters that I wished to present to the President and I did not propose to be hurried unnecessarily by one of his underlings. I therefore inquired of Mr. Bierut, who surely must have noted Modzelewski's hint that I had overstayed my welcome, whether the President had further time to give to me. Mr. Bierut told me reassuringly that I should feel free to take up as many matters as I desired.

After having touched briefly on these eight matters on which we would be in a position to give economic or financial assistance, I told President Bierut I hoped the Polish Government would give us permission to establish consulates in Poznan, Kraków, Lódz and Gdansk; to establish a radio station within our Embassy premises so that we might communicate rapidly with Washington through the United States European Theater Commander at Frankfurt, General Eisenhower; to establish a weekly courier plane service between Berlin and Warsaw; to admit American newspaper correspondents in accordance with the terms of the Potsdam decision; and to permit a Congressional subcommittee (consisting of Mrs. Frances P. Bolton, Mr. Karl E. Mundt, Mr. Thomas S. Gordon, and Mr. Joseph P. Ryter) to come to Poland in September 1945 to meet leading members of the government and study for themselves existing conditions.

The President stated that the Polish Government would be glad to give approval of my requests, and would give careful and sympathetic consideration to our eight offers of economic or financial aid to Polish reconstruction.

But although President Bierut impressed me as a suave, agreeable and courteous person, and displayed a wish to please, it was disquieting that his eyes rarely met mine. He impressed me as a shifty and opportunistic individual who was not master in his own house. It seemed to me that in the problems which we discussed he acquiesced too readily without exploring the details. I was soon to learn to my sorrow that the tactics of a Soviet-controlled government are to give sweeping promises which are rarely, if ever, implemented into action.

CHAPTER TEN

The Dark Road Ahead

ON THE day after this first official conversation with President Bierut, my wife and I attended a reception, at his personal invitation, in honor of two distinguished leaders of the Red Army, Marshal Zhukov and Marshal Rokossovsky.

Accompanied by Mr. Keith and Lieutenant Tonesk we arrived at the Belvedere Palace and proceeded to the same Pompeiian Room where I had presented my credentials the day before. Now it was filled with Soviet and Polish officers and members of the diplomatic corps. President Bierut soon arrived with the two Soviet marshals. After making what seemed to me an eloquent speech, Bierut presented the marshals with the highest Polish decoration—*virtuti militari*. The ceremony was in commemoration of the "liberation" of Poland by the Red Army and the part which these two officers had played. Rokossovsky's command was then estimated as numbering about three hundred thousand.

Zhukov who radiated strength, energy and good humor, wore a white tunic of light wool and dark blue trousers. Rokossovsky, taciturn and expressionless, wore the regular Soviet gray field tunic and was more massive and less ebullient than Zhukov. He also gave the impression of granite strength. Of Polish forebears, Rokossovsky spoke the language of the country and was reputedly, for that reason, picked for the command of the Red Army in Poland.

After the presentation of decorations, refreshments were served and I was invited by the President to sit at his table, next to Marshal Zhukov.

Through Tonesk's interpreting I told Zhukov of my hope that some arrangement might be made for a more efficient means of communication with Berlin and asked for blanket authority for our weekly plane to fly over the Soviet zone as well as for our motor convoys to come to Poland. The Marshal smiled cordially but shook his head decisively. He answered that we should make the request through our political adviser in Berlin each time we wanted to fly to Warsaw. When I went on to argue that I felt the Soviet and United States military authorities should be mutually helpful in matters that concerned our common aim, I realized that Zhukov had no authority to grant my request.

During my conversation with the Marshal he observed that General Eisenhower was to visit Moscow on August 11 as a guest of the Soviet Government. I said I hoped General Eisenhower might visit Warsaw en route, as I thought he would find it highly interesting to see for himself the extent of the destruction.

Marshal Zhukov said that he would like to do anything possible for General Eisenhower, for whom he had the highest regard, but unfortunately such a visit would not fit in with the plans. Then he asked me what the United States intended to do for the general in recognition of his services as commander in chief of the Allied forces in Western Europe. I said that I had just come from the United States, where I had seen the reception which had been accorded General Eisenhower in Washington, probably the greatest welcome which had ever been given to a returning American. In my opinion he had received the highest honor that anyone can be given in the United States—the wholehearted acclaim of the country. When Zhukov seemed skeptical of my interpretation of the greatness of this honor, I added that President Truman had publicly announced that General Eisenhower could have anything in the power of the President to grant; but Eisenhower had said he wished nothing. The Marshal observed laconically, "General Eisenhower is a very modest man."

After luncheon an informal concert was given in an adjoining room, during the course of which Mr. Michal Fogg, the owner of a popular Warsaw restaurant, sang Polish songs. Here it was that I heard for the first time a song of nostalgia, "Warszawa," written during the

Nazi occupation of Warsaw and the Russian occupation of the east of Poland. Fogg, a small, trim man with spectacles, sang in Polish with great feeling. Many of the Polish women present were in tears. The song was written by an emigré in a Siberian prison and voices his dreams of the streets of Warsaw, his longing to be home and to see his country free. Little did the Russian marshals know its significance. Since I came home I have heard it has been banned by the government.

On this occasion I had the highly educational experience of a conversation with Mr. Zygmunt Modzelewski, Vice-Minister for Foreign Affairs, with whom I had had a brief interview as I passed through Potsdam. Though Mr. Modzelewski had been present at my meeting with President Bierut, he had remained silent throughout. He was a Communist trained in Moscow and had spent many years in France. Earlier that year he had served as Polish Ambassador in Moscow. A nervous individual with quick perception and extraordinary memory, he could at times be most gracious, I was to learn later, in granting a general promise, never to be fulfilled. At other times he was most disagreeable in flatly denying what seemed to us a reasonable request, such as the right of the Embassy to visit claimants to American citizenship, jailed because of their alleged connection with the Polish underground. Modzelewski had been known as "Fischhaupt" during years of service as a member of the Soviet trade mission in Paris. Despite this pseudonym he was not of the Jewish race. Like so many others of the Communist minority of the new government, he had been virtually unknown in Poland before the war. He had emerged from the Soviet revolutionary machine and been planted as an important official in Poland. There was no doubt he was a Pole. But he was subservient to his Communist masters in the Kremlin, probably through Berman, who, in my opinion, was Moscow's chief representative within the Polish Government.

At this reception, I asked Modzelewski when a representative of the Polish Government would be sent to Paris, as arranged the previous day with President Bierut, to select from our stock of surplus property equipment the items most desired by the Polish Government. To my complete surprise he replied that the Polish representative had already left Warsaw, but had gone to London and not to Paris! I expressed astonishment that arrangements for his departure could take place without notice to our Embassy. I said that we wished to help the Polish Government to the extent of our ability, but cooperation on the part of the Poles would be an essential factor. Modzelewski suggested, somewhat coldly, that I send a telegram to Paris so that a United States Government representative could proceed to London to meet the Polish representative there. I remonstrated that, from our experience, telegrams between Warsaw and Paris would take at least five days in transit. Modzelewski then dumfounded me by stating that in the case of telegrams of such great interest to the Polish Government he would be able to arrange for transmission to Paris within forty-eight hours! This virtual admission that the Polish Government was holding up our official telegrams, except those in which it might be primarily interested, was too much for me. I told Mr. Modzelewski emphatically that this was an unheard-of procedure.

At this juncture I made my first of many appeals to Berman. He listened with apparent sympathy and regret for Modzelewski's attitude. He promised that a representative would be sent to Paris at once with full authority to conclude an agreement on the delivery of the one thousand trucks.

I asked myself then, if the Polish Foreign Office adopted an obstructionist and obviously unfriendly attitude in a matter in which the United States Government was proposing to accord a favor, what would its attitude be in cases in which the protection of American interests was involved? The answer in all its unpleasant reality was to be shortly forthcoming and was to be reiterated on many occasions during the eighteen months I was in Poland.

I had had since my arrival several conversations with Robin Hankey, an earnest, conscientious and keen career diplomat who had shown the utmost kindness to us from the start. He had received instructions from London to act in concert with his Soviet and United States colleagues in Poland in protesting to the Polish Government against the continued deportation of Germans from that part of Germany now under Polish administration. Hankey's telegram from London indicated that the Allied Control Commission in Germany could not cope with the influx of any more refugees from Poland. He had been directed to see the Foreign Minister as soon as possible but before doing so was to consult Lebedev (the Soviet Ambassador) and me. He asked whether I had received any instructions. I told Hankey that I had received none; in fact, I said, I had received no telegrams whatever from the outside world and we had not as yet been able to set up a radio transmitter to send and receive official messages.

Hankey had been unable to see the Soviet Ambassador, whose offices were then located on the other side of the river, near the Foreign Office. He had no car. He had not time to walk the eight miles to Praga and return, and he laughingly said that he felt it undignified for the British chargé d'affaires to ride to Praga in a cart used for carrying cattle—the only vehicle available at the moment.

In a report Hankey gave me afterward, Rzymowski asserted that as a result of the Potsdam decision he understood the position of our authorities, and said the Polish Government did not propose to aggravate the confusion in Germany by expelling a large number of Germans. Hankey quoted Rzymowski as saying, however, that it would be necessary to get rid of the Germans in Stettin and Silesia, owing to the desire of the Polish Government to reconstruct those areas.

It was not until days later that I received instructions from Washington to impress on the Polish Government the need of using the most humanitarian methods in effecting deportations of Germans from territories now under Polish occupation. Rzymowski gave me virtually the same answer he had given Hankey—that the Polish Government fully appreciated the situation but that no Germans could be left in Stettin and Silesian areas.

This question of definite demarcation of Poland's western frontiers was to become, toward the end of my stay in Warsaw, one of the sorest questions plaguing our relations with Poland.

My initial progress was very limited. The principal members of the Polish Government—President Bierut, Premier Osóbka-Morawski, Mr. Modzelewski, the keyman in the Ministry of Foreign Affairs, and Mr. Hilary Minc, the Minister of Industry, who had the final word on all matters dealing with economics and finance—had gone to Moscow right after the reception for the Soviet marshals on August 5. They were to be gone for two weeks. During that period I could not transact important business. But I was none the less able to continue meeting Polish officials, foreign diplomatic colleagues and private individuals, all of whose comments helped to give me a more comprehensive understanding of how much Poland had suffered and of the present outlook.

One of my calls in this interim was on Marshal Rola-Zymierski, a very affable, heavy-set officer who had attended the École Militaire de Guerre in Paris and accordingly spoke excellent French. He received me in his quarters at Wlochy, a suburb about ten miles west of Warsaw. He was jolly in manner, friendly in approach, hospitable in his way of living, and I always managed to maintain a cordial relationship with him until the end of my stay in Warsaw. Unlike some of the Communist members of the government, he did not interpret a difference of opinion necessarily as a cause for unfriendliness. He had the dual position of Minister of National Defense and Marshal of the Polish Army. Although it was he who took the salute of the troops, received such important military visitors as Marshal Tito and was a prominent figure at all governmental functions, he was evidently, however, merely the façade to mask the Soviet steps to organize the Polish Army and militia under the direction of Soviet officers. The real directing force within the Army came from General Spychalski, a lithe, quiet-spoken, nonmilitary-looking officer whose training had been in Russia. Semitic in origin, he did not have the

physical appearance of the average Polish officer. At political meetings of the armed forces it was he and not Zymierski who made the
important address. A member of the Polish Workers (Communist)
Party, he was the Polish counterpart of the political commissar in the
Soviet Army.

There was also Lieutenant General Korczyc, Chief of the General
Staff, reputed to be an officer of the Soviet Army, and later spoken
of as the real head of the Polish Army, rather than Spychalski.

The Minister of Finance, Mr. Dabrowski, whom I first visited on
August 18, was a slight, pleasant-mannered gentleman, obviously not
an initiator of policy. I was anxious to question him on a speech he
had made on August 9 at a meeting of the managers of credit institutions.

Dabrowski had been reported as stating that Poland had no need
to return to the gold standard and did not require gold as foreign-
exchange coverage. According to the press report of his speech, Poland's currency would be for internal use only; therefore the Polish
Government did not intend to establish a general rate of exchange for
the zloty in relation to other currencies. If necessary, Poland would
establish a special rate of exchange for any single transaction or group
of transactions.

The most significant parts of Dabrowski's speech were those which
indicated Poland's adoption of the Soviet economic policy: complete
control of all commercial and financial transactions. Thus, the Ministry of Foreign Trade (under the Communist Minister Jedrychowski)
would be the general importer and exporter and would control all
international trade through the issuance of licenses. Further governmental control would be provided through the stipulation that all accounts relative to foreign trade should be settled in zlotys through
the National Bank of Poland. Special rates were to be fixed for remittances from abroad.

Dabrowski confirmed to me the accuracy of the press reports, but he
did not appear concerned when I said that publication of this news
might undermine confidence of Polish recovery in United States eco-

nomic and financial circles. The maintenance of multiple rates of exchange would lead to confusion and would discourage the investment of American capital in Polish reconstruction.

The Minister, in response to my urging, promised that a rate of exchange would be fixed in the near future for the diplomatic corps, perhaps one hundred fifty zlotys to the dollar. As the open market rate was two hundred zlotys and prices had risen proportionately, I said this would not solve the situation. Having learned that unlimited quantities of Polish currency had been issued in Moscow, primarily for the use of Soviet troops in Poland, I enquired the amount of it. The Minister replied that this figure was confidential!

On August 21 I called on Premier Osóbka-Morawski and mentioned my apprehension that the policies which had been confirmed to me by his Minister of Finance would hardly work out to Poland's advantage and might result in Poland being unable to qualify for financial assistance from the United States under our existing general requirements. The Prime Minister said he knew nothing about the financial policy of the government and modestly admitted that he was not an economist. Thus did he naïvely indicate that the government of which he was the head had not been the author of a far-reaching financial policy.

Under date of September 6, 1944, when Poland was still being theoretically governed by the Soviet-controlled Committee of National Liberation, a decree was issued providing for agrarian reform. This was one revolutionary change on which almost all Poles—except the large landholders—could agree; for in the prewar years there had been much criticism of the landed gentry because of their power. The ostensible purpose of the legislation was to increase the size of the small farms, to provide farms for the landless, to establish fruit and vegetable-producing areas near the towns, to provide land for agricultural schools and experimental stations, and to provide land for the extension of towns, and for the establishment of military reservations.

The land to be redistributed was to be acquired, without compensation from the national treasury, from German citizens, traitors, deserters, collaborators with the Nazis, and those guilty of offenses punishable under decrees issued by the Committee of National Liberation. Furthermore, the edict provided that the property of persons owning cultivatable land exceeding fifty hectares (one hundred twenty-three and a half acres) should be confiscated. Thus the large landowners were liquidated as such by a stroke of the pen. The maximum area permitted an owner was fifteen hectares, but, in practice, the limit was generally five.

The legislation, primarily social and political in its purpose, had serious economic drawbacks, so one Socialist cabinet minister told me. He said that the Polish peasant, unless his work was directed by an overseer or unless he had been educated in foreign agricultural schools, was inefficient in marketing his produce. Under the prewar system the large landowners had organized their properties on a very businesslike basis and were able to produce the maximum output at the best prices obtainable. Under the new system agricultural production, especially of beet sugar, had greatly dwindled. My informant hoped, however, that little by little, through the importation of farm machinery and the necessary technical assistance from American agricultural experts, the output would reach its prewar level.

In an interval between days of making official calls was one memorable visit to Majdanek, the concentration and asphyxiation camp maintained by the Nazis about one mile east of Lublin. Because of the unexpected arrival of the Red Army in July 1944, the Nazis had not had time to destroy the camp, with all its horrible incriminating evidence. Although the camp at Oswiecim had a far greater number of victims, totaling millions, the Germans had had plenty of time to blow up the asphyxiation chambers and crematory machinery there, so that little remained to be seen now. Our guide was Krzysztof Radziwill of the Polish Foreign Office. We were particularly fortunate to have him conduct us through the camp, for he had spent two years in Majdanek as a prisoner of the Nazis. Even before we reached the camp, we could note his excitement in contemplating his return as a free man to the place where he had endured so much mental suffering.

As he took us through the various buildings in this concentration camp over a mile square, he trembled with emotion as he described the horrors he had witnessed at this or that spot. He showed us the room adjacent to the shower baths where the inmates who were marked for extermination undressed, believing that they were about to have their weekly showers. With an expression of horror which our guide was unable to conceal, he pointed out to us a heavy metal door containing a thick circular glass window.

He said to us, "Through this glass window I was obliged to watch the victims who were herded in here, like so much cattle, after undressing. Once they were in the room, the cyanide gas was released from a hole in the ceiling. They would ordinarily die in a matter of seconds; but often they struggled in resistance. When they struggled, the sight was something terrible: human beings fighting like animals without any hope of escape." Radziwill then showed us where the bodies of the victims were put into ovens and cremated. Piles of ashes were carted to Germany as fertilizer.

We were shown a large room filled with shoes, over two hundred thousand. We were told that these were the shoes of the dead, which were to have been sent to Germany for the use of the living. They included tiny shoes for babies who, like their parents, had been asphyxiated and cremated by Nazi barbarism. The superintendent presented me with two pairs of these infants' shoes which I sent to the Department of State for use in the Nuremberg trials, as well as two cans of cyanide gas which the Germans, in their hasty retreat, had failed to remove—deadly evidence of their dastardly crimes.

But to me the most revolting incident was one which Radziwill described when he showed us a part of the camp within the shadow of the main dormitories. "Here," he said, "one Christmas Eve, a Christmas tree stood with all its ornaments. The entire personnel of the camp was brought out as though all were to celebrate the anniversary of the birth of Christ. But the most awful mockery then took place. Without any warning, certain of the inmates were securely pinioned to stakes which had been driven into the ground in front of the tree, and then were mercilessly beaten to death with clubs."

After this description we did not feel like conversing. Silently in the dusk we drove back to Warsaw by the shell-pocked road over which the Russians and the Germans had fiercely fought as the Red Army advanced in 1944 and 1945. As we approached the Vistula from the east, the ruins of Warsaw on the other side of the river formed a low, black, uneven mass against the sun's afterglow. No friendly light gleamed from that lifeless pile. Warsaw was a city of darkness. It, too, appeared to have died along with the poor creatures of Majdanek.

CHAPTER ELEVEN

Our Initial Difficulties

I HAD been warned by colleagues in the Department of State fully familiar with Soviet methods that as the Red armies advanced into Poland from the east, the Soviet Secret Police (NKVD) would quickly and thoroughly organize the internal police administration, and would liquidate, through arrests or deportations, any elements considered unfriendly or politically dangerous. I learned also that an essential factor in Soviet technique is to keep all foreign elements away from the region to be organized by the NKVD.

As the Russian mentality conceives that espionage is an everyday required duty on the part of all Soviet citizens and of Communists generally, it is assumed that all foreigners, even those having only humanitarian functions, are secret agents working malevolently for a foreign power. Thus Poles who claimed American citizenship or who had contacts, through relatives, with the United States were doubly vulnerable.

If we required confirmation of secret-police activities in Poland, we obtained it immediately on our arrival.

The NKVD had not as yet been able to organize the country so efficiently as was later the case. There were still Poles who were willing to talk freely of what had happened since 1939, including the deportations to Siberia from 1939 to 1941 when the Russians were in control of all of Poland east of the Molotov-Ribbentrop Line.

Despite the suffering which the Poles had endured under the Nazi occupation and especially in Warsaw, many of the Poles with whom we spoke amazingly admitted that they preferred Nazi occupation to their present plight. Under the Nazis, they said, there were great brutality, complete deprivation of liberty, and even murders, but at

A SOVIET CONVOY, LADEN WITH LOOT, PASSES THROUGH GUTTED WARSAW

Photographers risked arrest to take pictures such as this.

MY FORMAL INTRODUCTION TO THE POLISH
PROVISIONAL GOVERNMENT
Front row, left to right: Modzelewski; Bierut; Lane; Rzymowski; and Dorsz.

RED ARMY MARSHALS HONORED FOR "LIBERATING" POLAND
Front row, left to right: Zhukov; Bierut; Rokossovsky; Osóbka-Morawski. (Soviet
Ambassador Lebedev stands behind Rokossovsky.)

least the Nazis had matters well organized. If a Pole was arrested for political reasons, his family generally knew in what town, prison and cell he was confined. They knew that food could be sent to him on such and such a day, and when it was possible for him to receive visitors. Under the NKVD system, however, a person disappeared, usually clandestinely. If he was heard of again it was a great stroke of good luck. In most cases there was no word from the Russian or Polish authorities confirming the arrest of the unfortunate person or his fate. He might have been temporarily detained in a Polish prison; he might have been sent to a Siberian slave camp; or he might have been "liquidated."

During our early days in Warsaw even the word of our Polish friends was not needed to convince us of the terrorist methods employed by the Soviet Army and secret police. At that time Red Army convoys were continually passing through Warsaw on their way eastward to Russia. Some of these convoys of primitive horse-drawn carts, filled with all types of loot, might have come from the Soviet-occupied zone of Germany. But some, we were able to ascertain, contained loot taken from Poland, even from parts east of the former boundary between Poland and Germany. Livestock, industrial machinery, or any property which served to give a livelihood to owners unfortunate enough to live on the route of the convoys moving east, was in danger of confiscation.

The danger was not only the relatively minor one of lost property. Tragic cases of the violation of women and even of young girls came to our attention. The Soviet Ambassador, Mr. Lebedev, admitted to me that he was most perturbed over the robbery, rape and murder which had been perpetrated by undisciplined members of the Red Army. He said that these occurrences were bound to affect adversely the relations between the Soviet Union and Poland, but, because of the sudden relaxing of military discipline at the end of the war, it was a development which, however regrettable, was not unnatural.

In addition to the terror created in Poland by the returning Red Army, the newly formed Polish Security Police—Urzad Bezpieczenstwa, colloquially known as "U.B."—was making itself unpleasantly known. Like the NKVD, the Russian counterpart, the members of the U.B. were distinguished by blue collar tabs and hatbands. Many an arrest by these uniformed agents was witnessed by members of the American Embassy on the streets of Warsaw during those early days. Later, more subtle and terrifying methods were employed, such as arrests in the middle of the night; and the person arrested generally was not permitted to communicate with the outside world, perhaps for months, perhaps for all time.

From the very moment of our arrival we were besieged by applicants for passports, by those claiming American citizenship through birth or naturalization, and for visas, by those of Polish nationality desiring to leave for the United States. For six years there had been no legitimate way for Polish citizens to emigrate. Now, with the Soviet police state replacing that of the Gestapo, these poor people longed to go to America, the land whence their relatives wrote to them of freedom and whence they used to send remittances.

Our "reception rooms" for visitors consisted, at the outset, of the bedrooms of the members of our staff. The hotel manager, though very considerate and co-operative, pleaded that he could not, for the time being, allocate further space to our Embassy; to do so he would be forced to eject from the hotel premises other diplomatic and Polish officials.

We had been fortunate enough to be able to re-employ some former Polish members of the staff of the Consulate General, women familiar with our passport and visa regulations. They came to us virtually in rags. They had lost their homes, all their possessions, including their modest savings, as a result of the Nazi occupation. They appeared undernourished and sickly. But their spirit was unconquerable.

When our "offices" opened for business on August 1, 1945, on the second floor of the Polonia Hotel, these valued Polish employees helped our officers in classifying the varying requests—for visas, passports, employment, information about families in the United States, veterans' compensation, or financial assistance—and in giving advice to the applicants who started forming in line before eight o'clock every morning.

We could give these hapless individuals friendly advice and moral support, but there was generally little we could do for them in a practical sense. Applicants for visas would have to obtain, in the first place, Polish passports; and the Polish Government was not permitting the emigration of Polish nationals, except those of Jewish race and certain other rare instances. Applicants for passports would be obliged to wait for months before we could, with our very limited staff, process the passport applications. These, by the beginning of 1947, amounted to fifteen thousand. And as these applications included only heads of families we estimated that about 50,000 persons were involved.

For weeks in these makeshift quarters our staff listened to the pitiful stories of misery, resulting from destruction of their homes, loss of their families and hopelessness as to the future. It was to escape the despair of ruined Poland that these poor people wished to join their friends and relatives in the United States.

Many of the applicants brought discouraging news of a different character. Fathers, husbands, brothers or sons had been imprisoned since the arrival of the Red Army in Poland. They had been arrested by the Russian NKVD or by the Polish U.B. In almost all cases of arrests of native-born or naturalized American citizens, the accused had been members of the Home Army, or Polish underground, during the Nazi occupation. They had, as such, been subject to the discipline of a well-organized military force which received its orders, by clandestine radio, operating under the very noses of the Nazis, from the Polish Government-in-Exile in London.

Owing to the wholesale destruction of documents, incident to the burning of Warsaw and to the devastation throughout Poland generally, the families of many of the arrested persons were unable to furnish proof of the American birth or American naturalization of their imprisoned relatives. On receiving the information as to date of birth, baptism, naturalization or issuance of passport, the Embassy would immediately take steps to verify the claim of citizenship through the Department of State from the respective state authorities in the United States. If the evidence was confirmed, the Embassy would bring to the attention of the Polish Foreign Office, orally and in writing, the information we had received about the individual: the date and place of his arrest, and the evidence supporting his claim to American citizenship. In several cases the persons arrested were charged with military offenses and were under sentence of death.

After we had approached the Foreign Office on repeated occasions, however, we finally received official confirmation of our already firm belief that the reason for the arrests of these American citizens—or "claimants to American citizenship," as we prudently termed them in our notes to the Foreign Office—was that they had been members of the Polish underground movement. The Polish Government termed them members of "illegal or terroristic organizations." For the most part they had been members of the Home Army, or "Armja Krajowa," known generally as the "A.K." This underground, unlike the People's Army, or Armja Ludowa (A.L.), had been fully as resentful toward the Soviet Government for its share in the spoliation of Poland in 1939 as toward the Nazis. The A.L., a left-wing group, looked at Soviet actions through rose-colored glasses.

The political implication in the Polish Government's denunciation of the A.K. was apparent. On Sikorski's death in 1943, Mikolajczyk, as Premier of the London Government-in-Exile, had directed the operations of the underground against the Nazis. The terrorization of its former members through arrests and through even more dire punishment would have as its aim the breaking up of a political force in sympathy with Mikolajczyk and the discrediting of Mikolajczyk himself.

In our oral and written communications to the Foreign Office we had asked, in accordance with the general provisions of the Treaty of 1931 between the United States and Poland, permission to visit these claimants in jail—to ascertain their welfare and to render such assistance as might be possible. In my talks with Polish officials I said that I was merely requesting what would be granted as a matter of routine procedure in case a Polish consular officer in the United States wished to visit one of his nationals detained for any offense. But permission was not forthcoming. I therefore decided to approach the Minister of Security, the highest authority on matters involving persons under arrest.

Of all the cabinet ministers on whom I was to call, I had been most anxious to meet Mr. Stanislaw Radkiewicz, Minister of Public Security. I would not have been surprised if my formal request for an interview had been refused. The Embassy had learned that it was almost impossible for even Polish officials to talk with him on matters of business. I was gratified, therefore, when I received an appointment for September 27.

Accompanied by Tonesk, I proceeded to Radkiewicz' headquarters—at that time established in Praga on the east side of the Vistula River—a large gray building, to which general access by automobile was prevented by the use of road blocks. Our car, flying the United States flag, was allowed to pass the barriers. After having been passed by men in U.B. uniforms, armed with tommy guns, we were met by a U.B. officer who led the way to the office of the reputedly inaccessible Radkiewicz.

If his customary technique, as we had heard, was to instill terror in the hearts of his callers, to us he showed great cordiality and urbanity. He was a good-looking man, apparently of Russian Semitic origin, with carefully combed oily black hair, a keen, mobile, aesthetic face. He opened our conversation by remarking, with understandable logic, that Poland had been so disorganized by the Nazis that the new government had been forced to call on one of her allies for assistance in the reconstruction of the country. The United States and England were far away; Russia was Poland's closest neighbor. Also after World War I, Poland had been disorganized as a result of German occupation. Then she had turned to France for assistance in reorganizing the Army. Now she had turned to Russia, as France was in no position to lend assistance. He frankly admitted that the Russians had lent him two hundred NKVD instructors, who would organize the Polish Security Police along Soviet lines.

I told Radkiewicz of my apprehensions over the arrests of American citizens. I said I had discussed the situation with the President, the Prime Minister and with various members of the Foreign Office, and I pointed out that maltreatment of American citizens could perhaps more easily than any other factor seriously prejudice the relations between Poland and the United States. Therefore, it would be to mutual advantage if Mr. Radkiewicz would give his personal attention to all cases involving claimants to American citizenship, so that a complaint could not be justifiably made against the Polish Government that it was not properly protecting our nationals. The Minister said that at the moment no Americans were under arrest in Poland, and he could assure me that in the event any Americans were arrested he would see to it that the Embassy would be advised at once. The promise was never carried out.

This was the first and last time I was able to see Mr. Radkiewicz in his office. Some months later, when the question of arrests of claimants to American citizenship had assumed a far more serious character—because of an increased number of arrests reported by families and because of the inability or unwillingness of the Polish Foreign Office to get permission for American Embassy officials to interview prisoners in the presence of Polish Government officials—I tried vainly to secure another interview with the Minister of Public Security, or with the Deputy Minister. Over a period of a week Lieutenant Tonesk called repeatedly by telephone. He was given a variety of reasons why the Minister could not see me: Mr. Radkiewicz was out of town; he was ill; he was in conference; he was very busy.

On October 19, when I again took up with Modzelewski the serious situation created by our inability to visit American citizens detained in jail, I was agreeably surprised. Modzelewski, after expressing the opinion that many of the men arrested had misrepresented themselves as United States citizens in order to obtain our protection, said we could visit all bona fide United States citizens—in other words, those whose citizenship had been confirmed by the United States Government. He said that all our notes on the cases of arrested Americans had been referred by the Foreign Office to the Ministry of Justice, which was the competent authority in matters of this nature.

The Minister of Justice, Dr. Swietkowski, a scholarly, benevolent and serious-appearing official, a member of the Polish Socialist Party, received me on October 26. He offered his assistance in effecting the release of our nationals but warned me that the police system had unfortunately for the time being supplanted judicial procedure in Poland. He said, however, that all arrangements for the release of foreign nationals should be made by the respective diplomatic missions with the Foreign Office. When I told Swietkowski of Modzelewski's statement that all our diplomatic notes relating to arrests had been referred to the Ministry of Justice, the Minister calmly said that the Foreign Office had not informed his ministry of the arrests of any American citizens.

If, as now seemed probable, Modzelewski was deliberately evading our requests by setting us off on a wild-goose chase through another ministry, what were his assurances worth? It seemed advisable to smoke him out without delay. Therefore, on that same day, October 26, I called on him and presented a note stating that of the thirteen American citizens then under arrest, none had been allowed to communicate with the Embassy while in detention. Furthermore, our note continued, we had received disquieting reports that the persons arrested had been imprisoned for alleged political offenses, had usually been held incommunicado and had on occasion been physically maltreated by the authorities in an attempt to extract information. I asked to be given the basis for the charges against the accused, inquired whether the accused had freedom of access to the Polish courts, as guaranteed under Article I of the Treaty of 1931, and asked what steps had been taken to effect their release in the absence of charges.

I also requested a written confirmation of Modzelewski's statement of October 19 to the effect that officers of the United States Embassy would be permitted to interview those persons whom the Polish authorities held under arrest and whose claims to American citizenship had been approved by us.

This note was not answered for five months! Then on March 21, 1946, the Foreign Office addressed a note to the Embassy, asking us to give the basis for the claims to American citizenship of the persons arrested. We had already given this information when we presented each case to the Polish Government. But we were glad to furnish it again. Finally, on April 27, 1946 (immediately after the grant by the United States of a ninety-million-dollar credit to Poland), Modzelewski informed the Embassy in writing as of that date, after a lengthy dissertation on the differences between the Polish and United States citizenship laws, that each arrested person claiming American citizenship should submit answers to a questionnaire, on the basis of which his citizenship would be determined. But independently of this procedure, Modzelewski assured us that whenever the Embassy would be particularly interested in having direct communication with the arrested person claiming American citizenship, a meeting with the prisoner would be made possible.

Yet, with the exception of the case of Mrs. Dmochowska, an employee of the Embassy who was arrested in August 1946, we were not permitted to visit, throughout my incumbency as Ambassador, any one of the arrested American citizens, whose number had increased to a hundred by the time I left Poland. One of this number, Stanislaw Tupaj, born in the United States and recognized as an American citizen by the Department of State, was condemned to death and executed without having recourse to the assistance of United States consular authorities.

After fifteen months of our continual insistence to the Polish Government the Foreign Office proposed to us in December 1946 that a commission be set up, composed of two members of each government.

This commission was to determine the citizenship of the arrested claimants and to arrange for the American Embassy to visit those whose American citizenship was confirmed. At last the commission held its first meetings in June 1947. But our citizens, up to October 1947, were still unable to enjoy their Embassy's protection, to which they were entitled by treaty!

One major difficulty in dealing with the thousands of applicants for protection, passports and visas was the critical housing situation in Warsaw. A month after our arrival the Polish Government offices which had been in Praga were little by little being moved across the river to Warsaw and, understandably, prior preference of accommodations was given to the government. Foreign embassies and legations were obliged to wait until buildings could be reconstructed and then formally allocated by the Polish Foreign Office. The Soviet Embassy, however, had no difficulties. Its magnificent new building on Aleja Szucha, later renamed the Avenue of the First Red Army— the first Soviet force to enter Warsaw—was constructed without delay and was ready for occupancy a few weeks after the arrival of the Soviet Ambassador.

Our chief concern was to find premises where the Embassy business could be transacted. The management of the Polonia Hotel was objecting to the long line of applicants which clogged the corridors. But, although the inhabitants of Warsaw showed energy and stoicism in making available a room or two from the rubble which was all that was left of their homes, they evidenced no enthusiasm in rebuilding: the municipality might, as it did in many cases, expropriate the property without compensation and divert it to government use. Finally the Foreign Office allocated to us a small building at 17 Emilia Plater Street. Our rent was paid to the Polish Government. The owners, who lived in England, received nothing. The assembling of four Nissen huts which the Naval Attaché had brought to Warsaw helped to alleviate our problem of office quarters; but when I left

Warsaw we estimated that unless we received funds to employ additional personnel and to rent adequate office space it would require from six to ten years to dispose of the pending applications.

By the end of September it was apparent that the Polish Government was unwilling, despite its prior assurances, to fix a rate of exchange which would enable our staff to subsist even on a modest scale. In August the average minimum weekly expenditure for meals and lodging per person of the Embassy, at the current diplomatic rate of eleven and one-half zlotys per dollar, was four hundred and eighty dollars. And the average weekly income per person was less than fifty dollars! At the same time the hotel management was courteously but firmly insisting that we would have to leave our hotel rooms unless we paid our indebtedness, amounting to over two million zlotys. I asked and obtained permission from the Department of State to sell United States yellow-seal currency on the open market to meet our official and living expenses. Modzelewski, while obviously not approving the course, which I told him I had been authorized to take in view of his not having fulfilled his promise, stated that we would be contravening no law or regulation. Under this arrangement the United States Government and members of the Embassy staff obtained a zloty equivalent on their dollar drafts of a rate ranging from three hundred to thirteen hundred, during the next six months. But a draft negotiated in a bank would net only one hundred zlotys to the dollar—the normal rate of five and three-tenths, which corresponded to the Soviet ruble rate, plus an "equalization rate" of ninety-four and seven-tenths. If it had not been for this practice, which was resorted to by almost all foreign diplomatic missions, we could not have retained our personnel in Poland or operated our mission within the budget fixed by the Department.

I attempted to persuade the Foreign Office to fix a reasonable rate of exchange applicable to all transactions; otherwise, American relatives of persons in Poland would be discouraged from sending remittances. In the year before the war these remittances were estimated at twenty million dollars, a valuable contribution to Poland's foreign-exchange surplus. Later we learned that when the government wished to invite foreign investments in Poland, for instance for the building of a hospital, a subsidy in zlotys was paid to the investor in addition to the amount realized from the sale of the draft at the rate of one hundred to one.

Another difficulty under which I labored was the censorship of the Polish press, which prevented me from reporting accurately to the Department of State the true conditions in Poland. Under the Yalta agreement, the American Ambassador had an international obligation to report to his government. And implicitly the Polish Government had an obligation to permit him to do so.

We learned soon after our arrival in Warsaw that the Polish newspapers obtained all their news from the government-controlled Polpress, a press service which also distributed releases of government statements, photographs, etc. All the newspapers in Warsaw published articles written identically, and the Polpress releases were usually interspersed with editorial comment favorable to the Communist-controlled regime. The most important Warsaw dailies were *Glos Ludu*, the organ of the Polish Workers Party (PPR); *Kurier Codzienny*, organ of the Democratic Party (SD); *Robotnik*, organ of the Polish Socialist Party (PPS); *Rzeczpospolita*, allegedly independent but with strong pro-government leanings; and *Zycie Warszawy*, dealing principally with local Warsaw news and also allegedly independent. The last two newspapers were published by the nationalized newspaper co-operative, Czytelnik, the editorial responsibility of which rested in a government-nominated editorial college. Although these two papers bore the names of prewar Warsaw newspapers, they were now controlled by members of the former Lublin Government. No changes in the editorial personnel had been made under the Polish Provisional Government of National Unity.

It was interesting to note that the general editorial policy of all newspapers stressed friendship for the U.S.S.R. and reviled the London Government-in-Exile which, regardless of withdrawal of recognition by the United States and United Kingdom, still continued as a private body in London.

It was not until October that *Gazeta Ludowa,* the organ of Mikolajczyk's Polish Peasant Party, was able to obtain permission to circulate.

I had a personal experience with the lack of freedom of the press shortly after my arrival. On August 9 I gave an interview to *Zycie Warszawy* at its request. What I said was innocuous in tone and expressed the cordial friendship entertained by the American people for Poland; I mentioned America's great interest in the holding of free elections in Poland. When the draft of the interview was submitted to me for approval, I pointed out that it did not contain this reference. The reporter shrugged his shoulders. I said nothing more, for I did not wish to make any trouble for him with the authorities. But this incident confirmed my belief that the stooge Polish Government had no intention of holding free elections, unless it was sure of winning them.

It was likewise depressing that the editorials in the Warsaw press in August 1945 belittled the United States' offer of economic and financial assistance as enunciated in my remarks to President Bierut on August 4. The Communist line of the papers was that the United States had a surfeit of goods which it could not use in any case and that we were therefore serving our own selfish interests by giving this help to Poland. The press had followed the Soviet line also in describing the victory over Japan, emphasizing the Soviet Union's enormous contribution—for less than one week, in Manchuria—and minimizing our effort—for more than three and a half years throughout the South Pacific.

But of all our trials and troubles, the development which caused me the greatest concern was a telegram from the Department of State early in September stating that only forty-three out of one hundred messages sent by us to Washington by radio had been received. As our telegrams were serially numbered, lack of receipt could easily be verified by the addressee. Obviously they had been held up in Moscow, for we were able to confirm that they had actually left the Warsaw post office on the day of filing. Even communication with my own government was being blocked!

As reference to our file copies indicated that the most important messages sent in our first month in Poland had not been received in Washington, I determined to fly to London and report personally to Secretary Byrnes. He was then taking part in the first session of the Council of Foreign Ministers, as established by the Potsdam agreement.

When I called on Modzelewski on September 10 to acquaint him with the reasons for my brief absence, he expressed pleasure that I would report "objectively" to Secretary Byrnes on the freedom of speech in Poland and would thus give the lie to calumnies that had appeared in the foreign press. I told him that my report would be candid and would therefore include an account of the censorship of the press, of which I gave him several examples that affected the United States. He strongly refuted my contention and said that I had been misinformed about conditions in Poland. The press, he averred, was completely free!

Colonel York flew me out of Warsaw at 10:00 A.M. on September 12 in the C-47 recently allotted to the Embassy. It was an unconverted Army transport plane which, from its battle scars, had evidently been through its baptism of fire long ago. Its bucket seats were not comfortable at all for passengers. But it was a comfort to feel that one could communicate with the outside world by plane, if not by telegraph. At noon we arrived at the enormous Tempelhof airdrome, administered by the United States. Its hangars were all destroyed, but the administration building was intact. Even after only six weeks in Poland my landing in territory under American control gave me the feeling of suddenly regaining freedom. The U.B. was not in control here! Due to our diplomatic position in Warsaw we ourselves had not been in physical danger. But all of us felt the mental strain of continual surveillance and of the never-ending fear lest some of our Polish friends be imprisoned because they had the temerity to speak to us.

Miss McNulty and I had lunch in a delightful homelike atmosphere, quite different from that of the spy-infested and garish dining room of the Hotel Polonia. We were guests of Ambassador Murphy in his tastefully furnished house in a residential quarter of Berlin little damaged by the war. Murphy gave me the good news that General Eisenhower had accepted an invitation from the Polish Government to visit Warsaw and would probably arrive on September 21. I was elated to know that the Polish Government had decided to pay tribute to our army leader whose exploits, like those of General MacArthur, had gone unsung in the Communist-controlled Polish press.

About three hours later, after a sunny flight over Germany and Holland, we landed at Bovingdon airport near London. In England I sensed the atmosphere of security and freedom. The British had suffered grievously during the war, as the ruins in the city and along the docks testified. But their nation had not been controlled by an alien police force, Gestapo or NKVD.

Among Polish circles news of my arrival spread rapidly, even though my telegram of September 8 to the Embassy in London, sent four days before, was not received until after I got there! That evening I met a group who besieged me with questions about their families, the condition of Warsaw, the food situation and my estimate of the future: would Poland regain its freedom? It was painful to have to tell the truth—that until the Red Army was withdrawn, there was little hope of the Poles having independence. But I did not divulge to these private individuals my fear that the NKVD and U.B. held the reins of power so tightly that no democracy in our sense of the word was possible for Poland for years to come.

Secretary Byrnes received me the next afternoon at four o'clock in his suite at Claridge's Hotel. Trim, vigorous and supple, he expressed with flashing eyes his indignation over our inability to communicate regularly with the outside world. His query of me, however, why I had allowed such a situation to arise, indicated that Mr. Byrnes, like all those Americans who had not lived in a Communist-controlled police state, could not visualize the restrictive measures taken. I told the Secretary, however, that our own radio station had at last been established—at Konstancin, twelve miles from Warsaw—and I hoped we would have no further trouble.

I related to him briefly the results of my observations during our first few weeks in Poland: the economic needs, the wonderful spirit of the Polish people in adversity, the lack of freedom of the press and the terroristic activities of the U.B. In response to my suggestion, he authorized me to use his name in urging the American press associations, through their offices in London, to send representatives to Poland at the earliest possible moment. Because of the acute housing scarcity in Warsaw, newspaper correspondents would be obliged to defer their arrival for a week or two.

That evening I dined with Maynard B. Barnes, the energetic and forthright United States representative in Bulgaria, whose vivid account of arrests, censorship and other police-state activities reminded me of my own Warsaw experiences. As I was later to verify from other colleagues in countries behind "the Iron Curtain," the technique in all Soviet satellite nations is virtually identical: only the names, places and languages differ.

In accordance with Secretary Byrnes's desire, Larry Allen and Charles Arnot, of the Associated and the United Press respectively, were members of our party as we left Villacoublay on the afternoon of September 17. (The International News Service had no representative available at the moment.) Dr. Bauer and Mr. Grady of the American Red Cross, although they had no Polish visas, also were on board the plane.

The next day, just as we were about to take off from Tempelhof for Warsaw, I received a phone call from Frankfurt that General Eisenhower would arrive in Warsaw on the twenty-first at about 11:00 A.M. and would return to Berlin the same afternoon.

Some minutes before eleven o'clock on a beautiful sunny morning General Eisenhower's four-motor plane circled over Okecie airport. It was a good thing that it did not land immediately, for the Polish authorities in charge of the reception had not yet arrived, and the Embassy had not yet been advised, despite our frantic appeals to the Foreign Office early that morning, regarding the program for the few hours which General Eisenhower would spend in Warsaw.

On the stroke of eleven, the door of General Eisenhower's plane opened. Smiling, he emerged, followed by his Chief of Staff, Lieutenant General W. Bedell Smith, and by Ambassador Murphy. After greeting them, I introduced them to General Spychalski who, in the absence of Marshal Rola-Zymierski, then vacationing in the Crimea, was temporarily in command of the Army. The band played the two national anthems, General Eisenhower reviewed the guard of honor, and our party proceeded to Warsaw without knowing our exact destination. General Eisenhower, General Spychalski and I, accompanied by a Polish naval officer acting as interpreter, drove in an open car which Hitler had used when he visited Warsaw after its capitulation in September 1939. I suggested to General Spychalski that we drive first to the Polonia Hotel to permit General Eisenhower to meet the members of the Embassy staff and then go to the old part of the city and to the Ghetto, so that the general might see for himself the extent and intensity of the destruction. Spychalski readily acquiesced.

When General Eisenhower walked out of the hotel onto the sidewalk, after meeting our official family, he was greeted by spontaneous cries of *"Niech Zyje!"* ("Long life to you!") from a crowd of several hundred which had suddenly assembled when word of the American military leader's arrival spread about. As General Eisenhower edged his way through the crowd without any police protection whatever, I thought of the reception of the Soviet marshals on August 5 who, even as they walked through the Lazienki gardens behind the President's palace, were flanked by armed guards.

General Eisenhower proceeded to the tomb of the Unknown Soldier, erected after World War I. This had been blown up by the Nazis before they left Warsaw. After drawing himself stiffly to attention and saluting, he placed on the broken marble slab a bouquet of roses—red and white, the Polish national colors. The flowers had been presented to him by an elderly woman at the airport. I noted that in the ruins of the tomb there still remained references to past battles in which the Polish Army had fought, including the engagements with the Soviet Army in 1920 when Warsaw was threatened. Later on, these battle names, which stood for Polish hostility to Russia in the past, were permanently removed.

We then went to the Stare Miasto, the oldest district in the city, whose medieval buildings had been utterly destroyed by the Germans during the Polish insurrection the year before. Here, because of the rubble, we were forced to leave our automobiles and walk through ruins. The Rynek, or market place, formerly one of the most beautiful architectural gems in Europe, surrounded by houses with multicolored façades, was nothing but a mass of crumbled stone. We walked by the hollow shell of St. John's Cathedral, where I had represented the United States Legation in 1919 at the consecration of Monsignor Ratti—then Apostolic Nuncio, later Pope Pius XI—as Bishop. I showed to General Eisenhower, through an arch which was still standing, a magnificent view of the Vistula River below and Praga beyond, with the dome of the Russian Orthodox Church glittering in the sunlight.

I explained to him that during the insurrection of 1944 this part of town had been initially held by the Polish Home Army, which was daily expecting the Soviets to join forces with them from the other side.

Emphasizing that he was speaking purely as a soldier, the general observed, "What a perfect bridgehead!" Evidently even such a famed military strategist could not understand why the Russian armies had not come to the aid of Warsaw.

We then made a tour of the destroyed Ghetto, razed and pulverized by the Nazis in April 1943, both from the air and from the ground, by planes, tanks, incendiary bombs and cannon. This was in retaliation for the insurrection of the Jewish population in protest against the tortures and asphyxiations at Oswiecim, Majdanek and Buchenwald. The ruins covered four square miles. There was utter desolation throughout. Not even the walls of a single house remained to show that this was once a humming part of a great city. Ex-President Hoover said to me, when he visited Warsaw in March 1946, "This should be left forever as a monument to Nazi bestiality."

Long before we had completed our melancholy tour, General Eisenhower's customary smile had vanished. And as we turned away from the last of the dreadful examples of destruction, he observed grimly that of all the great cities of Europe that he had lately visited none had been so completely wiped out as Warsaw.

At the Belvedere Palace President Bierut, his cabinet and high Army officials cordially received General Eisenhower. Bierut presented to him, on behalf of the Polish Government, one of the highest Polish decorations—the Order of Grunwald. He had already received the order of *virtuti militari,* but from the London Government!

In an extemporaneous speech of thanks, ably interpreted by Tonesk, General Eisenhower modestly stated that he considered this honor to be a tribute primarily to the United States and to the American Army, which had fought with the Poles, our gallant allies, and he spoke eloquently of the invaluable support which the Poles had rendered his command.

Groups of cheering school children in Polish national costumes paraded before the general as he stood on the front steps of the palace. But no regimented tribute could match the unbridled enthusiasm which the ragged men, women and children had given to Eisenhower in front of the Polonia that morning. If his visit accomplished nothing else, it showed, through that spontaneous demonstration, the deep-seated affection and admiration of the people of Poland for the United States, as personified by this military hero.

CHAPTER TWELVE

Political Freedom—Moscow Style

AT POTSDAM the Polish Provisional Government of National Unity had agreed, in accordance with the decisions of the Crimea Conference, to the holding of free and unfettered elections as soon as possible. This commitment was in fact embodied in the text of the Potsdam Declaration. Furthermore, as the British Ambassador told me, President Bierut had given assurances to the British Foreign Secretary, Mr. Bevin, at Potsdam that elections would take place in Poland early in 1946.

Two early developments during my stay in Poland gave me grave doubt of the sincerity of the Polish Government as to fulfilling its obligations in the vital matter of the elections.

When President Bierut received the American Congressional Subcommittee—consisting of Representatives Bolton, Gordon, Mundt and Ryter—at the Belvedere Palace on September 27, 1945, I accompanied the delegation. One of the congressmen, who said he had an especial interest because he represented many constituents of Polish descent, asked the President when elections would be held.

Bierut replied, reasonably, that elections could not be held until spring, because of the intensity of the Polish winters, which would prevent peasants in the outlying districts from getting to the polling places. He referred, also, to the serious lack of transportation as a result of the Nazi occupation, which too would make it difficult for the peasants to vote. Bierut expected that elections probably would not be held until May or June—the thaws in the early spring would render the roads impassable.

Had I, as Ambassador to Poland, been informed by the Department of State of all that had transpired at Yalta, I could have made

an appropriate observation to Bierut. But it was not until the publication of Mr. Byrnes's account of the Yalta conversations* that I learned
what Molotov had said there concerning the proposed Polish elections
in reply to Mr. Roosevelt's question: "How long will it take you to
hold free elections?"

"Within a month's time," Mr. Molotov replied.

But when President Bierut (more than six months after Yalta)
made excuses to the congressmen that the elections were to be delayed
until May or June, the cynical thought occurred to me that the real
reason for postponing elections for eight months would be to permit
the Security Police to organize its machinery and prevent, through
arrests, censorship or other means, the activities of the two opposition
parties, the Peasant Party, headed by Witos, and the Christian Labor
Party. As it turned out, the elections, when they were held finally in
January 1947, took place in the coldest month of the winter and at a
time when the snowdrifts in certain parts of the country prevented
all travel.

Another development which concerned me was the remark made by
President Bierut when the British Ambassador, Mr. V. Cavendish-
Bentinck, presented his letters of credence on August 25. Bentinck
and I had served together in Warsaw in 1919. A friendship of many
years and the fact that we saw eye to eye on the attempts of the Polish
Government to evade its international obligations, resulted in our
always speaking with the utmost frankness to each other.

Bentinck told me that when he broached the subject of the elections
to Bierut, on that occasion, and complained that freedom of the press
was being denied to the opposition parties, Bierut replied that the
control of the press was a matter for the Polish Government to decide
and was not the concern of foreign governments. When Bentinck
referred to an undertaking which Bierut had made at Potsdam on
August 1 that there would be freedom of the press in Poland, Bierut
replied that the Polish Government, although bound by the Yalta

---

* Byrnes, *op. cit.*, p. 32.

agreement, was not committed by any statements made at Potsdam, which were merely general expressions of policy!

In my initial talk with Bierut on August 4 I had, for reasons of delicacy, not mentioned the forthcoming elections. In view of the two foregoing developments, however, I decided that I should lose no further time in sounding him out as to the intentions of his government. I accordingly set forth to him, in an interview on September 24, at which Tonesk acted as interpreter, my deep concern over the lack of freedom of the press and over the apparent inability of some of the political parties—I had in mind the Witos Peasant Party and the Christian Labor Party—to reach the public through press and radio. I said I was disturbed also over the arrests of persons for political reasons, which would make it impossible to hold free elections in the proper sense of the term.

The President surprised me by admitting that the press was not entirely free, although he qualified this admission by asserting that out of one hundred and ten newspapers published in Poland twenty per cent were Catholic-controlled and therefore opposed to the government. (Nevertheless members of the Christian Labor Party informed me that they were unable to obtain newsprint for a paper which they desired to publish in Warsaw. Some members of the hierarchy stated openly that they were able to obtain newsprint for only fifteen thousand copies of the leading Catholic newspaper, while each government-controlled newspaper was able to publish fifty thousand copies.) Although the President denied that there was any joint editorial policy imposed by the government, he said it could not tolerate attacks made by "Fascist" elements which were attempting to destroy it.

I replied that the use of the term "Fascist" was often very elastic; that some well-informed persons had even gone so far as to define a Fascist as a person not in one hundred per cent agreement with Communism. I feared that this was the interpretation being used by the Polish Government. Bierut did not comment on my observation but admitted that "Fascists" were in prison. Further, he said that

Fascists would continue to be imprisoned; for he did not propose that his government should be destroyed by its enemies.

As I reported in a telegram to the Department of State on that day, this admission on Bierut's part clearly implied the real policy of his government in regard to freedom of speech and free elections. Although the interview with Bierut was characterized by cordiality and frankness, I did not fail to stress my view that lack of personal liberty, danger to private individuals, and lack of freedom of speech might eventually create in the United States a regrettably severe popular attitude toward the Polish Government. I earnestly begged the President to do all in his power to avert such a trend.

A disquieting incident involving the freedom of speech of American correspondents had in fact taken place the same day, September 24, when the Foreign Office informed the Embassy that the correspondents of the Associated Press, United Press and the *New York Times,* all of whom had recently arrived, should submit their dispatches to the Polish Government for approval before filing, despite the fact that the Tass agency was sending its dispatches without reference to Polish authorities.

Calling immediately on Modzelewski, I referred to the Polish Government's undertaking at Potsdam, "that representatives of the Allied press shall enjoy full freedom to report to the world upon developments in Poland before and during elections." He advanced the specious argument that nobody in Poland was talking about elections and that consequently this commitment was not applicable to the present case. I stated that we had a right to demand that the Polish Government adhere to its Potsdam commitment; I could think of nothing which would more seriously damage the Polish Government in the eyes of the people of the United States than censoring the dispatches of American press correspondents. My insistence had its effect, because from that time on until May 1946 no further censorship of the sort was attempted.

Having been in Warsaw for two months without an opportunity

to obtain a first-hand impression of conditions throughout the rest of the country, I decided to visit Kraków, the academic and cultural center of Poland; Katowice, the center of the mining industry; Wroclaw (Breslau), which lay within the territory placed under Polish administration by the Potsdam conference; and Lódz, the heart of the textile industry then outranking Warsaw as the largest city in Poland, with a population of almost one million.

Traveling south and accompanied by Lieutenant Colonel Andrew Wylie, USMC, our Naval Attaché, Larry Allen of the Associated Press, and Tonesk, I stopped briefly at Radomsko, the furniture manufacturing center. Here a curious crowd of men, women and children gathered about our automobile, attracted by the American flag and the uniforms of Wylie and Tonesk. This sign of friendliness for the United States was repeated daily during our trip. It was not until months after that these spontaneous demonstrations no longer were made. True, the novelty of the first American automobiles had worn off. But by that time the people had been warned by the U.B. not to have contact with foreigners, especially members of foreign embassies.

We passed through the famed city of Czestochowa with its thirteenth-century shrine, around which the towering cathedral had been built. I inquired of one of the priests of the cathedral whether freedom of worship had yet been infringed. He replied in the negative, but said that U.B. agents took notes on all sermons, indicating that repressive measures might be taken if any utterances from the pulpit were distasteful to the government.

Stopping for a moment in the streets of Zabrze, near Kraków, I found an extremely large crowd surrounding our automobile. But on this occasion, although the people professed to be great admirers of the United States, they were not Poles, but Germans. Zabrze, formerly named Hindenburg, had been a German city.

One woman approached me, caught hold of my arm and begged me to use the influence of the United States to prevent the Polish Government from obliging German children to attend Polish-speaking schools. The woman, who appeared to be the ringleader for the crowd, berated the Poles as a race for their inhuman treatment of the Germans.

Having just come from the desolation of Warsaw, which had been deliberately leveled by the Nazis, and having seen the horrors of Majdanek, I felt that her attack on the Polish nation was most incongruous, and I forcefully gave vent to my amazement. The crowd slowly dispersed, some of them sobbing.

In Kraków, one of the most beautiful medieval cities in Europe, I called on Archbishop, later Cardinal, Sapieha. He was nearing his eightieth year, but his was a most intense, energetic and sparkling personality. I happened to be the first American official whom he had seen since before the war; he had had practically no contact with the outside world since 1939. During the Nazi occupation he had refused to call on Governor Frank, who had installed himself in the Wawel, the famed medieval castle, where Marshal Pilsudski and all the kings of Poland were buried. Throughout Poland, Archbishop Sapieha was venerated because of his devotion to the people and his strong stand of moral resistance against the invader. By many he was termed the Cardinal Mercier of World War II.

It was on this trip that I saw Witos. I saw other Polish political leaders, including Professor Kutrzeba, who was one of those invited to Moscow and who died shortly after of an incurable illness. I spoke through my interpreter to many persons in the shops, restaurants and on the street. All gave me information confirming the opinion which we had already formed from our two months in Poland: Poland was a police state governed by the Kremlin. I was everywhere assured that not more than five per cent of the people supported the Provisional Government. The Peasant Party and the Christian Labor Party together represented over eighty per cent of the electorate. Anyone not supporting the government was in danger of arrest, I was told. Former members of the underground were particularly vulnerable.

The government in October 1945 had, so it claimed, shown an attitude of tolerance toward the Home Army and other underground organizations by granting an amnesty to their members, provided they would make their identity known and surrender their arms. This amnesty, the opponents of the government claimed, was primarily to obtain the names of the members of the underground. The information, they felt sure, would later be used to bring about their arrest. Their apprehensions on this score were, alas, proved correct in many instances.

From Kraków we traveled to Wroclaw, making a detour by way of the Oswiecim concentration camp, to visit what was left of that inhuman creation of the Nazis. Parts of the metal crematories still remained, but most of the camp, including the barracks, the asphyxiation chambers and the quarters of the Germans, had been blown to bits by the Nazis before they retreated. The area which this concentration camp covered was many times larger than that of Majdanek, but no harrowing souvenirs, such as babies' shoes, were left as a reminder to the visitor of the horrors which had occurred there.

Wroclaw we found half destroyed and in great confusion. Germans were being forcibly deported daily to German territory. It was obvious that the Poles did not consider that they were occupying Wroclaw temporarily, subject to final approval by the peace conference. All German signs were being removed and replaced by those in the Polish language. Poles were being brought into Wroclaw from other parts of Poland to replace the repatriated Germans. In Wroclaw again I found the Poles willing to talk to us. They too confirmed what we had heard at Kraków about the police-state methods in force.

And when we arrived at Lódz, where we made tentative plans to establish a consular office to handle visa applications—a project which eventually we abandoned because of the difficulty of obtaining personnel—I learned of the attempts to force the populace to join the two principal government parties, the Workers and the Socialist. Those who joined were given preference ration cards entitling them to receive certain choice UNRRA supplies and assuring them of continuance in their jobs which were, throughout Poland, under government control.

No wonder that Molotov, in the meetings of the Moscow Commission, had strongly objected to our observers going to Poland and finding out what the Polish people actually thought of the Lublin Committee and of its Kremlin masters! Now, with the U.B. organized, it would become more difficult and more dangerous for the people to talk to the members of the United States Embassy.

The sensitiveness of the Polish Government toward the Soviet control of the country was evidenced when Modzelewski, after my return from this trip, sent for me on the evening of October 26. He complained to me that two press dispatches sent by American correspondents in Warsaw had indicated that Poland was under Soviet domination. Modzelewski said that if these correspondents went on writing in this vein they could not stay in Poland.

After reminding Modzelewski of the guarantees of the Potsdam agreement, I pointed out to him that in the United States there is complete freedom of the press and that even the President of the United States, regardless of his political affiliation, is from time to time subjected to severe criticism. In the same way, I observed, if there were true freedom of the press in Poland I could not rightfully make any objection to any articles which might appear in the Polish press unfriendly to the United States. The Minister of Propaganda, Mr. Matuszewski, I added, had assured me that the government controlled the material issued by Czytelnik, which had recently published in the satirical weekly *Szpilki* some very offensive cartoons about the United States. As, however, this material had been published with the consent and probably at the instigation of the government, I felt obliged to complain on the ground that such propaganda would, if persisted in, bring about a deterioration in the relations between the United States and Poland.

When Modzelewski heatedly denied lack of freedom of the press, I quoted President Bierut as having said to me that freedom according to our conception did not exist in Poland. I said to Mr. Modzelewski, with some asperity, that I assumed I should accept the opinion of the highest authority in Poland—the President—rather than his view.

A few days later I had occasion to speak to Jakób Berman about the denial of freedom of the press. He asked from what source I had obtained this impression, indicating that he considered I had got it from enemies of the government. I told him that I based my remarks on the distortions which editors of Polish newspapers had made of important speeches and statements in the United States. I referred specifically to the emasculation of President Truman's Navy Day address of October 27, 1945, outlining the twelve points constituting American foreign policy. For instance, no mention was made of the President's reference to our policy of not recognizing governments which might be imposed by force, nor to his support of the principle of "freedom from fear and want," nor to the strength of the United States Navy and Air Force.

Berman in this same conversation contradicted his disclaimer of censorship by saying that it would be suicide if the government permitted its enemies to attack it, for such attacks would surely result in its fall.

The Soviet-controlled mentality evidently cannot conceive that freedom of the press can exist even in the United States. When Rzymowski and Olszewski, Director of the Political Department of the Foreign Office and a Communist, returned to Warsaw from the United States after the former had signed the United Nations Declaration, they summoned me to the Foreign Office and complained to me for more than forty minutes of the "lying" accounts which American correspondents had sent from Poland about conditions there. Specifically they objected to an article sent by one correspondent which Rzymowski considered offensive personally to him. From their attitude it was clear that they could not, or would not, believe that the United States Government could not exert any control, even if it wished, over the publication of press dispatches.

The government stratagem beginning in December 1945 was to

inveigle the opposition, and principally Mikolajczyk's Polish Peasant Party, as its nucleus, to join the government parties in a single electoral list.* If Mikolajczyk would agree to such a solution of the political situation, the Polish Peasant Party would be allocated twenty per cent of the seats of the parliament to be elected and twenty per cent of the government ministries. It must have been plain to Mikolajczyk that if he agreed to join the electoral bloc, not only would his reputation for political integrity be irremediably hurt among his supporters but also he would have no assurance that a further step would not be taken after this initial capitulation to eliminate his party and himself completely from the parliament and the government. He and his followers did not accept the offer.

In December 1945 the National Council of the Homeland approved a government-sponsored plan to limit the number of political parties to six. Although the plan did not directly affect any group, at that time, it would effectively prevent the formation of any independent party in the future. Under instructions from the Department I therefore informed Bierut that this restriction of the number of political parties was, in the opinion of the United States Government, contrary to the letter and spirit of the Yalta decision.

Bierut replied angrily, with his eyes squarely fixed on his shoes, "I never knew before that it is customary for a foreign government to interfere in political and internal affairs of another country." He opined that the United States would consider it highly irregular if the Polish Ambassador in Washington should officially object to there being only two major political parties in the United States.

I replied firmly that in the United States there is no limitation on the number of political parties and furthermore the Polish Govern-

---

* The single electoral list—as employed by Soviet-controlled governments throughout eastern Europe—grouped together on one ballot all parties not in opposition to the government. A vote for the single list, even though it might contain one or more non-Communist parties, would be a vote for the continuation of the rule of the Communist-controlled government. This stratagem had the double advantage of giving the appearance of political unity and of not precluding, in the future, the elimination from the government of any non-Communist party which did not faithfully adhere to Communist dictation. The parties adhering to the single list were known as the "government bloc."

ment had no responsibility with respect to the setting up of the American political system, while on the other hand the United States had a direct responsibility with respect to Poland under the Yalta agreement, which was the precursor of the formation of the Polish Government.

The increasing tensity in the political situation was evidenced by an incident which took place in Grójec, a town halfway between Warsaw and Radom, on December 1, 1945. The populace stormed the local jail in an attempt to free some political prisoners. The attempt failed. Thereupon the U.B. officials arrested four prominent residents of the city, none of whom was involved. Two of these persons were members of the Polish Peasant Party. The four were taken to a point in a forest some ten miles south of Grójec, stripped of their clothes and shot. One of the Peasant Party members, who had had experience with Gestapo technique, dropped as the shots were fired, feigned death and, after the secret-police officers had left the vicinity, dug his way out of the shallow grave in which he had been left. He finally reached his party headquarters at Grójec. The party demanded that the officials guilty of this outrage be punished. The government refused. No mention of the incident was published in the press, although it was common knowledge throughout the country.

During the Christmas and New Year season, it is customary in Poland to close virtually all places of work. All government offices followed this practice in the winter of 1945-1946 and we gladly took advantage of it to give the members of our staff a chance to leave the depressing atmosphere of Warsaw. Arrangements were made for those who wished to go to Zakopane, a beautiful spot in the Carpathians, near the Czechoslovak frontier, where the desolation of Warsaw and U.B. terroristic activities could be temporarily forgotten. The holiday spirit was, however, seriously dampened by a tragic happening. One evening in early January Zebrowski and Gubrynowicz, the new Chief of Protocol, brought the sad news that our Naval

Attaché, Andrew Wylie, had been killed by a fall from a blown-out bridge on the Oder River. I sent Lieutenant Commander Mrozinski, the Assistant Naval Attaché, to the scene of the accident. He left immediately in the company of Polish officials who rendered him every assistance in making a comprehensive investigation. He reported to me when he got back on January 7 that Colonel Wylie, while examining the condition of the bridge in a fog after nightfall to ascertain whether his car could safely pass, had plunged fifty feet into the icy waters of the Oder. The chauffeur had heard his shout, and then the splash as he hit the water, but the body was not recovered.

Rumors were current in Poland as well as abroad that Wylie had been the victim of foul play, but we found no evidence substantiating them. Both Mrozinski and I were convinced that Wylie's most regrettable death was purely accidental.

The political situation began to develop anew soon after the holidays. Mikolajczyk addressed the congress of the Polish Peasant Party on January 19, 1946. He refused to commit himself for or against the proposal that his party should adhere to the government election bloc; but he denied the charges which the government had made that the failure of the Polish Peasant Party to enter the bloc would be an anti-Soviet gesture, and he demanded a greater participation of his party in the National Council of the Homeland; it had only fifty-one out of four hundred forty-four representatives, despite its representing the majority of the electorate. The censor permitted only a small portion of Mikolajczyk's speech to be published.

The government-controlled press was then urging the adoption of a single election bloc as a necessity for Poland and as the only means by which political tranquillity could be attained. *Rzeczpospolita* went so far as to say that Poland must, through the adoption of the bloc, reject foreign interference in Polish internal affairs. This was an obvious reference to the efforts, however vain, which Bentinck and I were making to persuade the Polish Government to live up to its international commitments to the three big powers. The article was generally considered in Poland to be a trial balloon to ascertain how far the Yalta powers were prepared to go in their insistence on free elections. The Socialist Party stated that further delay of the Peasant Party in joining the electoral bloc would be "detrimental to the interests of the state and of the nation." The Polish Peasant Party was given by the Socialists until March 1 to join. After that date it would be considered to have refused.

But the pressure which was being exerted on Mikolajczyk was not merely verbal. Two members of his party had suffered violence at the hands of the Security Police: one Kojder had mysteriously disappeared, despite the efforts of the Ministry of Public Administration to ascertain his fate; Scibiorek, another leader, had been killed in Lódz because he had insisted on remaining loyal to Mikolajczyk. Later, the government was to charge that Scibiorek was killed by his own party. The United States Government was so provoked by these political murders, flouting the spirit of the Yalta decision, that Secretary Byrnes gave the press a statement bitterly denouncing the outrages.

Ambassador Lange immediately retorted with a statement to the effect that Byrnes was badly informed; moreover, many political murders had taken place in the American zone of occupation in Germany which had been condoned by our authorities. Whether or not Lange's contention as to happenings in Germany was correct, Polish obligations under Yalta were glossed over. And, while that part of Lange's statement which referred to our alleged guilt in Germany was published in the Polish press, Byrnes's speech did not appear in it.

To signify that the Polish Government had no disposition to allow any criticism whatever of its Soviet masters, Churchill's speech at Fulton, Missouri, was grossly censored. In the Warsaw account no mention was made of Churchill's references to the "Iron Curtain" in eastern Europe, to the police states east of the Elbe River, to the Communist fifth column, to the atomic bomb, to the Soviet desire to attain the fruits of victory without fighting, and to the Soviet respect for strength—and contempt for weakness.

The Polish Peasant Party members of the National Council of the

Homeland met on April 2, 1946, to set a date for the elections at the earliest possible moment. The resolution recommending early elections stated that over a year had passed since the liberation of Poland and the Yalta decision, and more than nine months since the Government of National Unity had been created. The resolution recalled that the controlling officials in the Polish Government had promised at the time of the formation of the government in Moscow in June 1945, and again in Potsdam in August 1945, that elections would be held not later than the first half of 1946. Parliamentary elections had taken place, or were about to take place, in nearly all European countries. Why then, these Polish Peasant Party members asked, had the controlling elements of the government decided to postpone the date of elections?

The censor forbade the publication of this resolution.

At the meeting of the National Council of the Homeland in April, on the initiative of the Polish Socialist Party it was decided, over the protest of the opposition parties, to hold a referendum on June 30, 1946, on three basic questions: abolition of the Senate; agrarian reform and nationalization of industry; the western frontiers. The feeling, among all parties, was that the frontiers as provisionally drawn at Potsdam should be made permanent.

Neither the government nor the KRN (the National Council of the Homeland) then gave any indication of the date of elections or of the text of the electoral law which, months before, so Modzelewski had told me, was ready for submission to the provisional parliament. If a referendum could be held before the last day of June, why could not the same machinery be used to hold elections on that date and thereby fulfill the commitments given to Mr. Bevin at Potsdam?

Obviously the Polish Government did not yet feel that it had sufficient control through the Security Police to risk an election which would determine the composition of the Sejm (parliament). The holding of a referendum, however, would give the government a chance to determine how efficiently its machinery could operate, and would reveal also whether the government actually did have popular support throughout the country.

THE DOOR TO THE ASPHYXIATION CHAMBER

200,000 SHOES OF MURDERED POLES

"THE SHOWER BATH"—WHERE THE VICTIMS
DISROBED

Państwowe Museum, Majdanek

THE EXTERMINATION PLANT AT MAJDANEK

ALL THAT IS LEFT OF THE WARSAW GHETTO

Former President Hoover (*center*) said that this should be left as a monument to Nazi bestiality.

THE NAZI SOAP FACTORY AT GDAŃSK

Box in the foreground contains human skin.

Unfortunately I was not able to find any record of Bierut's having given a commitment to the United States delegation at Potsdam regarding a definite date for the elections. Nor was the Department of State able to furnish, when I made the request, information on the Potsdam conversations on this subject.

Even before the KRN had made its decision to hold a referendum, and thereby postpone the elections, those of us in the Embassy chiefly concerned with the fulfillment of the Yalta decision were deeply apprehensive over the turn in developments.

I accordingly wrote a letter on March 1, 1946, to H. Freeman Matthews, Director of the Office of European Affairs in the Department of State, outlining as earnestly as I could the gravity of the situation.

We have been giving considerable thought to the political situation which is developing here and what our attitude should be in the event that "free and unfettered elections" are not held as promised, or if Mikolajczyk and members of his party are forced out of the government. The pessimism which I expressed to you in my letter of September 6, 1945, has been increasing as the months have passed and as I have observed the repressive measures which the Government has taken through the Security Police against those who were connected with the Armja Krajowa during the German occupation. In addition, as you are well aware, the Government has taken a violent line in the press against the PSL, Mikolajczyk's party, and has subjected Mikolajczyk's paper, *Gazeta Ludowa,* to rigid censorship.

Regardless of such freedom as may exist on the day elections are held, "free and unfettered elections" will not have been held in Poland in the broader sense of the term. Not only will supporters of Mikolajczyk have been, through their imprisonment, deprived of the privilege of voting, but the example of their imprisonment will undoubtedly indicate to those who have been fortunate enough to escape the wrath of the Security Police the fate which awaits them in case they take an active political part against the government.

This situation is no surprise to us. It is the logical sequence of the alliance between the Lublin Communist group within the government and the Soviet Union. We have always felt that it is to the interest of the Soviet Government that this puppet regime should remain in power to carry out the bidding of the Soviet Government, both in political and economic fields. On the other hand, the Bierut regime can remain in power only with the protection of the Red Army and the NKVD-controlled Security Police with its repressive and terroristic methods, to which I have referred above. The understanding may not be based on mutual admiration but it is based on mutual advantage, and I see no possibility at this moment that it will be dissolved.

From the foregoing you will appreciate that I consider Mikolajczyk's chances of winning the elections are virtually nil. As I pointed out in a recent telegram, I do not know by what means he will be defeated: it may be through expulsion of him and the ministers of his party from the government; it may be through the holding of rigged elections; it may be through an artificial creation of disorder which would require forcible measures to be taken, perhaps by the Red Army; or, most tragically, it might be through the physical elimination of Mikolajczyk. This last contingency must be considered as a possibility. No attempts have as yet been made on his life, but I know from what his closest associates say that they fear such a step might be taken. Of course with the recent death of Witos, Mikolajczyk is the only outstanding man of his party in the present government, and if he were eliminated some of the other elements, such as Kiernik and Wycech, who have already been reported to have indicated a willingness to join a single list with the other five parties, might be willing to compromise, thus contributing to the perpetuation in power of the Communist group.

The question naturally arises as to what our policy should be. I do not feel that we should show our indignation through withdrawal of the American and British embassies. By withdrawing we would be merely playing into the hands of those in control, as our influence would disappear from the scene. Furthermore, the Polish people, who through many subtle ways have shown to me their delight over the strong attitude which our government has taken with respect to the withholding of credits as long as present conditions prevail, would feel themselves abandoned by the two best friends they have left—the United States and Great Britain. (Please don't think that this recommendation is based on my desire to hold on to this job! Anyone who has been in Warsaw since the war will appreciate that this is not a bed of roses, and in fact there are few pleasant aspects connected with the post.)

I believe that in the next two or three years there is very little which we can do here which will make itself felt except to continue to show sympathy for the Polish people and to maintain our firm position regarding American rights. If the Yalta decision should be flouted through the holding of fictitious elections or through the elimination of PSL representation in the government, then I feel we should publicly make the facts known and abruptly terminate the credit negotiations in Washington with Rajchman and his delegation.

I feel that we should look at the situation in Poland from a long-range viewpoint and in connection with similar situations in other countries within the Soviet orbit. I believe it essential for the Congress and for the American public to be informed regarding conditions in Poland, Yugoslavia, etc. Education of the public cannot take place overnight. In my opinion, it will perhaps take a year or two. There will be attacks on us from the left-wing press and from some of the more radical labor elements to the effect that we are endeavoring to bring about hostilities with the Soviet Union. Our stand should, in my opinion, be based not on ideologies but on determination to protect American lives and property rights.

All of this, of course, boils down in the last analysis to a decision as to what our policy is going to be towards the Soviet Union. My own feeling is that unless we give publicity to what is going on in Poland and other nations in an analogous position, we will not be able to use our influence in these countries either politically or economically. With the withdrawal of the greater part of our armed forces from Europe we have lost one of the few arguments which are effective with a power such as the Soviet Union. In answer to the criticism which would undoubtedly be made that we are courting war with the Soviet Union in making the unpleasant facts known regarding Communist domination of the countries of Eastern Europe (and perhaps later the countries in Western Europe to an even greater extent than at the present time), I should like to say that the American public has a right to know the truth; that unpreparedness nearly cost us the last war, due to the isolationist attitude of a part of the people of the United States; that appeasement will be just as dangerous today as it was at the time of Munich; and that we run much more danger of war if we ignore the dangers of aggression than by honestly facing the facts.

All of this is so far-reaching in its implications and consequences that it deserves very comprehensive discussion with the highest officers of our government. Should elections be held in May or June, as at first contemplated, I should want to be in Poland continually up to that time. Should the Polish Government, however, as now seems probable, decide to defer the elections for six or eight months, I believe that it would be mutually advantageous to the Department and to us here if I should be called home, say in June, to discuss the situation with the President, the Secretary and others in the Department, so that we may plot our course boldly and so that I may be sure that our attitude here is in accordance with our government's views. I likewise feel that it would be very desirable for me to take part with officers of the Department in confidential talks with majority and minority members of the Foreign Relations Committees of the Senate and the House.

Would you please give the foregoing your very careful thought and let me have an expression of your views?

But because the referendum took place in June, I felt it advisable to remain in Poland and did not visit Washington until November.

CHAPTER THIRTEEN

Our Encounters with the Police State

FROM our earliest days in Poland information kept pouring in to us, not only to me personally and to the rest of our staff but to American newspaper correspondents as well, that a reign of terror was being imposed on the Polish people by the Security Police. Even if we had been so incredulous as to brush aside these reports we could not conscientiously have dismissed the information coming from relatives of American citizens who were then in prison. By February 1946 eighty-four claimants to American citizenship were in jail, almost all—so their relatives apprised us—for the "crime" of having once been members of the underground army clandestinely fighting the Nazis.

But this information which came to us officially from the families of persons born in the United States, persons whose citizenship had been confirmed by the Department of State, did not stand alone. There was also the admission which Bierut and Berman had made to me that the government would not permit its enemies to destroy it. The very policy of the government, as acknowledged by Bierut and Berman, was clearly demonstrated by repressive measures taken against the Polish Peasant Party through arrests, beatings and breaking up political meetings.

Over and above this evidence, advices came to us in the last months of 1945 so definite and so damning that they could not fail to convince one and all of us of the inexorable mesh of the Polish police state, from which a victim rarely if ever became disentangled.

Two United States Army officers, both understanding the Polish language, were in November 1945 superintending the repatriation of a trainload of Polish displaced persons from the American zone in

Germany. They had accompanied their convoy by train through Czechoslovakia and had turned over these "liberated" persons to the Polish officials on the Polish-Czechoslovak frontier. They reported to me in Warsaw that they had overheard U.B. officers (who interviewed all the returning displaced persons) force two of the repatriates, on threat of death, to sign printed statements in which they agreed to work as informers for the U.B. under assumed names. These printed forms, which the officers saw, stated that the penalty for divulging information to any persons other than the Security Police was death. Those who signed the forms were immediately imprisoned in cold, damp cellars for three days and then were told that they would be kept in prison indefinitely unless they would bring in information to the police immediately after their release. The United States Army officers reported that the U.B. was working at the frontier post under NKVD officers and using the NKVD technique.

By the end of 1945 various Polish members of the Embassy staff complained to us that they had been summoned individually and secretly to Security Police headquarters and had been told to sign forms promising to furnish the U.B. regularly with information about the activities of the American Embassy. In some cases these Poles had been threatened with death or with torture unless they acquiesced. One employee, in fact, who was required to report to the police once a week was beaten so badly on each occasion that he was unable to conceal his lameness and was forced to invent excuses for it, such as having been hit by an automobile, thrown off a streetcar, etc. Finally he told us what had happened.

According to State Department regulations, aliens are not permitted access to confidential material. The Polish citizens who were in our employ were accordingly confined in their work to the processing of passport and visa applications, the translation of newspapers, and other routine duties normal in any United States diplomatic or consular office. Even had the Embassy been engaged in nefarious irregular activities such as contact with the underground, as the government subsequently charged, these Polish employees would not have had access to such files.

The U.B., like its Russian counterpart, also took a keen interest in the work of American relief organizations, evidently believing that, like Soviet organizations operating abroad, they were acting as spies for the United States Government.

A revealing incident happened early in 1946, involving a Polish woman employed by one of the American relief organizations in Warsaw. She was approached by a U.B. agent and asked to proceed to U.B. headquarters to testify about a traffic accident which the agent said she had seen. As she had not witnessed any accident, she demurred; but finally she was persuaded to go to headquarters to testify that she had not seen the accident in question.

On arrival at U.B. headquarters she was subjected to an interrogation for four hours, during which she was threatened with a revolver and told that unless she signed an agreement to work for the U.B. she and her family would be shot. She was also told that if she ever discussed the interrogation with anybody, death would be the penalty to her family and to herself. When she finally signed the agreement she was instructed to report on all the activities of the relief organization for which she worked and especially on the communications sent to and received from the United States.

After ten or twelve cases of threats to our Polish employees had come to my attention and when I had been informed by the British and French embassies that they had encountered the same difficulty, I recommended to the Department of State that I be instructed to make a vigorous protest against this systematic terrorization which, if not stopped forthwith, would seriously affect the work of the Embassy and would make it increasingly difficult for us to employ Polish nationals. Already, in fact, Polish citizens had withdrawn their applications for employment, having been told by the police that it would be "inadvisable" for them to accept positions in the Embassy.

On comparing notes with the British and French embassies we

ascertained that the procedure toward the employees of the three missions was identical in almost all cases. If the employee refused to join the U.B., he was threatened with death and with the death of his family. Then the employee was usually given time to think the matter over, but was told that the penalty for divulging the interview at U.B. headquarters would be death. Without waiting for authorization, I had made oral representations to the Foreign Office on previous occasions, and I was told at the time that my complaints would be forwarded to the Ministry of Public Security.

Two months later, under instructions from Washington, I delivered a note to the Foreign Office on June 25, 1946, stating that the intimidations of the Embassy staff had made a most unfavorable effect on the United States Government and requesting that this procedure be stopped at once, as it would seriously handicap the Embassy in performing its functions.

As I presented my note to Olszewski, director of the Political Department of the Foreign Office, he looked at me with stony eyes. He said that the Ministry of Security had denied that members of the Embassy staff had been molested, and asked me to furnish the names of those members of the staff who had been questioned by the U.B. Naturally I refused, remarking that, in view of the threat of death which these persons had received, I would merely be making matters much worse for them. Olszewski then made the surprising suggestion that the Embassy should employ no Polish nationals whatever; hence, incidents such as those of which I complained could not arise. I pointed out that it is customary, not only for the United States Government but all governments, to employ aliens in nonconfidential positions. In Poland in particular the language problem was great and it would be difficult if not impossible to obtain for the Embassy a sufficient number of American citizens with adequate knowledge of the Polish language.

Our protest was disregarded and the intimidations continued. Finally the U.B. went so far as to arrest one of our number, Mrs. Irena Dmochowska, who had been employed as a translator. Her duties at the Embassy consisted solely of preparing a daily English summary of the local Polish press. She worked under Dillon's direct supervision. When Mrs. Dmochowska did not report for work on August 23, 1946, and sent no word why she failed to do so, Dillon called at her apartment and heard that she had disappeared. The next day, August 24, we learned that Mrs. Dmochowska was being held by the U.B., but our personal requests to a deputy of the Minister of Public Security, a colonel who would not even give us his name, were of no avail. We then appealed to the Foreign Office and a note was sent asking for Mrs. Dmochowska's release:

I have the honor to inform Your Excellency that according to information received by the Embassy, which has been confirmed by the chief of cabinet of the Minister of Public Security, Mrs. Irena A. Dmochowska, an American citizen and an employee of this Embassy, was arrested by the Security Police on the morning of August 23, 1946, and has since been under arrest without the Embassy having been permitted to interview her in accordance with the rights accruing to the Embassy under the Treaty of 1931.

In view of the fact that Mrs. Dmochowska is a member of my official staff and, as such, is entitled under international law to the privileges which accrue to an employee of a diplomatic mission, I have the honor to request that she be released immediately and an explanation furnished to the Embassy as to the reasons for the action taken against an American member of the Embassy staff.

That afternoon I called on Prime Minister Osóbka-Morawski, emphasizing to him the seriousness which these constant acts of intimidation were creating in the relations between the United States and Poland. I said that it would be unheard of in the United States for the police to arrest an employee of a foreign embassy, even for the most serious offenses, without first communicating with the Embassy. In this case it was only through accident that we had learned of Mrs. Dmochowska's detention.

I said that the terroristic activities of the U.B. could, in my opinion, have a more devastating effect than any other element in bringing about the deterioration of United States-Polish relations; that in the United States conservatives or liberals, rightists or leftists, might be very much in disagreement on matters of our foreign policy, but on one point they were all agreed: American citizens abroad must be protected. I gave my opinion that if the Polish Government should continue to show disregard for the liberties of American citizens in Poland, American public opinion might be permanently prejudiced against it.

After I had finished my argument, Osóbka-Morawski made no reply. His face, however, had assumed a deep flush, apparently of anger, and he stiffly bowed me out of the room without any of the polite amenities which he customarily used. Perhaps the Prime Minister resented my complaint about the activities of the secret police as being an attack on the government of which he was nominally the head. But, more likely, he was resentful because, although Prime Minister, he had no power over the activities of Radkiewicz or of his underlings in blue. Only a few weeks before, Osóbka's fellow party member, Wachowicz, then Assistant Minister of Public Security, had released from prison a member of the Polish Socialist Party who had been arrested on what Wachowicz considered unfounded political charges. Osóbka had sent his automobile to the jail to take the liberated man home. But on arrival at his house the luckless fellow was greeted by U.B. agents who rearrested him under orders from Radkiewicz. Then Radkiewicz demanded and obtained of Osóbka the dismissal of Wachowicz as his deputy.

Dillon was able to see Mrs. Dmochowska in the U.B. headquarters in the presence of an interpreter from the Foreign Office about ten days after her arrest, and was allowed to furnish her with food parcels and cigarettes. I finally was permitted to see her on September 12, in the evening, at 7:00 o'clock. I went to the new Security Police headquarters, which I found far more modern in its appointments than the office in which I had first met Radkiewicz. Our identification papers were closely checked, even though we were accompanied by

Lieutenant Rulski of the Foreign Office and by three different U.B. agents. At last we were led into the room of Captain Hummer, an evil-looking official who advised me that I was not to question Mrs. Dmochowska about her case and that I was not to address her in English.

Mrs. Dmochowska was soon brought into Hummer's office. She was evidently extremely nervous; her hands and her lips trembled; and her voice was so low in replying to my questions (which I put in English and which were translated into Polish by Stephen D. Zagorski of our Embassy staff who had succeeded Tonesk as my interpreter) that I could barely understand her. When I asked her if she knew why she was imprisoned she said she had a good idea; but she did not give me a definite answer. In reply to my question she said she had been well treated, and she begged me to tell her mother not to worry about her condition. But during all the questioning, which lasted the better part of an hour and which I purposely restricted to generalities so as not to make her position more difficult, Hummer's eyes pierced those of Mrs. Dmochowska continually as though he were conveying to her that she should not divulge any prohibited information.

I saw Mrs. Dmochowska once more, on October 5. On this occasion she again said that she was well treated, but had not been permitted to consult an attorney. I was told, after the interview, that she might choose defending counsel from a list of names which would be supplied her. The Foreign Office explained that, although the Polish Government did not accept our contention that Mrs. Dmochowska was an American citizen, permission was given me to interview her because of her having been employed in the Embassy.

She was finally brought to a public trial in January 1947, and there pleaded guilty to the charges: she had been in possession of a revolver, without having a permit; she had had knowledge of the murder of Scibiorek, and had not divulged the information to the police as required by law; and she had assisted persons connected with the murder to leave the country. On the strength of this "confession"—

which she undoubtedly made under duress—she was sentenced to five years' imprisonment. This sentence was later suspended in a general amnesty decreed in February 1947.

She did not, however, resume her duties at the Embassy.

The helplessness of the American Embassy in coming to the assistance of one of its employees who, according to our laws, was considered an American citizen, was clearly shown in this case. We were at the mercy of the Polish authorities who ignored precedent and international comity.

According to Polish Government officials with whom I discussed the necessity of evacuating Russian forces in Poland as soon as possible—so that free and unfettered elections could be held in accordance with the terms of the Yalta and Potsdam agreements—Marshal Stalin had at Potsdam agreed to withdraw all of them except a number sufficient to maintain two lines of communication between the Soviet zone of occupation in Germany and the Soviet Union. Bierut, when I asked him in October 1945 how many Russian troops were there, said he did not know; he would prefer to have no foreign troops in Poland, but because of gratitude to the Soviet Union, it would be indeed difficult to suggest that the Red Army withdraw. It was known that Marshal Rokossovsky was in command at Lignica of a force estimated at about three hundred thousand. At Wroclaw, only fifty miles from Lignica, a hundred thousand Soviet troops were quartered in October 1945, according to estimates obtained from many different sources there.

But as the months passed the number of uniformed Russians visible in Warsaw and other cities gradually diminished. As the Soviet Ambassador admitted to me, the misdeeds of the Russian soldiery were seriously hurting Soviet-Polish relations and the Polish people were fearing that the Red Army was to be a permanent occupying force. It was therefore understandable that the Soviet Government should wish to keep the Red Army out of the public eye.

While men in Russian uniforms decreased, those in Polish uniforms increased and it was significant that many of the latter spoke with a

Russian accent. Starting from a skeleton force brought in from Russia and trained under Communist methods, the Polish Army had, by the middle of 1946, grown to at least one hundred thousand.

In addition, militia or ordinary police force, used for traffic controlling and other normal police duties, had grown to the same size.

And yet another organization, known as the Volunteer Citizens' Militia Reserve (O.R.M.O.) and also numbering one hundred thousand, had been formed. This sinister group, composed of adherents of the Polish Workers Party, was used to break up political meetings, to damage buildings occupied by the opposition parties and, like the hoodlums of the Brown Shirts, generally to make life disagreeable for all those who did not toe the government line. Dressed in civilian clothes, they were identifiable by their red and white arm bands and the rifles slung over their shoulders.

The Polish Peasant Party organ, *Gazeta Ludowa,* had in an editorial in February 1946 protested the proposal of the Polish Workers Party to create the Volunteer Citizens' Militia Reserve. The article, which strangely enough was permitted to be published, particularly objected to a statement of agitators at recent factory meetings: "We have enough rifles to arm the best part of the working class, peasants and intelligentsia." It complained that an "internal security corps (KBW)" had been formed as an independent unit at the disposal of the Minister of Public Security to be used against "bandits" and that members of the Polish Peasant Party had been dismissed from the militia solely because of their party affiliation. The political nature of the O.R.M.O., which was directly under the supervision of Radkiewicz and not of the commander in chief of the Army, was disclosed by an editorial of *Glos Ludu,* the Polish Workers Party organ, which said that force had to be used against "murderers, bandits maintained by dollar-pound funds, and against the whole underground reactionary scum."

Most dreaded of all the military was the U.B. At the time of my departure from Poland in February 1947, it too was estimated to have at least a hundred thousand agents.

In all, the Polish Government had at its disposal a total armed force of at least four hundred thousand, not including Marshal Rokossovsky's men, which by that time may well have been reduced to a hundred thousand. My estimate is based on something more definite than conjecture, for Marshal Rola-Zymierski himself, in November 1945, had asked me to endorse his application for a credit from the United States to enable him to purchase out of United States Army surplus war equipment uniforms, overcoats and boots for three hundred fifty thousand men—a figure which included the militia and the Security Police. I told the Marshal and President Bierut that our government's refusal of the credit should be interpreted as disapproval of Security Police activities in Poland and of the Polish Government's control of the Polish people through force. The Department of State had in fact informed me that "of course" no United States funds could be used for Polish military purposes.

An incident illuminating the Soviet and Polish Government policy toward the United States and Great Britain took place on March 7, 1946, when Bentinck and I gave a joint showing of *The True Glory*, a film produced by the British and American armed forces. This well-known movie, which depicted the Normandy invasion and the conferences that led up to it, was a magnificent portrayal of solidarity between the British and American forces as well as of the overwhelming power directed against the Nazis. Invitations were sent to all Polish Government ministers and to the higher officers of the Army, as well as to all diplomats.

The invitations were naturally complimentary, yet requests for tickets were received from persons not invited, with offers as high as the equivalent of twenty dollars for a seat. A huge crowd swarmed outside the theater, clamoring for admission. This would be the first opportunity the Warsaw people had had to see motion pictures of their western allies in action. Until that date only Soviet films had been shown in the capital.

It was significant that few government ministers were present. And the reception which followed the picture was attended by no Communists, whether members of the Polish Government or of the Soviet Embassy.

Bentinck and I agreed that the Polish ruling clique stayed away from the reception because of resentment that this public demonstration of British-American solidarity had been so vigorously applauded by an enthusiastic crowd at the theater. Furthermore, we had been able, through the showing of this firm, to refute publicly the Polish Government's contention, as expressed in the editorials of the controlled press, that the Soviet Union, and the Soviet Union alone, had been responsible for the winning of the war.

Vice-Premier Gomulka, at a showing of a film of the taking of Okinawa, had asked, apparently with entire honesty, why American airplanes had not been used in Europe during the war!

None of the Polish Army officers who were invited attended *The True Glory*. I learned that strict orders had been issued to the general staff not to go. This directive reminded me, in reverse, of an incident which took place when I was in Belgrade in 1940 some weeks after the conquest of Poland. The German Minister, von Heeren, had, under instructions from his government, issued invitations to the Yugoslav general staff to attend a showing of the German army film of the invasion of Poland. Although I did not see the film myself, I was told that it was an awful but telling documentation of Nazi might and ruthlessness, and a dire warning to European countries, such as Yugoslavia, to beware of resisting Hitler's demands. Many of the general staff declined the invitation. The German Minister then insisted to the Yugoslav Minister of War that the officers be ordered to attend. They were thus obliged to witness the fate of Poland. Yet even this intimidation did not later deter the cream of the Yugoslav Army from overthrowing a government which had tossed away Yugoslav sovereignty by adhering to the infamous tripartite pact signed at Vienna on March 25, 1941.

Besides the intimidation of the Polish members of our staff, physical measures were taken from time to time either to cause annoyance or to impede our activities. For instance, in March 1946, entry into the rooms of Howard A. Bowman, American Consul at Poznan, in the Hotel Continental there, was attempted. Despite the fact that signs on the door of the room showed clearly it was the official quarters of the consul, U.B. agents endeavored to break in at two o'clock one morning demanding to make a search. Finally Bowman was able to persuade them to leave.

At about the same time U.B. agents, accompanied by Russians, tried to force their way into the quarters of Alexander Radomski, an attaché of the Embassy temporarily at the Grand Hotel in Lódz.

No reply was ever received to our complaints over these incidents, nor did we ever get satisfaction to a complaint about a Soviet general officer removing tools from the automobile of Lieutenant Colonel York at the point of a revolver.

The efficient organization of the secret police was shown by the May Day parade on May 1, 1946, in which, according to the estimates of the government press, one hundred fifty thousand persons took part. Highly effective measures were taken to insure the appearance of the paraders: the personnel of all factories, social institutions, local state farms and government offices were checked at the beginning and at the end of the parade. Workers were threatened with the loss of their jobs or of their rations if they did not present themselves. People were prevented from leaving the city during the parade by the militia guarding the bridges and all roads leading out of town. But in spite of warm sunny weather, the general aspect of the paraders and of the spectators was funereal, with only occasional shouts on the part of the government party whips of "Long live the people's Poland!" "Down with foreign agents!" "Long live red Madrid!" The chief purpose of the demonstration appeared to be political. Among the trucks (most of them had UNRRA markings) which took part, many carried political slogans. The principal floats caricatured Mikolajczyk and Churchill. One truckload of orphans, the oldest of whom

could not have been more than eight, prominently carried a sign reading, "We want a single electoral bloc." But no banners of the Polish
Peasant Party or the Christian Labor Party were to be seen. Under
the guise of celebrating May Day, the government underlined its
control, through Radkiewicz's organization, of all workers.

On March 14, 1946, the military police state had finally a chance
to show itself in all its sinister glory. On that morning the Office of
Protocol telephoned the Embassy that Marshal Tito was arriving at
11:00 A.M. at the station at Wlochy, some ten miles from Warsaw.
All the chiefs of mission were invited to be at the station on his arrival. The road was lined with soldiers on the whole route between
Wlochy and Warsaw. On the streets of Warsaw along which the
caravan of some twenty-five automobiles passed, including that of
Marshal Rola-Zymierski who acted as Tito's host, the troops were so
closely drawn up that no would-be assailant could come near. No
news had been published of Tito's arrival. He traveled in a closed
armored car and could not be recognized by the people. How different, I thought, was this to the spontaneous welcome which had
been given to General Eisenhower. How unnecessary it had been to
have military protection for him!

Because of the secrecy with which arrests were usually effected, and
as public trials were rarely held, we could not learn definitely the
number of persons who were held in prisons or concentration camps
in Poland for alleged political offenses. We estimated, however, in
1946, that over one hundred thousand Poles were being forcibly detained either by Polish or Soviet police officials. This estimate was
based on our knowledge that large concentration camps, constructed
by the Nazis, were still being used in Oswiecim, in Rembertów (near
Warsaw) and in Wolów (Wohlau), about thirty miles from Wroclaw, in the zone under the Red Army control. In addition, the
prisons in Kraków, Lublin and Poznan were filled to capacity with
political prisoners.

In Lublin and Kraków the crowded cells could be observed from the street by anyone passing by. And in Lublin, once a week, a line which usually numbered two or three thousand formed at the prison gate, before eight o'clock in the morning, to leave food and cigarettes for relatives or friends who were shut off from the outside because of political beliefs. Promptly at 6:00 P.M. the gates clanged shut. There were always many in the line when this disheartening moment arrived. But the prison rules were rigid. No exceptions were made, regardless of the hours one had stood in line. And those who had not yet reached the gate at that hour were obliged to wait another week before again trying to perform their errand of mercy.

A native of one of the Baltic States, whom I had known when accredited there, came to me one day in 1945 at my apartment at the Hotel Polonia, after having traveled two hundred miles by begging a lift from truck drivers. He was a cultured, intelligent man, who spoke English and French well. He was now destitute. His clothes were ragged and he looked haggard and hungry. But a greater preoccupation haunted him: the danger of being arrested by the NKVD on the ground that, in Soviet eyes at least, he was a Soviet citizen and, as such, should have reported to the authorities.

We were able to clothe him and furnish him with funds. Some weeks later, a mutual acquaintance reported that he had been seized by the Russian secret police on the small farm where he was living in hiding. Later I received a letter from him written in the Russian camp at Wolów. Through one of the relief organizations, I made further inquiries and learned that he had been moved to the east. No definite word of him was received again.

One of the chief reasons for the bitterness of the Polish people toward the Lublin core of the Polish Government was its having acquiesced, prior to the formation of the Provisional Government of National Unity, in the Soviet authorities deporting Polish nationals to the east. These Poles had probably been outspoken enough to criticize the Russian part in the Nazi-Soviet scheme for the spoliation of Poland in 1939, which led to the outbreak of the war; or to condemn the brutality of the Soviet-controlled Polish police state. Through an agreement signed in 1945, the Soviet Government had been accorded the right to deport those persons who were considered dangerous to the Red Army.

In the summer of 1947 a Polish woman living in Poland sent a heart-rending letter to her relatives in the United States, describing the fate of her son who had been sentenced to four years' imprisonment on the charge that he had made derogatory remarks about the Russians. Here is a translation of the pertinent part of the letter, with the excision of passages which would identify and hence endanger the sender:

We bring you very bad news. Why did not the Lord take me from this earth so that my sorrow, grief and terrible worry would be buried in the grave with me!

During the last nine years I shed enough tears to bathe myself in them. Then in May our eldest son was taken to prison from the army. For seven weeks we had no word from him, and we worried. Our letters to him were returned to us. Finally we received information that he is in prison in ———, that he will have another trial in July, that he will need a defender. Although our son was forbidden to write, I received this information through a young friend of his. So I, his mother, went to ——— to help him. What did he do to deserve arrest and jail? I could not see him nor speak to him.

I went to the office of the District Attorney in ——— to ask what caused my son's arrest. The District Attorney asked me to wait while he consulted the books. Then he told me that he had violated a section of the law.

I could hardly wait for the day of the trial. I hired an attorney who asked for thirty thousand zlotys, and I gave it to him because we wanted to help the boy. There were four judges, and he was brought into the room like a criminal. He was a pathetic sight. I hardly recognized him. What a sight! If I did not die then it is because a human being is often harder and more enduring than a horse. Then his accusing witness came and made the following accusations: 1. That my son had said, in his presence, that much coal is being sent to Russia. 2. That better lands were being taken from us and we were being given poorer land instead. 3. That he had listened to the American radio. 4. That if he had to drive in a wagon with a Russian he would drive off the road into a ditch, even if he broke his legs. For these words he was sentenced to four years in prison.

When I heard the verdict, I was stunned. Seeing this, one of the judges suggested that the verdict be appealed to the highest court in Warsaw. We did appeal. I went to Warsaw, hired an attorney, who asked one hundred thousand zlotys. We paid the money and begged him to defend our son. Today he wrote us with sorrow that the highest military tribunal refused to review the case, thereby confirming the verdict of the lower court. His only relief would be pardon from the President of Poland.

Please tell us how we are to survive this sorrow. We have spent all our money. We wanted to help the boy, and everything was to no avail. Dear Lord, what are we to do?

Would you not be willing to ask the American consul to intercede for us with the President of Poland because here there is no justice.

I visited ——— in a prison in ——— twice already. I could visit him only five minutes in the presence of a guard, and behind an iron gate. ——— begs us to do all we can to get a release for him, for he will not be able to stand this incarceration for four years. He is getting a nervous breakdown.

I did not write you immediately because we felt sure that so many thousand zlotys would help him, but in the end nothing counted.

CHAPTER FOURTEEN

American Assistance

It will be recalled that in my first official talk with President Bierut on August 4, 1945, I had outlined eight ways in which the United States Government could be of help to Poland. Two of these were the extension of aid through the United Nations Relief and Rehabilitation Administration, known as UNRRA, in which the United States Government had a seventy-two per cent financial participation, and the American Red Cross, a United States Government affiliate.

The first UNRRA mission, headed by the Soviet delegate Menshikov, had arrived in Warsaw a few days before the opening of the American Embassy. Menshikov had signed an agreement with the Polish Government giving the latter complete jurisdiction over the distribution of UNRRA goods. Menshikov had then departed, leaving his staff to supervise the unloading of the first shipments of supplies to come by sea (which were expected in early September) and to await the arrival of the new head of the UNRRA mission, yet to be appointed. The first ship bringing UNRRA supplies to Poland was the SS *Nishmaha*. It arrived in Gdynia on September 6. A reception commemorating the event was held on board the vessel. Jedrychowski, Minister of Navigation and Foreign Trade, and I went to Gdynia for the occasion, passing through Gdansk on the way.

Gdynia had been sadly bombed during the initial Nazi invasion in September 1939, especially on the water front, but much of the residential portion was still intact.

Gdansk (Danzig), ten miles away, was almost as badly ruined as Warsaw. We were told by residents that the Germans boasted before they retreated that if they could not possess Danzig, no other nation would have it. They had accordingly destroyed it as they had destroyed

213

Warsaw, house by house, not even sparing the Gothic St. Elizabeth's Cathedral, one of the most beautiful churches in northern Europe. We were also told that when the Russians arrived in Gdansk, full of vodka, they finished off what little of the fiendish job of destruction the Nazis had left.

In Gdansk we were shown a most gruesome reminder of Nazi bestiality—the soap factory. There we saw the remains of human bodies, still lying in vats of alcohol, the fats from which were to be converted into soap. Dried human skin was still stretched out in the laboratory for the manufacture of lamp shades. It was a most revolting sight, which I immediately wished I had not seen.

The first UNRRA shipments which followed the arrival of the *Nishmaha* brought immediate hope to the Polish people. For six years they had had no new clothes; even the most elementary comforts had been denied them. Blankets, condensed milk and other necessities were, however, no more welcome than horses, mules and tractors, for in Poland, primarily an agricultural country, the economy had been gravely disrupted because of the loss of draft power.

In the months to follow, the UNRRA organization expanded greatly: branches were set up in the principal cities and co-operation with the government was efficiently maintained. A young Canadian officer, Brigadier Charles Drury, who had a brilliant war record, was appointed director of the mission. Tactful, suave, yet energetic, Drury did a creditable job, as far as he was able.

But, as the agreement with the Polish Government gave UNRRA no control over the distribution of goods imported by UNRRA, Drury could not prevent supplies being used for political purposes. Certain types of supplies, such as blankets, could be purchased only by those persons holding a specified type of ration card issued solely to government employees or to members of the Workers and Socialist parties. And, although over ninety per cent of the Polish people were Catholic, Catholic schools, hospitals and orphanages had difficulty in obtaining UNRRA supplies. One municipal official, in fact, told the bishop of his community that UNRRA supplies were not intended for "reactionary" organizations, such as the Roman Catholic Church. UNRRA supplies, chiefly canned foods, appeared in many of the Warsaw shop windows at outrageously high prices, and some goods were even peddled on the sidewalk in front of the Hotel Polonia. One American UNRRA official naïvely begged me, on the visit of an American Congressional committee, to ask the police to put a stop to this practice so that Congress would not obtain the wrong impression of UNRRA! But in many cases the resale of UNRRA goods was understandable and did not imply any irregularity. Certain products sent to Poland, such as orange juice, were not normally used by the Polish people. Recipients would sell such items in order that they might purchase other articles which were more vitally needed.

Although we had experienced great delay in getting official permission for the American Red Cross mission to function, the Red Cross activities had in fact been proceeding unofficially since February 1944, when Donald Castleberry, a member of the American Red Cross mission in Moscow, arrived in Poland without either a Soviet exit visa or a Polish entry visa. He had established a close relationship with the Polish Red Cross, which had sole responsibility for the distribution of much-needed medicines and hospital supplies. But as time went on, the efficient personnel of the Polish Red Cross who had, even during the Nazi occupation, greatly alleviated the suffering of the Polish people, were little by little replaced by persons with Communist sympathies who had little, if any, technical knowledge. And one of the first allowed to resign was the president of the Polish Red Cross, General Szeptycki, the hero of the Battle of the Vistula against the oncoming Red Army in 1920.

Although the Red Cross had begun its operations with a relatively modest budget of one million dollars it had increased its activities within a year to such an extent that its expenditures totaled approximately seven million.

The Joint Distribution Committee, under the able direction of Mr. William Bein, a naturalized American citizen of Polish origin, performed a humanitarian service of the highest order in ministering to

the needs of the unfortunate members of the Jewish race who had
suffered so much, and whose future held out so little for them.

Henry Osinski, directing the work of the American Relief for Poland, had been one of the earliest American arrivals in Warsaw.
Through his tact, knowledge of the Polish language, and efficiency,
he had built up an organization which reached persons in all parts of
Poland, regardless of race or religion. But on one occasion a member
of the government strangely complained to Osinski that too much of
his organization's supplies were being distributed by Caritas, a Catholic relief agency!

The National Catholic Welfare Conference, under George Szudy,
the Committee for American Relief for Europe, known as C.A.R.E.,
headed by Mr. Wm. C. Macdonald, and the Quakers brought help in
the form of food and clothing to the needy people of Poland.

But more important than the material help which all these humanitarian organizations so generously gave, I felt that they were also
accomplishing a mission of permanent, although intangible, value:
the rebuilding of the bridge of understanding and affection between
the American and Polish peoples, which had been closed to traffic
during the Nazi occupation.

In relief, as in other matters, I felt that a sharp distinction should
be drawn between the Polish Government and the Polish people; and
I thoroughly agreed with a member of the Roman Catholic hierarchy
who said to me with the greatest earnestness before I left Warsaw in
the winter of 1947, "Please, Mr. Ambassador, do not allow your
country to crucify the Polish people for the crimes of their government!"

To canvass the possibility of the Polish Government's obtaining
credits from the Export-Import Bank, Mikolajczyk called on President
Truman at the White House on November 9, 1945, accompanied by
the Polish chargé d'affaires, J. Zóltowski.* Mikolajczyk's pleas for

---

* For an account of Mikolajczyk's conversation with the President, see text of *aide-
mémoire,* furnished to Department of State by the Polish Embassy in Washington, in
Appendix.

assistance were backed by Dr. Ludwig Rajchman, the Polish Government's financial representative in the United States, and by Mr. Zóltowski in an interview which they had with Assistant Secretary Clayton and Mr. Durbrow on December 5.

Dr. Rajchman also indicated that Poland had an urgent need for fats. Because of shortage of fats, as well as of other critical materials, the Polish Government had established a ration system, granting priorities to special categories in the following order: (1) miners, (2) radio operators, (3) textile workers, (4) hospital workers. Mr. Clayton said that our government would give very careful consideration to the Polish Government's request.

At this meeting Dr. Rajchman explained the needs of the Polish economy, stressing that Poland needed thirty thousand railway cars, primarily gondola cars, to handle coal shipments. He added that road-building machinery, port facilities, raw materials, especially cotton, and telecommunication equipment also were vitally required, and he made an earnest plea for the granting of sufficient credits to purchase these types of goods in the United States. Rajchman stated that the Polish Government had not made and would not make any arrangements with any country which would give that nation a monopolistic or privileged position in economic matters; and that, although the Soviet Government had endeavored some time ago to conclude an agreement which would have given it a privileged position, the Polish Government had not accepted it.

When I first called on the Minister of Education, Mr. Wycech, a member of the Polish Peasant Party, he gave me a most illuminating yet depressing account of the state of Polish education as a result of the studied and efficient Nazi program to destroy the heart of Polish culture. What made the exposition particularly impressive was that Wycech, a modest schoolteacher, used no histrionics in reciting the facts. He told me how the Nazis had imprisoned or murdered almost all outstanding intellectual leaders in the universities; how they had burned all volumes which might be considered a means to keep Polish nationalism alive; and how they had transported to Germany, or deliberately destroyed, all laboratory equipment, thus putting an end to any further scientific advance of the Polish people. During that conversation and in later interviews with Mr. Wycech we talked over the possibility of sending perhaps fifty young Polish students who wished to specialize in various fields of scientific and academic education to the United States so that they might serve as the nucleus of modern educational methods in Poland.

In December 1945 Dr. S. Harrison Thomson, who had arrived from Prague as cultural attaché of the Embassy, discussed this proposition in detail with the Minister in the hope that we might encourage an exchange of students, as well as of professors, between the United States and Poland and bring about a closer understanding between our two peoples. Thomson, a professor of Central European History in the University of Colorado and a keen student of Central European affairs, was an enthusiastic and valuable member of our staff. Restricted though he was by primitive quarters—a Nissen hut—he organized a library open to the public which offered the Polish people their first opportunity since 1939 to read American periodicals, fiction and technical works. Concerts of phonograph records were given twice weekly, and American films were shown from time to time.

Our efforts, however, to bring about closer intellectual co-operation were disappointing. In almost all cases of applicants for scholarships in the United States, the Polish Foreign Office refused to grant visas. Although our cultural center was always crowded and no political propaganda against the Polish Government or against the Soviet Union was displayed, the Security Police officers who patrolled the premises, ostensibly to protect our personnel, warned many of our visitors that it would be better for them if they did not come there. Taking another leaf from the Soviet book of rules, the Polish Government was endeavoring to prevent the people from being enlightened in what Western democracy stood for.

As for radio broadcasts beamed to Poland as the "Voice of America," my opinion of their value differed radically from that of the authors of the program in the Department of State. First, from a practical standpoint, no broadcast from the United States could receive wide dissemination in Poland: there were few radio sets in operation after the Nazi occupation, and those on sale were arranged so that only Polish Government stations could be heard. Second, I felt that the Department's policy to tell the people in Eastern Europe what a wonderful democratic life we in the United States enjoy showed its complete lack of appreciation of their psychology. And, especially in Poland, which had suffered through six years of Nazi domination, it was indeed tactless, to say the least, to remind the Poles that we had democracy, which they also might again be enjoying, had we not acquiesced in their being sold down the river at Tehran and Yalta. Indeed, after I left Poland, persons returning to the United States told me that very few Poles would listen to the "Voice of America" broadcast even if they had access to radio sets which could receive it.

But this opinion of mine is not to be construed as an objection in general against radio broadcasts to the Soviet Union or to other nations behind the Iron Curtain. If appropriate material is used which will bring hope and cheer, instead of intensifying despair, there is much of a constructive nature that we can do. But the wisdom of statesmanship, not that of salesmanship, is a requisite.

During the latter part of February 1946 it became plain that Poland was facing a very serious grain shortage which might lead to famine. Simultaneously Poland was facing an acute political crisis, due to the efforts of the Communist and Socialist parties to force the Polish Peasant and Christian Labor parties to join the single electoral list.

The grain situation was greatly aggravated by the world-wide shortage of food compelling UNRRA to curtail grain deliveries to European countries.

On February 23, 1946, at a lavish reception at the Soviet Embassy to commemorate Red Army Day, the Soviet Ambassador, Mr. Lebedev, and Vice-Premier Gomulka upbraided me, as the representative of the United States, because, so they said, UNRRA was cutting off food supplies to Poland to force the Polish Government to alter its attitude on the political situation. Gomulka said that the government had offered Mikolajczyk twenty-five per cent representation in the government and in the National Council of the Homeland, but that he obstinately held out for seventy-five per cent, a figure which in Mr. Gomulka's view was fantastic.

Lebedev argued that the United States was making a great mistake in using food as a political lever. My protestations that UNRRA was an international organization and that the Soviet Government was represented on the board of directors made no impression. Lebedev continued that the United States put up almost three-fourths of the money for UNRRA and it was absurd to assume that it did not control UNRRA activities. He said, with great heat, "Let's not be diplomatic. You know as well as I that the person who pays is the person who controls."

To me this conversation was significant, first of all because it showed such a lack of comprehension of the United States' approach to humanitarian problems; and, secondly, because it disclosed that the Soviet Government, which in fact had in Iran used starvation as a political weapon, considered the practice normal.

But before ending his attack on the United States, Lebedev said that if the United States would not aid Poland the Soviet Union would do so; and he added that two hundred thousand tons of grain were being delivered by the Soviet Government to Poland at that time. This grandiose gesture on the part of the Soviet Government was indeed ludicrous to those of us who knew the truth: Months before, the Red

Army had seized two hundred thousand tons of grain from Polish lands. Now the Red Army was returning it—not as borrowed material, but as a gift!

The world-wide food situation had assumed such tragic proportions that in March 1946 former President Herbert Hoover had, at President Truman's request, embarked on a tour of all the needy countries of Europe to study the critical food problems and to make recommendations to the President of the United States as to how the United States Government could best meet the needs.

Mr. Hoover, accompanied by my former chief Hugh Gibson, D. A. Fitzgerald, the eminent agricultural analyst, and other experts on relief, arrived in Warsaw on March 28, 1946. Mr. Hoover immediately paid a courtesy call on President Bierut, outlining the scope of his mission and offering his services and those of his staff to assist the Polish Government in the solution of the food problem. According to the estimates of the Polish Government and of Mr. Hoover's mission, it would reach the critical stage of starvation by the first week of May, unless sufficient grain supplies were imported in the meantime. The following day Mr. Hoover met with the Prime Minister, Vice-Premier Gomulka and Vice-Premier Mikolajczyk, together with Polish experts on health, food and agriculture, to devise means by which the tragedy of famine could be averted. Mr. Hoover hoped that the Polish Government would adopt food rationing as an essential measure; but the Polish Government demurred on the ground that the people had been so accustomed under the Nazi occupation to disobey regulations they would not observe any food restrictions which the government might now impose.

Mr. Gibson had telegraphed me before Mr. Hoover's arrival that Mr. Hoover hoped that social engagements would be reduced to a minimum and no lavish entertainment be given to his party. It must have seemed particularly incongruous to Mr. Hoover at the sumptuous dinner given in his honor at the Belvedere Palace on the evening of

March 29—ten courses of elaborate dishes—to recall the impassioned speeches of government ministers that very morning, stressing the danger of famine.

I had invited Prime Minister Osóbka-Morawski, as well as Vice-Premiers Gomulka and Mikolajczyk, to meet Mr. Hoover at a very small and informal dinner at the Hotel Polonia on the evening of March 30. Mr. Gibson and Mr. Maurice Pate, who had after the first World War served in Poland as a member of the American Relief Administration, and Lieutenant Tonesk, who was to act as interpreter, were the only other persons invited.

That afternoon Gubrynowicz, the Chief of Protocol, excitedly approached me as I was leaving the hotel with Mr. Hoover for luncheon and said that the Prime Minister would like to bring his own interpreter, Colonel Sosnicki of the Foreign Office. I said that, although I greatly regretted it, our party was unfortunately so small and intimate I would prefer not to increase the number, and I emphasized that Mr. Mikolajczyk, Mr. Pate and Lieutenant Tonesk were familiar with both English and Polish. Later that afternoon we received an ultimatum from the Prime Minister that, unless his interpreter were invited, he would be unable to come. At the dinner hour and after Gomulka and Mikolajczyk had arrived at my hotel apartment, a telephone call from the Premier's office said he had been detained on business and could not attend. It was obvious that the government desired to have on hand an independent interpreter to listen to any conversation of a political nature which Mikolajczyk might have with Hoover; but as a matter of fact, no matters relating to politics were discussed.

Gomulka, stout, vociferous in speech and violent in gestures, came to the hotel accompanied by two men in U.B. uniforms. Both stayed outside my sitting-room door until dinner was served when they followed us to the dining room and watched Gomulka from behind a partly opened door.

Mr. Hoover, on the other hand, walked about the streets and ruins during his stay in Warsaw without requiring any police escort. No official public demonstration was arranged for him, but when he entered or left the hospitals or schools (which we visited at his own expressed desire) he was cheered spontaneously and wholeheartedly. The sincerity of the cheering was similar to that which had greeted Eisenhower; markedly different from the regimented demonstrations in honor of the Soviet marshals and of Marshal Tito.

In the autumn of 1946 Poland again faced the possibility of a spring grain shortage, because of the impending liquidation of all UNRRA activities in Poland during the early months of 1947. At least this was the view of the Polish Government and of the UNRRA mission. But our agricultural experts, Clifford C. Taylor, economic counselor of the Embassy, and Edward R. Raymond, agricultural attaché, were of the opinion that Poland had sufficient grain on hand to meet its forthcoming needs.

I was concerned, however, by the discrepancy of nine hundred fifty thousand tons between our estimates on the one hand and those of the Polish Government and UNRRA on the other. On arrival in Washington in November 1946 I conferred with experts in the Department of Agriculture to make certain that Taylor and Raymond had been justified in reaching an estimate so much more optimistic than that given by the Poles and UNRRA. When I had set forth my apprehension, these agricultural experts smiled in amusement and told me that in the case of all other countries in Eastern Europe a similar situation had arisen: UNRRA and the respective government had agreed on an estimated grain supply far smaller than the figures of the experts in the various American embassies.

In 1947 Colonel Harrison of the Department of Agriculture made an investigation in Poland and submitted a report which, as the Department of Agriculture subsequently informed me, substantiated the estimates made the year before by Taylor and Raymond; and I learned with some surprise that even the Polish Government had concurred in Colonel Harrison's findings.

This seemingly consistent concurrence between UNRRA and the

governments of the nations in which it operated was illustrative of what, in my opinion, was one of UNRRA's chief defects: a tendency of its leaders, and hence of its personnel, to whitewash the irregularities of the Communist-dominated governments, such as those in Yugoslavia and Poland, which had control over the distribution of UNRRA supplies. The attitude of tacit acquiescence was, of course, an incentive to the Communists to continue to use UNRRA goods, contributed in large part by the people of the United States, for their own political advantage.

Regardless of irregularities and inequalities in the distribution of UNRRA and other supplies given by the American people, the value of sending relief to Poland from the United States surmounts any question of misuse for political purposes. There is no doubt that the help furnished by UNRRA and other humanitarian organizations— Swedish, Swiss and British, as well as those financed by the United States—created a great spiritual bond between the Polish people and Western civilization. The distribution of packages was a constant reminder to the Poles that the West had not forgotten their plight and that the West, especially the United States, was helping as in the past.

The implication was that we would continue to help in the future.

LABEL ON CAN OF CYANIDE GAS LEFT BEHIND BY NAZIS AT MAJDANEK
With this type of gas 3,500,000 Polish Jews were killed at Majdanek and Oswiecim.

WARSAW SPONTANEOUSLY WELCOMES EISENHOWER

In contrast to regimented demonstrations in honor of Soviet Marshals and Marshal Tito.

"WHAT A PERFECT BRIDGEHEAD!" EXCLAIMED EISENHOWER

But the Red Army did not use it when the Warsaw insurrectionists needed their help.

CHAPTER FIFTEEN

Financial Appeasement

THE PROGRAM for the economic reconstruction of Poland was carefully formulated in the autumn of 1945 under the general supervision of Hilary Minc, Minister of Industry, a Communist. Before the war he had served in a subordinate capacity in the Polish Ministry of Finance. A man of medium height, with an inscrutable expression, he was generally affable. He spoke excellent French and impressed me, as he previously had impressed Will Clayton at Potsdam, with his extraordinary command of figures and production, required raw materials and financial data in general.

At my first interview with Minc on September 3, 1945, he outlined to me the terrific devastation which Polish industry had suffered. Although the textile mills in Lódz had not been destroyed, the greater part of the machinery had been taken to Germany by the Nazis. In Bialystok, another textile center, little remained of the mills. And Poland was without cotton to manufacture the clothing so vitally needed after almost six years of Nazi occupation.

The Nazis had also systematically razed the ports of Gdansk—which was now to be incorporated into the Polish state—and Gdynia. Port machinery would be vitally needed so that foreign commerce could again flow normally.

But most important, and important to the countries of Western Europe as well, was Poland's need for locomotives and coal cars so that Silesian coal, now Poland's greatest potential export, could serve to rehabilitate the economy of the country.

The agricultural condition was desperate due to the lack of seed and draft animals. And the hog industry, which accounted for the largest Polish prewar export to the United States, was nonexistent, owing to German depredations.

Minc, being a loyal Communist, did not mention to me that the Soviet authorities had removed from Gdansk the cranes and other port machinery which the Nazis had not destroyed; nor that they had appropriated for the Red Army much of the grain and livestock in the country, and had dismantled factories and moved the machinery to the Soviet Union. But Poland was in dire economic straits whether the Nazis, the Soviets, or both, were responsible.

In accordance with the initial conversation which I had had with President Bierut on August 5, I confirmed to Minc the desire of the United States Government to assist in Polish rehabilitation to the best of our ability. I suggested, provided the Polish Government would subscribe to the general principles embodied in the Mutual Aid Agreement of July 1, 1942 (elimination of all forms of discriminatory treatment in international commerce, and the reduction of tariffs and other trade barriers), that the Polish Government send a commission of experts to the United States to discuss with the authorities of the Department of State and of the Export-Import Bank the possibility of obtaining credits which were urgently needed to purchase essential materials.

On September 28 Minc and Lange, whose appointment as Ambassador to the United States had already been announced, came to call on me. Minc assured me—I felt at the time, with excessive glibness—that of course Poland would meet all our requirements. His government had decided to appoint as its representative, in negotiating financial and economic arrangements with the United States, Dr. Rajchman, then in Washington as Polish delegate to UNRRA. A few days later, on October 2, I returned Minc's call. I was accompanied by Marshall MacDuffie, of the Office of Army-Navy Liquidation Commission, who had come to Warsaw to assist in the possible allocation of surplus war property to Poland. When we were ushered into Minc's office, we found Marshal Rola-Zymierski with him.

It was at this meeting that Rola-Zymierski made the urgent request for a credit to clothe the Polish Army which, he said, including the militia and Security Police then numbered three hundred fifty thousand men. The Marshal appeared surprised when MacDuffie informed him that this was the first request received by the United States for surplus equipment to be used for the maintenance of an army. Minc told us, at this meeting, that he was intending to ask for a loan of five hundred million dollars from the Export-Import Bank to be used for reconstruction. If granted, this credit, in addition to the assistance from UNRRA during its first year in Poland (seventy-two per cent of four hundred fifty million dollars), would bring the total to over eight hundred million dollars to be received from the United States Government.

I determined to take advantage of the eagerness of the Polish Government for economic assistance and to use it as a lever by which we would obtain fulfillment of Polish commitments under the Yalta and Potsdam decisions, as well as an improvement of the situation of imprisoned American citizens.

Accordingly I called by appointment on President Bierut on October 4, and told him with complete candor that, unless the Polish Government co-operated with us in establishing a reasonable rate of exchange, restoring freedom of the press, and putting a stop to arrests by the Security Police, I should not feel that I could recommend the granting of credits by the United States to the Polish Government. I referred to Marshal Rola-Zymierski's request that these credits should at least be partly for the benefit of the U.B., and I observed that such credits would be interpreted in Poland as an acquiescence on the part of the United States in U.B. activities, which were repulsive to the American people.

Bierut endeavored to excuse U.B. activities on the ground that Poland was in a state of transition after six years of foreign occupation. He assured me that they would not be kept up permanently. He asked me whether I thought unwarranted the detention of one thousand Poles for political reasons. I replied that I considered it wholly unwarranted and stated that since I had last seen the President ten more persons claiming to be American citizens had been arrested on political grounds.

The President promised to investigate these cases, and to arrange for the immediate release of the accused if they had been jailed for political reasons. But it did not seem to occur to Bierut that through his question he had admitted that the number of arrests and not the principle involved appeared to the Polish Government of primary importance.

Wishing to ascertain how the Polish people in general would feel about our extending financial assistance to the government in the face of the suppression then existing, I took advantage of a trip throughout the country in early October to sound independent political leaders and businessmen in various centers. Among those whom I interviewed I found an impressive unanimity of opinion. Summarized, it was to the effect that we would be making a great mistake to grant a credit of half a billion dollars to the Polish Government: the Polish people would interpret our action as acquiescence in non-democratic and brutal practices. On the other hand, our refusal to give financial aid to an imposed government having the support of less than ten per cent of the people would be appreciated as a mark of sympathy for the people's plight.

Using these opinions as a premise, I urged the Department of State to make our views clearly and emphatically known at that important moment.

In reply, I was authorized in a telegram dated November 9 to "imply" to the Polish Government that, apart from economic considerations involved, the granting of credits could be seriously jeopardized if its record in the fulfillment of obligations were impaired by failure to adhere fully to its acceptance of the Yalta agreement and to its Potsdam commitments on the holding of elections and on the freedom of the Allied press. I was authorized to say that if the policies of the Polish Government should create conditions under which free and unfettered elections would be an impossibility, and this fact became known to the American people, it could not be ignored, under our system of government, when we considered the Polish application for credits.

I was heartened by the attitude which the Department took in this telegram, but the authorization to "imply" rather than to state our position on paper—to be a part of the record—caused me some apprehension. I accordingly re-emphasized my position in a telegram to Washington on November 13. In this message I argued against the extension of credits substantially as follows:

1. The Polish Government, being provisional in character, would presumably make political capital of the extension of a credit.

2. As long as the Polish economy was patterned along Soviet lines there was little hope of normal processes of international trade in Poland and little likelihood of the borrowing nation being able to service and repay the credits.

3. Extension of a credit at the moment when the activities of the Security Police were creating terror throughout the country would indicate acquiescence on our part.

4. The government's evident intention to compel the opposition to adhere to a single electoral list would, if successful, vitiate the purpose of the Yalta and Potsdam agreements.

5. As the Polish Government was not its own master and required the Red Army to maintain it in power, any credits extended would be under the control, if not actually for the benefit, of the Soviet authorities who were still taking eastward, by train and by trucks, huge amounts of material from Poland originating both from east and west of the Oder River.

6. We had recently noted a liberalization of restriction on the freedom of the press. This healthy change was attributed to the continued firmness of the United States Government and to the press dispatches of American correspondents. If we should now relax in our resistance to the spread of totalitarian measures (as an extension of credit would be interpreted), we would not succeed in fulfilling our publicly expressed policy—maintenance of a strong, free and independent Poland.

I called on President Bierut on November 14 to expound to him the Department's views. I said that our government in considering the extension of credits would be influenced by the consensus of the people. Consequently, if the American people felt that undemocratic processes prevailed in a foreign country, their displeasure would affect our government's position. I said that the United States was deeply concerned with the holding of free and unfettered elections in Poland, and that I did not see how they would be possible if the Polish Government continued to arrest political opponents with the aid of the Soviet Army and police.

Bierut responded, somewhat heatedly, that if Poland must accept the activity of the Allied powers in its internal affairs as the price for economic assistance, it would prefer not to have such aid. Perhaps it occurred to him then that his government had made commitments to the three powers in accord with the Yalta and Potsdam decisions. For, in a moment, he spontaneously stated that, of course, his government accepted the principles and provisions of the Yalta decision respecting Poland, and would fulfill them.

On January 3, 1946, the National Council of the Homeland passed a decree nationalizing all industrial property in Poland in which more than a given number of persons was employed. Minc made a speech on that date explaining that the decree legalized the position of the Polish Government, which had heretofore been administering, without legal authority, various foreign properties in Poland. He said that the decree emphasized Poland's desire for economic as well as political sovereignty and Poland's intention not to become a colony of foreign capital. This speech was interpreted generally as an attack on the United States.

The next day, January 4, I stated to the Foreign Minister, Mr. Rzymowski, in the presence of Olszewski, that I failed to understand the criticism which Minc and other government officials had made of the "capitalistic" policy of the United States at the very moment when Poland was requesting from us a credit of a half billion dollars. And at the same time I lodged a protest against the refusal, up to that time, of the Polish Government to grant visas to American citizens who wished to go to Poland to inspect their properties which were about to be nationalized.

On January 7 Berman told an American press representative that I had protested against the nationalization of American-owned property, and he said that I had no reason to do so. Berman's statement was without basis in fact.

The next day, realizing that the Polish Government was endeavoring to place us in an erroneous position before the public, I called a meeting of the American correspondents. I told them that I had made no protest over the nationalization decree and emphasized that Poland as a sovereign nation had a right to enact any legislation it desired. I added, however, that I had protested to the Foreign Office under Article 1, paragraph 4, of the Treaty of Friendship and Commerce of 1931, the Polish Government's refusal to permit American citizens to enter Poland to inspect their properties which were subject to the decree.

Under instructions from Washington I addressed a note to the Polish Government on January 18 expressing the belief that United States nationals were entitled to "adequate and effective compensation" for property nationalized, which would permit the conversion of proceeds into dollars as soon as possible. We proposed the establishment of a mixed commission to determine the amount of compensation to be paid. At the same time we reiterated our desire to establish a basis for durable and mutually beneficial economic co-operation.

But the Polish Government rejected the proposal for a mixed commission on the ground that it was an affront to Polish sovereignty! Months later, in December, it agreed to the setting up of a commission. But no decisions by the commission on compensation had been made up to October 1947.

Besides our desire to obtain adequate compensation for nationalized American-owned property, and to have a reasonable rate of exchange established, we also had been interested since our arrival in Poland in the conclusion of a bilateral aviation agreement which would give each country the right to institute transatlantic commercial air service to the other.

The Foreign Office had granted permission for a flight of an American Overseas Airlines C-54 plane to Warsaw. The plane arrived on the morning of January 20, but on the eve of this event we received a message from the Foreign Office that the permission granted was for one flight only. On taking the matter up repeatedly with the Premier, Berman and the Foreign Office, we were finally advised that because of the technical complexity of the problem it would be necessary for the Ministry of Communications to study it at length. On the other hand, an official of the Ministry of Communications had told us that his ministry was heartily in favor of our proposal but that the Foreign Office was holding it up for political reasons. This point of view was in effect confirmed by a statement made by Zebrowski to Mr. Keith, counselor of our Embassy, on January 25 that no action on the aviation agreement could be taken by the Polish Government until the more basic economic problems between the two governments had been settled. In other words, we were given to understand that the Polish Government exacted the extension of a credit as the price for an American airline coming into Warsaw. But later, after American credits had been extended, the Prime Minister explained his government's continued postponement of the aviation negotiations by the specious plea that the United States and the United Kingdom were not in agreement on aviation policy. This being the case, said he, Poland did not intend to have its hand caught in a trap.

It was clear from the three different excuses advanced—and I so told Osóbka-Morawski—that Poland did not intend even to discuss the negotiation of this agreement. Its consummation would have meant much to the economic development of Poland through faster and more efficient air-mail and passenger service to the United States. And, obviously, it would have been highly advantageous to the United

States. But it was plain that the Soviet Government did not wish our encroachment in this vital area of Eastern Europe.

While I was absent on a trip to Paris in January 1946 to attend a meeting of the economic counselors of our embassies in Europe, Rzymowski and Modzelewski, who were in London in connection with the organization of the United Nations, called on Secretary Byrnes and complained that I had protested against the decree nationalizing Polish industry and that I had refused to accept the exchange rate of one hundred zlotys to the dollar.

Mr. Byrnes, after reporting this conversation to the Department of State, authorized the Embassy in Warsaw to inform the Polish Government that I had recognized the government's right to enact the nationalization decree and had made no protest, except regarding the exclusion of American citizens who wished to inspect their properties. And as for the rate of exchange, the Embassy in Warsaw was acting with the approval of the Department of State in declining to accept a rate which was unrealistic.

But in the meantime, on January 24, Olszewski had sent for Gerald Keith, who was acting as chargé d'affaires in my absence. Olszewski told Keith about a telegram from Rzymowski in London according to which Secretary Byrnes had accepted the rate of one hundred zlotys to the dollar and had authorized Rzymowski to advise the American Embassy in Warsaw of this fact. Keith was so astounded by this news that he wrote out, in the presence of Olszewski and Zebrowski, who acted as interpreter, the exact phraseology which Olszewski had used.

Mr. Byrnes, on receipt of Keith's message giving the text of Olszewski's statement, immediately instructed Keith to deliver a memorandum to the Foreign Office denying that he had made any such statement to Rzymowski and adding that should he have occasion to communicate with the American Embassy in Warsaw he would do so directly and not through a foreign government. Mr. Byrnes directed Keith to describe Olszewski's statement as a willful distortion of the facts.

The negative attitude taken by the Polish Government in the matter of the aviation agreement, the vicious criticism of the United States in the government-controlled press, and the misrepresentation of the statements made by Secretary of State Byrnes convinced me that it was imperative for us to take a strong stand in insisting on satisfaction on all matters which were then at an impasse. I advised the Department of State as follows:

We have now reached the time when our policy toward Poland must remain completely firm and conducted in such a way as to discourage the thought not only on the part of Poles but of their guiding authorities to the east that we do not intend to be backed farther against a wall. Every time that we make a move which is interpreted as a partial retreat, the area in which we can operate will be decreased and optimism of those opposing our principles will be increased.

But early in March 1946 I received the disquieting news from Washington that, despite my repeated objections, the Polish Government was to be granted the utilization of a fifty-million-dollar credit for the purchase of surplus war material. It was understandable that our Army and Navy authorities wished to dispose of this material regardless of price, as it was deteriorating because of weather and otherwise would be a complete loss. But because of the important international implications I felt that we were making a grave error.

I therefore let the Department know, under date of March 14, that I regretted this step, for the Polish Government would undoubtedly use the credit to bolster itself politically. I feared, too, that it would greatly weaken our stand in making representations on internal conditions if the news of our granting a credit to Poland were announced, especially as in the past few days the following instances of the Polish Government's disregard of its pledges at Potsdam had taken place:

the temporary arrest of Polish Peasant Party members in Warsaw to prevent their attendance at a political meeting on March 10; the surrounding and searching by Security Police of Polish Peasant Party headquarters on March 12; the attempts to prevent the circulation of *Gazeta Ludowa,* the Polish Peasant Party organ; and the increasing number of arrests, principally of former members of the Home Army.

The United States Government, desirous of regularizing the financial operations of the Embassy in Warsaw, had sent, in March 1946, Mr. William Taylor, of the Treasury Department, and Mr. James Gantenbein, of the Department of State, to Poland with a view to reaching an understanding with Poland on a realistic rate of exchange. These officials had had conversations with the Foreign Office and with the Minister of Finance. It was agreed that Mr. Taylor should return for a further meeting with the Minister of Finance on April 18.

On the evening of April 17 a circular note from the Foreign Office was received by the American Embassy as well as by other diplomatic missions in Warsaw, stating that exchange transactions must from that day be conducted through the National Bank, or other authorized banks, and that transactions outside of this channel, being illegal, would be punishable in accordance with the law.

Persons convicted of accepting yellow-seal currency from the United States Embassy in the future would be liable to imprisonment of twenty years. This would put an end to our selling United States yellow-seal currency on the open market, which we had been doing, with the permission of the State Department, for the past six months.

The receipt of this note put an end to Mr. Taylor's negotiations with the Minister of Finance and came as a tremendous blow to the Embassy staff. It meant that, at a time when the open market rate was about six hundred zlotys to the dollar and the official rate was only one hundred, our personnel would not be able to subsist on their salaries. Few members of the staff were from then on able to afford to eat in the hotel or in restaurants. They were forced to resort to eating (in their bedrooms) tinned food from the United States Army commissary and, hence, purchased in dollar currency. And during the next eight months while this unrealistic rate, unilaterally imposed by the Polish Government, was in effect, our work was seriously affected by resignations. Moreover, we were unable to hire locally Polish personnel, when the maximum we could offer was five thousand zlotys a month, the equivalent of six dollars in purchasing power.

The Polish Government's action smacked of the Soviet technique to confront one with a *fait accompli* immediately before the commencement of negotiations. But undoubtedly it had uppermost in mind the serious hindrance which the enforcement of this directive would have on the legitimate activities of the United States diplomatic and consular establishments in Poland.

My anxiety over the rate of exchange was as nothing in comparison with my bitter disappointment on Easter morning, April 21. Then I received the depressing news from Washington that the Department of State intended to grant two credits to the Polish Provisional Government, totaling ninety million dollars: one for fifty million dollars to acquire surplus war property in Europe, and another for forty million dollars from the Export-Import Bank to purchase locomotives and coal cars.

According to the Department's telegram the Polish Government had agreed to accept our "proposals for expansion of world trade and employment"; it would continue to accord to nationals and corporations of the United States the treatment provided for in the Treaty of 1931; it would make adequate and effective compensation to American nationals and corporations whose properties were nationalized; it would make available to the United States Government full information about economic treaties entered into by Poland with third parties; and would agree to hold elections within the calendar year.

I telegraphed that I felt great concern over the Department's apparent intention to grant the credits in spite of the bad faith so clearly shown on so many occasions by the Polish ruling clique.

Acceptance of the Provisional Government's promises, I continued, would imply misunderstanding of the entire situation in Poland, and be the utmost discouragement to the Polish people, who still kept hoping that we would maintain a firm attitude. I concluded:

With the greatest earnestness of which I am capable I beg the Department not to approve the extension of any credits at this time. When the terroristic activities of the Security Police come to an end, when freedom of the press is restored, and when American citizens are released from Polish prisons—not until then should United States public funds be used to assist the Polish Provisional Government of National Unity.

My advice was in vain. Word came that the Department on April 24 had agreed to exchange notes with the Polish Government.*

On April 25 I wired that the Department's decision to extend the credits was most discouraging to me, for it indicated either that it had little confidence in my evaluation of the Polish situation or, for reasons not disclosed to me, did not wish to do what I recommended.

I particularly regretted that the extension of a credit was to be announced right after the Polish Government's arbitrary action of fixing an unrealistic exchange of one hundred zlotys to the dollar while negotiations were on to determine a fair rate. The extension of the credit would be interpreted by the regime as encouragement to continue its unfriendly policy toward the United States and to flout the Yalta and Potsdam decisions.

As the notes between the Department of State and the Polish Embassy had presumably already been exchanged, I supposed further recommendations on my part would be futile. I ended:

I do wish, however, now to place on record my final protest as American Ambassador to Poland that we have agreed to extend credits to a government which has not only assumed in its controlled press an attitude hostile to the United States but has likewise refused to accord to us the rights to which we are entitled by treaty. To the best of

---

*For text of Polish notes see Appendix.

my recollection the Polish Provisional Government has up to date not acceded to any important request which the United States Government has made of it.

Although the Polish Government had, in the conversations both in Washington and Warsaw, insisted that political and financial questions should not be linked, the government-controlled *Rzeczpospolita* said in an editorial on April 27:

Polish people received with deep satisfaction the news concerning the granting of a loan to us by the United States of America. We have no intention of belittling the significance of the material help received, but in our opinion the moral and, for this reason, the political side of the loan has an even greater meaning.

The editorial made no mention of the conditions attached to the credit, nor did the Prime Minister when he announced it before the National Council of the Homeland on April 26 in justification of his foreign policy, nor even, I learned indirectly, when he told the cabinet meeting about it. Among these conditions were provisions that the text of the notes should be published in full in Poland and the United States, and that there should be no restrictions on the transmission of press dispatches in Poland.

That spring Stanislaw Banczyk had resigned in disgust from the Communist-controlled Peasant Party. Then he had joined Mikolajczyk's Polish Peasant Party and had become its vice-president. In a speech before the National Council of the Homeland, on April 26, he denounced the activities of the Security Police; the government administration, the militia, the Army and the Security Police should serve the interests of all the people and not merely the Polish Workers' Party. Larry Allen, of the Associated Press, said that his dispatch giving the text of this speech was not received by his home office in New York.

Because the text of the notes exchanged in Washington had not been published by May 1, and as we had not received the promised information regarding Poland's economic treaties, I determined to fly to Paris and discuss with Secretary Byrnes the Polish Government's complete disregard of its solemn commitments.

On May 6 I saw Mr. Byrnes in his suite at the Hotel Meurice. The Secretary was attending the third meeting of the Council of Foreign Ministers and was experiencing, through the intransigent attitude of Mr. Molotov, the difficulties of dealing in a constructive manner with a Communist government.

I proposed that, in view of the failure of the Polish Government to live up to its obligations, we should suspend immediately the delivery of any further surplus war material and that the Export-Import Bank credit should not be made available until Poland carried out its obligations.

The Secretary approved and the necessary action was taken. The Polish Government was duly informed of the reasons for it.

Mr. Byrnes instructed me to seek an interview with President Bierut as soon as I got back to Poland, to acquaint him with the motives behind our suspension of deliveries of surplus war material and to impress on him the seriousness which we attached to the fulfillment of Poland's commitments, not only with regard to the loan but with regard to the elections as well.

But, though I made three attempts to see Bierut, he declined to receive me. The atmosphere of government officials was chilly. For all that, the suspension of the deliveries and of the Export-Import Bank credit had its effect: A telegram from Allen on the Banczyk incident was passed and no other case of censorship of American dispatches was reported to us; the texts of the notes exchanged in Washington were published on May 16 with the excuse that publication had been delayed because of "technical reasons"; and, within a few weeks, the treaty material was furnished us by the Foreign Office.

In my opinion, these minor gains in no way compensated for the loss of prestige suffered by the United States when we granted credits to a government which had not kept its word to us and which seized on our leniency as warrant for proceeding to even greater attacks on the freedom of its own citizens—and of our citizens.

CHAPTER SIXTEEN

Referendum and Pogrom

THE referendum scheduled for June 30, 1946, was, according to the law passed by the National Council of the Homeland in the latter part of April, to determine: (1) whether Poland would have a unicameral or bicameral Congress; (2) whether principles underlying nationalization of industry and agrarian reform should be incorporated into the constitution; and (3) whether Poland's permanent frontier should remain on the Oder and western Neisse rivers.

The three points to be voted on were noncontentious in so far as most Poles were concerned, with the possible exception of the first point which had as its aim the elimination of the Senate as a legislative body. As the majority of the Polish people were agriculturists, they were generally apathetic to the nationalization of industry, but in favor of agrarian reform, for they felt that the division of the large feudal states would be a progressive step toward economic recovery and would furnish every peasant with at least a small parcel of land. As to the third point, the people, who had already lost that portion of their country east of the Molotov-Ribbentrop Line to the Soviet Union, naturally desired the compensation in the north and in the west which had been promised in the Yalta and Potsdam decisions. Furthermore, the Polish Government had been permitted by the Potsdam Conference to deport Germans in that north and west territory under Polish administration. In the light of this permission the Polish Government and people assumed that, although the terms of the Potsdam decision provided that the frontier would be finally settled by the Peace Conference, there was no intention that the Germans were to return there. Otherwise, why would the deportation of the Germans be specifically authorized?

In the month before the holding of the referendum there was speculation in diplomatic circles in Warsaw whether the government and
the opposition would agree on the questions involved and whether, if
they did not, the government would permit the balloting and the
counting of the ballots to be conducted fairly and justly.

The opposition consisted at that time of the Polish Peasant Party of
Mikolajczyk and the Christian Labor Party of Karol Popiel, who had
formerly held a portfolio in the Polish Government in London. These
two parties finally decided to oppose the government's position on
question number one on the ground that the elimination of the Senate
would be contrary to the Constitution of 1921 and would, in effect,
remove a valuable brake which might be used against a Communist-
controlled Sejm, or Chamber of Deputies. These parties therefore
urged their members to vote negatively on this question, but affirmatively on questions two and three.

Because of the significance of the procedure which might be followed in the referendum, our government urged that as many representative American newspaper and press association correspondents
as possible be sent to Warsaw to report developments. Over a dozen
were on hand. The Embassy arranged for teams of observers to be
sent on referendum day to various districts of Poland (Kraków,
Poznan, Gdansk, Kielce, Radom, Bialystok, Bydgoszcz, Lódz, Wroclaw, Szczecin, Lublin, Radomsko, Katowice and the environs of
Warsaw), and invited correspondents to accompany them. Thus we
could obtain the most accurate picture possible of the methods employed, intimidation, if any, and the reaction of the people to the
elections.

Even before the day of voting, the opposition parties were impeded
in their efforts to campaign against the elimination of the Senate.
Posters of the Polish Peasant Party were rarely in evidence, for in the
majority of cases they had been torn down, or the bill stickers had
been threatened or manhandled. And the two opposition parties were
allowed little, if any, time on the government-controlled radio. The
advice of Mikolajczyk to his followers to vote No on question number

one was not permitted by the government censor to be published. The Polish Peasant Party had to resort to word of mouth to advise its members of party policy. Three thousand of the party were arrested at Poznan and prevented from voting. And arrests of many other party members were reported throughout Poland. On the other hand, the government campaign slogan—"3 Razy Tak" (Three times Yes)—was posted or painted on thousands of buildings. This crude propaganda, costing the country millions of zlotys, was also spread by truckloads of subsidized men who, on the eve of the referendum, drove through the streets of the various cities shouting the political battle cry at the top of their voices.

During the morning I drove about Warsaw to observe the crowds which, orderly and good-natured, awaited their turn to vote. I visited several voting booths and noted that there was no evidence of intimidation of any sort. In the afternoon my wife and I visited neighboring villages, such as Konstancin, where the outward peacefulness of a summer Sunday gave no sign that a heated political battle, with international implications, was being waged. After returning to the Hotel Polonia I soon began to receive the first-hand reports of our observers as they came back from the districts they had visited. Some reports, because of the distances involved, were delayed for several days.

The voting which was heavy and amounted often to ninety per cent of the electorate apparently was conducted in an orderly manner with no overt intimidation. Members of the Embassy, watching the crowds outside the booths awaiting their turn to vote, were even invited by the election officials to enter the polling places. In fact, from all reports the day passed quietly and without major disturbances. The voter could mark his ballot secretly, but there was widespread fear, as our observers reported, that fraudulent means would be used in counting the ballots.

There were, indeed, provisions in the referendum law that could give rise to collusion or dishonest practices; for instance, a blank ballot was to be regarded as an affirmative vote on all three questions;

and provision was made that government organizations as well as government-controlled industries would vote in bodies. They were urged to vote three times Yes as groups. Since disobedience was punishable by loss of jobs, they voted solidly for the government's policy.

Some of our people ascertained that, in a practical manner, there were definite impediments to impartial observation. Steven Zagorski, Administrative Assistant, and Edward R. Raymond, Agricultural Attaché, had driven to Kielce to watch the procedure and the attitude of the people. They were arrested by the Security Police while they were having luncheon and, despite their protests of diplomatic immunity, they were held at headquarters for over three hours on the charge that they had distributed "antistate" handbills. They were released at last with apologies but not until the voting was over.

In the vicinity of Bialystok Lieutenant Colonel Frank Jessic, Assistant Military Attaché, was arrested by Polish troops on the charge of traveling in a forbidden area and photographing Russian troops.

John Scott, correspondent of *Time* magazine, who had come to Poland to report the referendum, was arrested near Poznan a few days before it and was held and cross-questioned for five hours by two Soviet officers. He understood Russian perfectly and was impressed by the fact that the phone conversations between these officers and the Minister of Public Security which eventually resulted in his release were conducted in Russian.

The most venal phase of the referendum procedure was in the counting of ballots. The law provided that they be counted at the polling places in the presence of representatives of all parties. But high government officials and the Security Police gave illegal orders to the electoral authorities to remove the ballot boxes, before the tabulation of votes, from the polls to the district commissioner's headquarters.

In Kraków the electoral commission appeared to have advance notice of the government's intentions. The ballots were tabulated and the results reported before the instructions were received to remove the ballot boxes. The government was forced to admit that in Kraków the voting was eighty-four per cent No on question number one.

With this exception, the government claimed a sweeping affirmative vote on all three questions. The four "government bloc" parties—Polish Workers Party, Polish Socialist Party, Democratic Party and Peasant Party (not to be confused with Mikolajczyk's P.S.L.)—had obediently followed the prescribed line. On the controversial question of the abolition of the Senate, the government claimed a victory of over eighty per cent; whereas, according to figures which our observers compiled independently of one another, the opposition voted No in approximately the same percentage. Even on the other questions many voted against the government on the ground that any resistance should be regarded as a healthy political sign.

The referendum served the dual purpose of testing out the electoral machinery and the possibility of diverting it to fraudulent uses. But, more important, it served as an excuse for the postponement of the elections for a further indefinite period, and so enabling the Security Police to exert an even tighter control over the country.

I reported to the Department a summary of the conclusions of our observers on the results of the referendum:

The only evidence obtainable that the referendum ballots were accurately counted, as the government press reported, came from the official statements of government officials.

The following factors indicate that the balloting was not accurately counted and reported:

(1) There is no conclusive evidence that the government enjoys more than a very minor support of the electorate. Modzelewski and others in the government have, in fact, admitted, either to this Embassy or to other diplomatic missions, that the government does not enjoy more than twenty per cent support of the electorate.

(2) The Embassy's observers reported that in the twelve different regions of the country visited, the vote, as indicated by conversations with voters, was No on the first question of the referendum.

(3) Mikolajczyk, who enjoyed a universal reputation for integrity, had publicly charged that there had been a falsification of the election results. Barcikowski, the chief of the electoral commission, stated however that the charge could not be accepted, as the referendum law made no provision for filing such charges!

On August 19, pursuant to instructions from Washington, I delivered a note to the Foreign Office, of which the following are the two pertinent paragraphs:*

The United States Government considers that it had no responsibilities in connection with the referendum held in Poland on June 30. Nevertheless, as the Polish Ambassador in Washington informed my Government on April 24, 1946, this referendum was a measure preparatory to the election, and the methods by which it was held bear a relation to the preparations for holding the election itself. The official representatives of the United States Government in Poland have reported that the voting in the referendum appeared to have been generally carried out in a correct and fair manner but that the methods used in tabulating the ballots and reporting the vote have given rise to charges of serious irregularities, including removal of ballot boxes from polling places in contravention of the referendum law. . . .

In view of the foregoing, my Government wishes to emphasize its belief that *inter alia* it is essential for the carrying out of free elections that (1) all democratic and anti-Nazi parties are allowed to conduct election campaigns freely without arrest or threat of arrest. The parties recognized as "democratic and anti-Nazi parties" include the following: The Polish Workers Party (PPR), the Democratic Party (SD), the Polish Socialist Party (PPS), the Polish Peasant Party (PSL), the Peasant Party (SL) and the Labor Party (SP); (2) all such parties are represented on all electoral commissions and ballots are counted in presence of representatives of all such parties; (3) results will be published immediately by local districts; and (4) there shall be an adequate system of appealing elections disputes. . . .

The United States Government had accordingly made it clear that it was aware that fraudulent practices, employed in the referendum,

---

* For the full text of the note, see Appendix.

might again be used in the elections, for which we, as well as the Polish Provisional Government, had an international responsibility.

One did not have to live more than a few weeks in Warsaw to become cynical about the designs of the Lublin group to remain permanently in power. And as the referendum was officially stated to be a forerunner of the elections it was generally anticipated that the government would score an overwhelming victory, no matter by what means it was achieved. Few people therefore were surprised by the government's announcement that the electorate had overwhelmingly voted affirmatively on the three questions to be decided.

But there was one aftermath of the referendum—a very tragic one—which had not been expected. In Kielce, in southeastern Poland on the Warsaw-Radom-Kraków road, a violent anti-Jewish disturbance had taken place on the morning of July 4. Forty Jews had been killed, as well as several members of the Polish Army and militia. The news of this pogrom reached me that afternoon during the Fourth of July reception which we were holding in the dining room and garden of the Hotel Polonia. As the first accounts were so conflicting I sent representatives to Kielce to obtain as objective and factual a report as possible. At the same time I personally interviewed members of the government, leaders of the opposition, prominent members of the Jewish community, representatives of the Joint Distribution Committee and members of the Roman Catholic hierarchy. It was on the basis of our investigations in Kielce and of these conversations that I reported my findings to the Department of State.

Kielce is a charming old town situated on a hill overlooking the fertile valley to the south, famous for its sixteenth-century cathedral. Before the war it had a population of about sixty thousand, twenty thousand of whom were Jews. During the war, however, due to the Nazi policy of exterminating the Jewish race, almost all the Jews had disappeared. In July 1946 only about two hundred fifty Jews were living in Kielce, most of them in one apartment house; half of them had been repatriated from Russia.

For many weeks before the pogrom, a strong anti-Semitic feeling had been developing in Kielce with credence being given to vicious rumors, such as: the Warsaw Government was dominated by Jews; the few Jews living in Kielce all had been repatriated from the Soviet Union and were not Polish Jews but Russian Communists; Jews were receiving preference in the distribution of UNRRA and other relief supplies; the Jews were engaged in the ritual murders of Polish Gentile children. These rumors must have reached the government, for we learned from government sources in Warsaw that as far back as May the Security Police in Kielce had been warned by the Ministry of Public Security that trouble was brewing and that an uprising might be expected.

Almost all the sources available to us were in agreement that on July 1—the day after the referendum—a small Polish boy about eight years old had disappeared from his home and did not return until the evening of July 3, when he told his family that he had been kept a prisoner in the cellar of a Jewish home and had seen the bodies of Polish children there. The boy's father took him to police headquarters at Kielce on the following morning—July 4—where the boy told his story. He accompanied members of the militia to the house where he had been held, and pointed out the man who had been responsible for his detention. The militia then arrested the Jew and, under instructions from the U.B., encircled the house, entered it and searched for weapons.

Quickly, as a result of the militia's action, the report spread throughout the town that Jewish ritual murders of Polish children had been committed, and a crowd of about four thousand indignant persons gathered outside the apartment house where the accused Jew, as well as over a hundred others of his race, resided.

There was discrepancy in the reports as to whether the Jews in the building had opened fire on the militia from the windows of the house when they insisted on being admitted. Most of the Gentile sources we consulted insisted that the Jewish tenants had become terrified by the presence of the militia and the gathering of the crowd, had lost their heads and fired in self-defense. Jewish sources, on the other hand, were equally insistent that no shots were fired by the Jews but that they had been ordered downstairs by the militia, who were unable to maintain their formation and were powerless therefore to prevent the Jews from being brutally clubbed to death by the infuriated crowd. But almost all sources agreed that the militia had been responsible to a great extent for the massacre, not only in failing to keep order but in the actual killing of the victims, for many had been shot or bayoneted to death.

Although the violence of the pogrom might have given the impression that the tragic happening was due primarily to uncontrolled racial passions, both government and antigovernment sources admitted that it was not spontaneous, but a carefully organized plot.

Premier Osóbka-Morawski told me on July 10 that underground "bands" had been responsible for the outbreak and that "reactionary and clerical elements" had been infuriated by the result of the referendum. In reporting Osóbka's remarks to the Department of State, I gave it as my personal opinion that it would be more accurate to say that the people generally were infuriated by what they regarded as the falsification of the referendum results.

Berman also, in a talk I had with him on July 11, held that the Kielce pogrom was part of a general plan on the part of the underground bands—specifically the National Armed Forces (N.S.Z.) and Freedom and Independence (W.I.N.)—to create dissension against the government throughout the country; and that it was a direct result of dissatisfaction over the outcome of the referendum.

Vice-Premier Gomulka, Secretary General of the Communist Polish Workers Party, on July 7 gave the government's official view, which endeavored to link Mikolajczyk with the instigation of the pogrom:

The policy of negation pursued by the Polish Peasant Party and the National Armed Forces, having been unable to win a victory in the referendum, is now tending to push the struggle into the abyss of civil war and anarchy. Evidence of this is the pogrom of the Jews in Kielce. The Polish fascists who until now were so enthusiastic whenever they saw M. Mikolajczyk have now surpassed their masters, the Nazis, in spreading anti-Semitism in Poland.

On the other hand, independent sources held that the pogrom was prepared by the government to provoke difficulties for the opposition, especially among Jewish circles in the United States. The government, they claimed, figured that the falsifying of referendum returns would be overshadowed by the more spectacular and tragic event of the pogrom—with all those American and British correspondents in Poland!

Whether or not this conjecture was correct, the correspondents were quick to grasp the news value of the Kielce murders. So, emphasis in the United States press was placed on the anti-Semitism still existing in Poland, rather than on the significance of the rigging of the referendum.

An American citizen of the Jewish race in whom I have the greatest confidence for intellectual honesty and loyalty to the United States, expressed to me his private opinion that the pogrom could have been averted had the chief of the Security Police in Kielce not given the order to search the apartment house, and had the senior U.B. officer and the Roman Catholic clergy taken some action to calm the mob.

When I visited Cardinal Hlond, the Primate of Poland, on July 8, he was deeply indignant over the Kielce massacre. He said he would give a statement to this effect to the American press correspondents in Warsaw, in order to allay the unfortunate impression that the hierarchy had condoned it. The absence of the Bishop of Kielce, Monsignor Kaczmarek, at the time of the pogrom had created the belief in the minds of some people that the Church was indifferent to the tragic fate of the murdered Jews.

But the statement which the Cardinal gave to the correspondents on July 11 provoked further violent attacks against the Church. Cardinal Hlond indicated in it that the Polish Government was itself responsible for much of the anti-Semitic feeling in the country through the unpopularity of its policies and actions in which the Jews played a prominent part. The government-controlled press immediately interpreted this statement as a defense of the pogrom.

The trial of the twelve persons charged with responsibility was held in Kielce from July 9 to July 11 before a military court. The prosecution indicated that "reactionary" bands had been accountable for the uprising, but as the defendants were all civilians the jurisdiction of the court was questioned by some of the lawyers for the defendants. Nine of the defendants received death sentences, which were immediately carried out, while a woman, a man and a youth of about twenty years of age who appeared to be of an abnormally low mentality, received sentences of ten years, seven years and life imprisonment, respectively.

The Prime Minister informed me on July 10 that the Vice-Governor, the chief of the Security Police, and the chief of the militia at Kielce had all been arrested under the Premier's personal orders because of their having permitted the pogrom to take place; and Ambassador Lange, who was in Warsaw on a consultative visit, told me that the government considered the militia largely responsible. Yet no members of the militia were brought to trial.

My belief, after sifting various reports which came to me, including those from Polish-speaking members of the Embassy whom I had sent to Kielce to attend the trial, was that the underlying cause of the pogrom was the growing anti-Semitism which, even our Jewish sources admitted, was caused by the great unpopularity of the Jews in key government positions. These men included Minc, Berman, Olszewski (whose real name was said to be Specht), Radkiewicz and Spychalski. Our Jewish friends said that the Jews in Poland had little regard for the government and resented the implication that the Jews in it were representative of their people. I told the Department of State that, from the reports received, I believed there was bitter feeling within the militia against the Jews because the Security Police, controlled by Radkiewicz, dominated the militia and the Army, and a Russian general, Kiziewicz, dominated the Internal Security Police (K.B.W.). It was known, furthermore, that both the U.B. and K.B.W. had, among their members, many Jews of Russian origin.

Although I had no definite proof that the government instigated the Kielce pogrom, I wondered, in view of the unbelievably inefficient manner in which the U.B. and the militia had handled the affair, whether it might not have seriously welcomed the opportunity to denounce, as responsible parties, its principal critics, including the Roman Catholic Church, Mikolajczyk and the underground movement.

Before the war anti-Semitism had become more active in Poland, but chiefly for economic reasons—jealousy of the Jews' acknowledged superiority in the realm of commerce.

But, were it not for the unpopularity of the Jews within the Provisional Government of National Unity, the anti-Jewish feeling was bound to have diminished. Because of the decrease of the Jewish population, through the Nazi extermination of Polish Jews at the Oswiecim, Majdanek and Buchenwald concentration camps, and during the razing of the Warsaw Ghetto in April 1943, the Jews could no longer be considered an economic menace. From a prewar population of four million Jews, Poland in August 1945 had only fifty thousand left. Perhaps two hundred thousand more were to be repatriated from the Soviet Union. Warsaw, which had had a population of three hundred fifty thousand Jews, had only five thousand after the war.

As Polish Jews were being repatriated from the Soviet Union in the winter of 1945, often in open freight cars, a serious situation confronted our military authorities in the United States zones of occupation in Germany and Austria. In December 1945, for instance, three hundred Jews were arriving daily in our zone in Bavaria and two hundred and fifty in our zone in Berlin, claiming they had fled for fear of persecution because of their race, religion or political beliefs. They intensified the United States Army's difficulties of housing and feeding by the influx of about fifteen thousand displaced persons a month.

Their exodus from Poland was voluntary, for there was no incentive for them to remain: their relatives and friends had disappeared; there was no opportunity to enter their former occupations; and there was the traditional fear of anti-Semitic hatred. As Dr. Sommerstein, the head of the former Jewish Party, put it, Poland was now a Jewish cemetery. Besides, having experienced in the Soviet Union the terrors of a Communist police state, they had no inclination to live under the Polish variety. In fact we were informed by Jewish relief officials that not more than five per cent of the repatriated Polish Jews were Communistic in their viewpoint.

Shortly after our arrival in Warsaw the government-controlled *Glos Ludu* announced on August 14, 1945, that a serious anti-Jewish demonstration had taken place in Kraków, that some Jews attending a synagogue service had been beaten, and that the synagogue had been set on fire. In its issue of the fifteenth, *Glos Ludu* stated that "reactionaries" were responsible for the outbreak as a protest against the agrarian reform measures of the government.

Some independent sources, however, claimed in talks with members of our Embassy that anti-Jewish demonstrations were Soviet-inspired so as to give the Red Army a pretext to remain indefinitely in the country for the purpose of preserving order. But an investigation which I myself made in Kraków in October 1945, through numerous interviews, convinced me that the alleged Kraków pogrom was an isolated demonstration of ill feeling which broke out because of the irresponsible acts of young hoodlums who had stoned some Jews leaving the synagogue.

Although it was most difficult for a Polish Gentile to obtain permission to leave the country unless he had legitimate business abroad which would benefit the government, Polish Jews might leave quite freely, without passports and without any restrictions at the frontier. Those who were being repatriated from Russia were generally assembled at Lódz and then traveled in groups to the Czechoslovak frontier whence they would proceed to Austria or Germany. Many of them had no definite ultimate destination. All they desired was to leave Poland and, after the Kielce pogrom, the exodus increased to the rate of seven hundred per day.

In August 1946, because of the critical phase of the housing situation in our zones in Austria and Germany, I was instructed by Washington to try to obtain the co-operation of the Polish Government in curbing the exodus of the Jewish emigrants in their own interest. The government informed Mr. William Bein, director of the Joint Distribution Committee in Poland, and me that attempts were being made to settle seventy-five thousand Jews in Silesia but that it could not force the Jews to remain in Poland where they feared they might be the victims of further outbreaks. However, I could not escape the conclusion, because of the Polish·Government's tacit permission to the Jews to leave the country without observing the usual passport and visa requirements, that it welcomed their exodus. This feeling was confirmed when Schwalbe, Vice-President of the National Council of the Homeland, told me he thought the Jewish infiltration into the American zone of Germany was a carefully planned maneuver to influence the United States Government to put pressure on the British Government to open up Palestine to Polish Jewish displaced persons.

The result of the referendum, the Kielce pogrom and the executions of the defendants combined to bring about a noticeable increase in political tension. This was aggravated by the refusal of Prime Minister Osóbka-Morawski to permit a meeting of the Christian Labor Party scheduled for July 19. Mr. Popiel, the president of the party, in the face of this negation of freedom of assembly, suspended the party's activities. Thus only Mikolajczyk's Polish Peasant Party remained in the field in opposition to the government.

That the government intended to continue to consolidate its position, regardless of any protests which the United States and British governments might make under the Yalta and Potsdam decisions, was evidenced by a statement made by President Bierut to W. H. Lawrence, staff correspondent of the *New York Times,* on July 19. In this interview he came close to saying that I was *persona non grata,* charging that I had little understanding of the Polish people and could not or would not appreciate their problems. This attack was unprecedented in that a chief of state criticized an accredited representative of a friendly government through the press, rather than through official channels. It was dismissed by the Acting Secretary of State, Dean Acheson, on August 3, with the dry comment: "Ambassador Lane continues to enjoy the complete confidence of this government."

The general view in Washington, as interpreted by the Associated Press, was that relations between the United States and Poland were destined to become more tense as the elections drew nearer.

CHAPTER SEVENTEEN

The Frontier Question

SOVIET troops had entered Warsaw on January 17, 1945. Other Red Army forces reached the Oder River near Wroclaw (Breslau) on January 23, took the port of Memel on January 28 and captured the ports of Danzig and Gdynia before the end of March.

On the heels of the Red Army as it advanced through territory which had been German before the war came emissaries of the Soviet-created Provisional Government of Poland. These emissaries, with the sanction of Moscow, set up a civil administration in the occupied territory, including Danzig. Although the Soviet Union had pledged its word to the United States and Great Britain that the frontiers of Poland should not be settled until the peace conference, it well knew that by this action the puppet government's hold would be so greatly strengthened that the chances of dislodging it would be reduced to zero.

The Soviet Government and the Soviet-controlled Polish Provisional Government had, however, received encouragement from both Churchill and Roosevelt to justify the turning over of former German territory to the Poles for administration purposes.

Churchill, in his speech to the House of Commons on February 22, 1944, speaking of the Tehran Conference, had said:

I took occasion to raise personally with Stalin the question of the future of Poland. . . . Here I may remind the House that we ourselves have never in the past guaranteed, on behalf of His Majesty's Government, any particular frontier line to Poland. . . . The British view in 1919 stands expressed in the so-called Curzon line. . . . Marshal Stalin and I also spoke and agreed upon the need for Poland to obtain compensation at the expense of Germany both in the North and in the West.

President Roosevelt in his last appearance before the Congress on March 1, 1945, had also referred to the provisions for the new Polish frontiers.

The Department of State, however, evidently felt that the Soviet Government had exceeded its prerogatives. On April 8, 1945, it notified that government, through the American Embassy in Moscow, that it had received several press and radio reports, attributed to responsible officials of the Provisional Government functioning in Warsaw, to the effect that certain Soviet-occupied territory, including the free city of Danzig, had been formally incorporated into Poland. The Department requested to be informed regarding the actual status of the territory in question.

The Soviet Government replied on April 17 that the departure of the German population in the wake of retreating German troops had left behind only a Polish population, for the government of which a Polish civil administration had been set up locally. The note asserted however that this action had no relation to the question of boundaries.

The reply of the United States Government, dated May 8, expressed its failure to understand the statement that the establishment of the Polish civil administrations set up in these territories had no relation to the question of the future boundaries of Poland; the impression was created by this and other statements made by the Soviet Government that the territories remained effectively under Soviet military occupation, but that the local administration was set up only as a matter of convenience to indigenous Polish officials who were in no way the agents of, or responsible to, the Provisional Government functioning in Warsaw. The United States Government added that it was unable to reconcile the Soviet Government's assertion with the numerous reports and public statements to the effect that the Warsaw Government had formally decreed the incorporation into the Polish

POLICE-STATE PROPAGANDA FOR THE REFERENDUM
"3 Razy tak" meant "Vote Yes on all three questions."

THE CROWD GREETS MIKOLAJCZYK
Leader of Polish Peasant Party leaving polling place after voting on referendum.

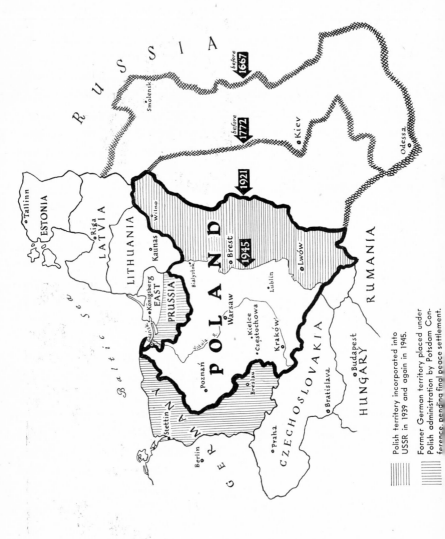

Polish territory incorporated into USSR in 1939 and again in 1945.

Former German territory placed under Polish administration by Potsdam Conference, pending final peace settlement.

state system of the territories in question, besides appointing Poles from within Poland to govern such enemy territory as integral parts of Poland.

The note stated further that reports from Poland, ascribed to official sources there, indicated that the Warsaw Government was (1) establishing its complete state apparatus and enforcing its laws in those areas, (2) already engaging in a large-scale transfer of Poles from other areas to these enemy territories, and (3) planning to extend the administration over additional enemy territory under Soviet military occupation. The reports from Warsaw had declared that these and similar acts attributed to the Polish Government then functioning in Warsaw had been effected with the full knowledge and approval of the Soviet occupation authorities.

The United States Government concluded, therefore, that changes such as those mentioned in the status of occupied territories, based on unilateral action without prior consultation and agreement among the United Nations concerned, disregarded the principles underlying the agreements for the control and occupation of Germany. It emphasized that the territories in question and all other Soviet-occupied enemy territory must remain under Soviet military occupation pending agreement, after full and complete consultation and deliberation among the Allied powers concerned. In delivering this note, our chargé d'affaires at Moscow, Mr. George F. Kennan (in accordance with the instructions he had received from Washington), stated to the Soviet Government that the United States Government would recognize the western frontier of Poland when delimited in accordance with the applicable decisions of the Yalta Conference, but that we insisted meanwhile no transfer of any Soviet-occupied territory be made to the government then functioning in Warsaw.

The Vice-Commissar for Foreign Affairs, Mr. Vishinsky, replied on May 16 only with respect to the establishment of a Polish civil administration at Danzig. Mr. Vishinsky said that it was quite natural that the Polish civil administration, acting under the direction of the Polish Provisional Government, was functioning according to Polish law. He denied that this condition could be considered as disregarding the principles on which were based the agreements for the control and occupation of Germany. He added that as it was recognized by the Yalta decision that Poland must receive substantial additional territory in the north and west, the possibility of a Polish administration functioning in this territory not only was not excluded but was presupposed. He emphasized as self-evident that, as envisaged in the Yalta decision, the final determination of Poland's western boundary would be made at the peace settlement.

And thus, when the Big Three met at Potsdam the United States Government was again faced with a *fait accompli* as a consequence of the Soviet Government's action in turning over former German territory to a government which was admittedly provisional, had not as yet been recognized by the United States or British governments and had not been legalized by any popular election. Yet were not the former public utterances of Churchill and Roosevelt an indication to the Soviet Government that it could proceed, unhampered, with its plan for the organization of the Polish administration of former German territories?

At Potsdam in August 1945 it was reaffirmed by Generalissimo Stalin, President Truman and Prime Minister Attlee that the final delimitation of the western frontier of Poland should await the peace settlement.

But, although the language of the Potsdam agreement again made it clear that the western frontiers had not been definitely established, the Polish Government continued to show by action and statement that it regarded the matter of the frontiers as permanently settled. Through the press and through the display of posters and photographs the government endeavored to encourage Poles repatriated from the Soviet Union to settle in what was formerly East Prussia or in the western territories of Pomerania or Silesia. And, as the Potsdam Powers had given to the Polish Government permission to deport the German population from the former German territories now under

Polish administration, it was believed certain in Poland that these territories would not revert to Germany. The transfer of population involved some six million persons, which indicated that the three major powers would not further complicate the situation by later demanding that the Poles who had moved into the newly acquired territories should be evicted. One of the first instructions, in fact, which had been sent to the British and United States embassies was to insist to the Polish Government that the deportation be effected in the most humanitarian manner possible.

But we noted that the Polish Government endeavored on almost every possible occasion to make it clear that Polish claims to the western frontiers had been definitely approved.

For instance, when President Bierut received my credentials as Ambassador to the Polish Provisional Government he was careful to say to me:

You came to us in the moment when the Potsdam Conference—in which the President of the United States of America has played such an important part—confirmed our rightful claims to base our frontiers on the Oder and western Neisse and gave us confidence, as Your Excellency stated in your address, that Poland will take its place as one of the great free nations of the world.

Later, on April 12, 1946, the Foreign Office informed our Embassy that on the next day a special train would leave for Szczecin (Stettin) to celebrate the first anniversary of its liberation from the Germans. Feeling confident that the presence of the diplomatic corps would be used for political purposes, I begged to be excused on the plea of being indisposed. Keith and Tonesk, who represented the Embassy on the trip, brought back accounts of the regimented celebrations there which made it clear that they were primarily political. Boy Scouts, who were to march in the parade and who had cheered Mikolajczyk when he appeared at the reviewing stand, were forbidden to take part.

But the most significant action from the point of view of the importance of the Polish western frontiers was the speech made by

Modzelewski. He said that the Polish Government viewed with great satisfaction the presence at Szczecin of representatives of all the diplomatic missions accredited in Poland, as their attendance confirmed the intention of their governments to support Poland's new western frontiers.

It was true that the United States Government had requested and received permission to establish consulates in Wroclaw and Szczecin, both of which cities lay in the newly acquired western territory, as well as in Gdansk, Kraków, Poznan and Lódz. And although we never opened consular offices in Wroclaw and Szczecin, our action did indicate our concurrence with the Polish claim to this territory.

The Polish people keenly felt the loss of the territory east of the Curzon Line. That loss was one of the factors which contributed to the bitter hostility toward the Soviet Union. While the eastern territories, including the cities of Lwów and Wilno, meant more, sentimentally and materially, to the Polish people than did the territory to the west, the loss of the former justified to the people the need for the acquisition of the latter. Moreover, the Polish people could not understand why, when Poland had been ravaged by the Nazis for almost six years after a war of aggression which started because Poland would not bow to Hitler's demands, Germany should not be made to contribute territory to compensate Poland for what had been lost in the east.

On September 6, 1946, I was summoned to the Foreign Office to see Olszewski who was then acting as Foreign Minister in the absence of Rzymowski and Modzelewski. When I entered his office, he immediately asked whether I had read the speech which Secretary Byrnes had delivered that morning at Stuttgart. I said no, and Olszewski began to read those portions of the speech which affected Poland and which were a reiteration of the statement in the Potsdam decision that the western frontiers would await final delimitation at the peace conference.

Olszewski said with considerable heat that the Polish public would be greatly shocked by Mr. Byrnes's statement, for it indicated that the population in western Poland might later fall under German domination. I said that judging from the portions of the speech which Olszewski had read to me Mr. Byrnes had merely reaffirmed the Potsdam decision; if the Polish people were under the impression that the Potsdam decision provided for the permanent incorporation of the western lands within Poland it was because the Polish Government and the local press had so prepared them. As an instance I cited Modzelewski's speech in Szczecin in April in which he referred to the presence of foreign representatives as an acknowledgment by their governments of the definite incorporation of the western territories.

I said I earnestly hoped that the government press would not distort Mr. Byrnes's speech and give to it an unjustified meaning which would merely result in a worsening of American-Polish relations; and I reminded Olszewski that on several recent occasions, as in the case of the shooting down of our aviators in Yugoslavia, the press had not correctly presented the American point of view.

Olszewski, with his customary brusque manner, roared, "Telegraph to Mr. Byrnes and ask him whether his speech means that the United States has changed its policy toward Poland." I brushed this aside by saying that I would undoubtedly receive officially a copy of Mr. Byrnes's speech and would then be glad to talk further.

All the Warsaw press of September 7, with the exception of the *Gazeta Ludowa,* bitterly attacked the Byrnes speech. Most of the editorials interpreted it as an attempt to rebuild a powerful Germany to serve as a policeman for Western capitalism. The organ of the Communist Party, *Glos Ludu,* said in an editorial, "American reaction is searching for agents to combat democratic movements and seize candidates for such a task in the names of Hitler, Himmler and Göring."

On Sunday, September 8, a mass meeting was held in the government auditorium, known as *Roma,* under the slogan, "Our answer to the defenders and guardians of Germany." All government parties took part and Byrnes was violently attacked by the various speakers.

Gomulka, Vice-Premier and Minister for the Western Territories, orated that he preferred "open enemies" to "masked friends" and boasted that international capitalism could in no way hurt Soviet-Polish friendship. Cyrankiewicz, a prominent member of the Polish Socialist Party who had been influential in persuading his party to join the single electoral bloc and who was later to be Prime Minister, said, "Peace cannot be dictated by the United States. It is safe and far from the German danger."

Although the diplomatic corps was not invited to attend the meeting as a body, the French Ambassador, M. Garreau, accompanied by his military aide, was conspicuously present and applauded the speeches hostile to the United States. Undoubtedly this action was taken on his personal initiative. He may not have recalled that Mr. Byrnes was in Paris at that time as the official guest of the French Government.

After the mass meeting a crowd of about fifteen hundred persons surrounded the Polish Peasant Party headquarters on Jerusalem Street, three blocks from the Hotel Polonia, and broke all the windows with stones. Then fifteen or twenty of the ringleaders, armed with clubs and guns, beat up ten members of the Polish Peasant Party who were in the building, and destroyed party records, typewriters and office furniture. The Volunteer Citizens' Militia Reserve (O.R.M.O.), members of which were on duty at the headquarters, made no effort to stop the rioters. The crowd then gathered in front of the Hotel Polonia and shouted insulting epithets against the United States and Mr. Byrnes. My wife and I and some members of the Embassy staff had gone on that Sunday morning to the home of Second Secretary M. Williams Blake, about fifteen miles from Warsaw, and were not present to receive the jeers of the government-instigated mob. It was not until our return in the early evening that we heard of the hostile demonstration.

As was indicated by the attack on the Polish Peasant Party headquarters, the government intended to have Mikolajczyk and his party bear some of the onus for the United States attitude. *Glos Ludu* on

September 8 editorialized, "We paid blood to regain these lands, and will not give them up even for American dollars." The editorial linked Mikolajczyk and the Polish Peasant Party with the alleged attempt to deprive Poland of its newly acquired territory. Furthermore, the central committees of the Polish Workers Party and the Polish Socialist Party published in the Warsaw press of September 13 an open letter to the Polish Peasant Party which attacked it for its silence on the frontier issue and for having the same views as the "supporters and protectors of Germany." Mikolajczyk's party had in the referendum urged its members to vote affirmatively on question number three, relating to the permanence of the western frontiers, but now the party was asked by this open letter to answer four questions:

1. Are you prepared to protect our boundaries in opposition to Byrnes and Churchill?

2. Are you prepared, in the name of our sovereignty, to protest against meddling of Anglo-Saxon reactionary circles in our affairs?

3. Are you prepared to prosecute reactionary bands and bandits?

4. Do you accept our proposal for an electoral bloc?

On September 19 I told Olszewski how sorry I was that my fears about the distortion of Mr. Byrnes's speech by the government-controlled press were not unfounded. The press had calumniated the United States as pro-German and anti-Polish and had pilloried Mr. Byrnes as a "Fascist." Surely the attitude of the Polish Government and the Polish press would not deceive the Polish people as to our real attitude. The United States was one of the greatest friends, if not the greatest of all friends, that Poland had.

Olszewski replied that he hoped the future would prove my statement correct. As I took leave I said that his remark was one of the most discouraging I had ever heard, for it indicated that the Polish Government did not appreciate the friendship which the United States had shown Poland consistently, and especially during the last year when through UNRRA, the American Red Cross and American private relief organizations of all sects Poland had been saved from economic ruin.

Though Mr. Byrnes was not specifically mentioned by name, there was no doubt in any mind that President Bierut referred to the Secretary of State in a speech during a session of the National Council of the Homeland in Warsaw on September 21. Bierut said that "certain Allied statesmen" were now showing sympathy for the Germans, but nobody could deny Poland's right to those lands which were given her after the destruction of the enemy. He remarked, with evident sarcasm, that, as Poland was not an imperialistic country, her rights, in the view of "certain statesmen," were not to be respected.

Deputy Mazur of the Polish Peasant Party took occasion at this meeting to launch an attack on the Workers Party and on the Security Police for having incited the crowd to resort to violence against the Peasant Party and its headquarters, immediately after Mr. Byrnes's Stuttgart speech. But the ensuing uproar in the auditorium of the *Roma* building prevented him from continuing his remarks.

When in October 1946 I had a chance to discuss the repercussions of Mr. Byrnes's speech with representatives of the Department of State who were then in Paris, I learned that its purpose was to smoke out Molotov's attitude on the eve of elections in Germany. The Soviet Government had previously, through the Communist press in Germany, held out the enticing bait to Germany of the return of the former German territories now temporarily under Polish administration. Yet at the same time the Communists—synonymous with the Soviet Government—were promising the Polish people their permanent possession! The speech finally did evoke a reply from Molotov. He took Poland's side but, significantly enough, he delayed this until after the elections in Germany. The result of the elections, incidentally, was a defeat for the Communists.

It was an unfortunate coincidence, however, that the National Council of the Homeland meeting at which the electoral law was discussed was held just after the Stuttgart speech. The Communist groups seized on the occasion, and Mikolajczyk and his Polish Peasant Party were bitterly attacked for friendship with the Western Powers. Undoubtedly the influence of the Peasant Party was greatly weakened at the meeting. The shouting down of Deputy Mazur was illustrative. And an electoral law was passed at the session, over the protests of the Peasant Party, which would, by not providing safeguards, admit in the elections a repetition of the fraudulent tabulation of votes in the referendum.

I subsequently recommended to the Department of State that we should remain silent on the Polish western frontier until we could reach an agreement with the Soviet Government. The British Ambassador shared my view.

Regardless of the opinion of some United States Government officials that it was vital to European recovery for the Polish western lands to be returned to Germany because of Germany's desperate need of agricultural produce, the practical fact was that this territory was under Soviet control. Unless we were prepared to use physical force— and surely there was no thought of that—we could not unilaterally change the frontier, and our espousal of the thesis (which was implied if not actually expressed in Byrnes's Stuttgart speech) that the western frontiers were not to be permanently Polish made a universally bad impression in Poland.

Even members of the Polish Peasant Party and of the hierarchy, who so generally opposed the Communist-dictated policy of the Lublin group which still controlled the Government of National Unity, were amazed—and told us so—that we should seemingly take the side of Germany, our former enemy, rather than that of Poland. Later, in December, after I had learned the purpose of Mr. Byrnes's speech, I could minimize their apprehensions. But I felt—despite my assurances—that the United States had suffered a severe setback in standing and prestige with the Polish people generally, whose friendship had been so important to us in the past and might be a critical factor in our favor should we be unfortunate enough to participate in another war in Europe.

Although the Polish Government had been bitter in its vilification of the United States, because we had seen fit to reiterate the provisions of the Potsdam decision to which it had agreed in August 1945, not a word ever appeared in the Polish press about the 1939 meeting of Ribbentrop with Stalin which precipitated World War II; or the Molotov-Ribbentrop agreement of the same year which resulted in the fourth partition of Poland.

The exhibition of a British war film in Gdynia in 1946 which began with a scene showing Stalin and Ribbentrop shaking hands in Moscow in 1939 was not allowed to continue. The lights in the theater were suddenly extinguished.

An incident in which I was a participant on March 9, 1946, was even more illustrative of the sensitiveness of the Polish Communists to any criticism that they had acquiesced in the Soviet Union's having unilaterally appropriated the territory east of the Molotov-Ribbentrop line.

That day I attended a luncheon at the house of Marshal Rola-Zymierski in honor of General Modelski's appointment as military attaché to the Polish Embassy in Washington. Earlier that day I had a somewhat bitter interview at the Foreign Office with Rzymowski and Modzelewski on the vexatious question of the imprisonment of American citizens for political offenses. I had emphasized that relations between the United States and Poland would surely grow worse unless the Polish Government evinced a sincere disposition to allow us to interview our own nationals under arrest. One of the guests at the Marshal's lunch told me afterward that Modzelewski, who was a guest also, had warned the assembled company before my arrival that I was in a very unpleasant mood that morning. He therefore suggested they try to placate me.

In accordance with the Slav custom, toasts were exchanged. They began at the start of the luncheon and kept up profusely. At first they were of an extremely friendly character in their cordial references to the United States, to the American Army and to me personally. But as the luncheon proceeded and the barriers of conventionality were loosened, many of the speakers expressed their real feelings. There were references to the size and the wealth of the United States, as contrasted with our refusal to contribute to the support of the Polish Army. Allusion was made to the suffering which the Soviet Union had endured during the war. Yet, the speaker said, the Soviet Union had come to the aid of the Polish armed forces in the reconstruction of the Polish economy.

Finally I had enough of these slurs against the United States. Replying to a toast of one general, I said that perhaps at times the United States Government might not have been as generous as we should like to be; perhaps at times we might not have fully appreciated the needs of other countries; but Poland could never rightfully accuse the United States of having appropriated Polish territory. Looking squarely in the face of Modzelewski, who sat opposite me at the table, I ended with the words, "Not even in 1939 had the United States taken part in the dismemberment of the Polish state."

Marshal Rola-Zymierski endeavored, by putting his hand on my arm, to deter me from finishing the sentence, for in the gathering there were also, besides Modzelewski, other Russian-trained Communists, including General Spychalski, Minister of Public Security Radkiewicz, and Olszewski, the Director of the Political Department of the Foreign Office. The luncheon broke up in polite good-bys. This incident indicated to me clearly—even more than the silence of the Polish press on the loss of the eastern frontiers—the subservience of the Polish Government to the Soviet Government.

From the defiant attitude which the Polish Government had assumed toward the United States after Mr. Byrnes's speech at Stuttgart, it was as clear as day that it would likewise defy us in the elections presumably to be held within the next few months. The falsification of the referendum results; the denial to the Christian Labor Party of the right of assembly; the forcible measures aimed at thwarting the political usefulness of the Polish Peasant Party—all were confirmation of the government's intent to remain in power at all costs. And as we knew that this intent was in harmony with the wishes of the Soviet Government there seemed little hope that the United States could accomplish anything to salvage the last remnants of the Yalta agreement with respect to Poland.

Since this was so, I suggested to the Department of State that I be summoned to Washington for consultation so that we might plan our next move.

CHAPTER EIGHTEEN

Consultation

THE Department of State approved my returning to Washington for consultation and considerately granted me leave of absence so that I might spend a few weeks in France and Italy en route to the United States. We made plans to fly to Paris on October 10, piloted by Lieutenant Colonel York.

At the airport of Okecie that morning we noted a poster prominently displayed in the waiting room which, even with no other warning signs, was proof enough of the Polish Government's hostility to us. It depicted a Polish soldier facing the west with a tommy gun pointed at a human hand, clenched like a vulture's claw, emblazoned with dollar signs and swastikas. The hand was endeavoring to reach across the Oder River. Here was a farewell reminder of the unconcealed sentiment of the Polish Government toward the United States!

Before my departure from Warsaw, I took repeated occasion to emphasize to the Polish Government how deeply concerned I felt over the deterioration of relations between our two countries. On September 24 I told Olszewski frankly that the government had shown a lack of desire to cultivate friendliness with the United States. I cited the Polish attitude of obstruction in citizenship cases; the matter of the rate of exchange; our difficulties in obtaining adequate housing for our offices and staff; and the continual attacks in the government-controlled press. The United States desired no material or financial aid from Poland—just friendship. But if this friendship were denied to us, we would not be the principal loser. A serious situation had been reached. It seemed inconceivable to me that the Polish Government should wish to make trouble with us, but if trouble came it could not be blamed on us at all. Significantly, Olszewski made no attempt to justify his government's attitude of hostility. After listening in silence until I ended, he bowed coldly, and that was all.

On October 3, I called on Prime Minister Osóbka-Morawski to take my leave. I repeated to him what I had said to Olszewski. I referred to our note of August 19 on the forthcoming elections and mentioned that it had never been answered, except through press statements to the effect that it was an interference in Polish internal affairs. I spoke of the antagonism of the press toward the United States, and reminded the Premier, who always gave me the impression of being our sincere friend, that even he had spoken recently at Katowice of Mr. Byrnes's "undermining the frontiers of Poland." I was aware that the Polish Government had incited the Polish people against the United States, after Mr. Byrnes's Stuttgart speech, and had instigated for the demonstration outside the American Embassy on September 8. Again, as in the case of my talk with Olszewski, I was accorded no explanation or excuse for the government's unfriendly attitude. The Prime Minister heard me through, in apparent sympathy, as though he wished he could change the state of affairs.

On October 8, just before I left, I sent a telegram to the Department of State for its consideration, pending my arrival, as to the basic position which the United States should maintain, recommending:

1. We should continue to make vigorous representations regarding the mistreatment of American citizens, and publish the facts.

2. We should insist that the Polish Government give prompt and adequate compensation for nationalized American property, and should refuse to be satisfied with mere promises.

3. We should emphasize our dissatisfaction with the Polish Government's policy of indifference toward the United States and toward our wishes, such as the negotiation of a bilateral aviation agreement.

4. We should not encourage the granting of further United States Government charitable assistance to Poland if the Polish Government continued its existing policy.

5. We should refuse to consider the request of the Polish Government for further financial assistance until the Yalta and Potsdam commitments were fulfilled, compensation for nationalized property was

actually made, and United States Embassy officials were permitted to visit valid claimants to American citizenship now in jail.

When I arrived in Washington on November 5, after an uneventful flight from Paris, I immediately had talks with Llewellyn E. Thompson, who had succeeded Durbrow as Chief of the Eastern European Division, and Elbrick, who as Assistant Chief of the Division was charged with Polish affairs. Elbrick's previous experience in Warsaw, both before the war and for four months as a member of my staff, had given him sympathetic interest in our problems. He had served as the invaluable link between our Embassy and the Department of State. I learned that Keith had telegraphed that, according to the feeling in political circles, the elections would probably not come off until the winter months.

Secretary Byrnes was in New York attending the meeting of the United Nations. On November 5, I expressed my view to Acting Secretary Acheson that we should withhold all further financial assistance from the Polish Government until the election commitments were finally fulfilled. Acheson's attitude was characteristically noncommittal.

During my first week in Washington, the greater part of my time was spent in trying to straighten out some of our administrative problems, such as adequate compensation for our staff and authorization to employ additional personnel. Also, I endeavored to obtain authorization to purchase real estate for our Embassy offices and residences, against the credit which we had extended to Poland for surplus-property material.

Shortly after our arrival in Warsaw my wife had chosen as a suitable house for us a medium-sized three-story building occupied by Count Adam Tarnowski, who had been the last Austro-Hungarian Ambassador to the United States just before our entry into the First World War in 1917. The house had been allocated to us by the Foreign Office, and we had been using the ground floor temporarily as an office for our accounting section. For more than a year a squatter who claimed that nobody in the Polish Government could evict him—obviously he had his understanding with "the right people"—had made it impossible for us to use the upper floors. Following his example, others had occupied rooms, so that when we finally left Poland at least ten squatters were in the house.

I had spoken to the Prime Minister, to Berman, to President Bierut's secretary and to many officials of the Foreign Office, but I was always told that it would be "very difficult" to take action. I might have evicted the squatters by force or by cutting off water and electric light, but I felt sure that such a move would not help the prestige of the United States. And so I informed the Foreign Office that I would continue to live, however uncomfortably, in the Hotel Polonia during the rest of my tenure in Warsaw.

On November 13 the Presidium of the National Council of the Homeland announced that elections to the constituent Sejm, to enact a new constitution and to choose a president of Poland (Bierut), thereby terminating the provisional character of the Government of National Unity, would be held on January 19, 1947.

When news of this came to us in Washington, Thompson, Elbrick and I had many discussions about it. We prepared a note to be submitted for Secretary Byrnes's approval.

Acting under instructions from the Department, Gerald Keith, as chargé d'affaires at Warsaw, accordingly delivered a note to the Polish Foreign Office on November 22, 1946:

I have been instructed to inform you that my Government has taken note of the announcement that the Polish Government of National Unity has fixed January 19, 1947, as the date on which general elections will be held in Poland. In this connection, my Government recalls that Ambassador Lange's note of April 24, 1946, stated that in accordance with the Potsdam Agreement of August 2, 1945, which provided that elections would be held as soon as possible, elections would take place this year. Although my Government is surprised that the Polish Government would fail, without explanation, to fulfill this formal assurance, its chief concern is not with any particular date but with the discharge of its responsibility under the decisions taken at the Crimea and Potsdam conferences with respect to the holding of free elections in Poland.

The importance which the United States Government attaches to the carrying out of these decisions has repeatedly been brought to the attention of the Polish Government. In his note of August 19, 1946, to which no reply has been received, Ambassador Lane outlined certain points which the United States Government considers essential for the carrying out of free elections. In view of the disturbing reports which it has received concerning the preparations for the elections, my Government has instructed me again to inform Your Excellency that the Government of the United States expects that equal rights and facilities in the forthcoming election campaigns and in the elections themselves will be accorded to all democratic and anti-Nazi parties in accordance with the Potsdam Agreement. My Government could not otherwise regard the terms of the Yalta and Potsdam decisions as having been fulfilled.

On November 19 I attended a dinner in New York in the apartment of Dr. Oskar Lange, Polish Ambassador to the United States, as well as Polish delegate on the Security Council of the United Nations. To this he had invited also the Polish Minister for Foreign Affairs, Mr. Rzymowski, and Wiktor Grosz, head of the press section of the Polish Foreign Office, who were in New York for the forthcoming meeting of the Security Council. Grosz was an influential member of the Polish Government, a Communist of the Jewish race, who had received his training in Russia. Brilliant in repartee, adroit in his interpretation of facts, he was a dangerous adversary. Ben Cohen, Counselor of the Department of State, and Herschel V. Johnson, deputy United States delegate on the Security Council, a close friend of many years' standing through our association in the Foreign Service, were also present.

After dinner we had an earnest but friendly discussion of Polish-American relations. I stressed again, as I had done so often, my apprehension over their decline, in spite of all our efforts to prevent it. I had heard that Cohen had been largely responsible for drafting Byrnes's Stuttgart speech; Grosz was said to guide the editorial policy of the Polish press on foreign affairs. Taking advantage of their joint presence, I bluntly asked Grosz to explain the deliberate distortion of Byrnes's speech by the Polish papers. I told the group that I had warned Olszewski, when he sent for me on September 6, that this distortion would surely result in turning the Polish public against us. The government apparently did not care whether it had our friendship or not. I cited our inability to visit Americans in jail; the Polish Government's failure to answer us definitely on compensation for nationalized American property; and its evasion in dealing with us on an aviation agreement. Grosz merely replied that I did not understand. Lange and Rzymowski made no reply at all.

As I drove with Cohen and Johnson to my hotel after dinner, I said I was amazed that Lange, Rzymowski and Grosz had refrained from answering my indictment on any count. By their silence they all seemed to admit my thesis. It looked like another illustration of the Polish Government following dictation from Moscow—to make trouble with the United States.

The next day I called on Secretary Byrnes by appointment at his suite in the Waldorf-Astoria. During this meeting, which was limited to only a few minutes because of his strenuous duties in connection with the Council of Foreign Ministers, I recommended that he reaffirm to Lange or Rzymowski the views I had expressed to them so strongly. I suggested that the Embassy in Warsaw be instructed to urge the Polish Government to settle without delay its points of serious difference with the United States. I followed up my conversation with a memorandum, dated November 25, citing our specific complaints. But although Mr. Byrnes was affable, he gave me no assurance that he would discuss the general situation with the Polish representatives.

Meanwhile, Keith had telegraphed from Warsaw that actions against the Polish Peasant Party were being intensified; that it had been arbitrarily judged illegal in twenty-five per cent of the states in Poland; that its meetings were being prevented; and that arrests were continuing. He hoped I would return as soon as possible since the local political situation was becoming daily more critical. I made plans to leave on November 28.

Before leaving I pointed out to officials in the Export-Import Bank and to the Department's representatives in the International Bank that under existing conditions Poland was not a safe banking risk: first of all, it was obviously not a sovereign nation—its policy was dictated by Moscow; secondly, because of the widespread unrest arising from the imposition of an unrepresentative government, there was no assurance that political stability could be achieved in the near future. Adoption of Soviet methods in restricting freedom of commerce with the United States would, from a practical point of view, hinder Poland from discharging the financial obligations to the United States which it had already contracted. And, even though I was unable to obtain assurances from the Department that energetic representations would be made to the Polish Government on the outstanding questions which were so darkly clouding our relations, I felt encouraged from my talk with President Truman, whom I saw on November 26, as well as from conversing with other high officials of our government, that there no longer appeared any intention on the part of our government to appease the Polish Government through financial means.

I arrived in Warsaw on December 12 to find that Keith had by no means exaggerated the political situation: it was boiling.

CHAPTER NINETEEN

The Elections

On the afternoon of December 19, Stanislaw Mikolajczyk, as President of the Polish Peasant Party, called on me by appointment in the new offices at Aleja Ujazdowskie 33, which had been allocated to us by the Foreign Office and into which the Embassy had moved while I was in the United States. He wished to deliver to me, as representative in Poland of one of the Yalta Powers, the official protest of his party against the many measures taken by the Polish Government to impede its normal activities in the elections. He said that identical notes, all dated December 18, were being delivered to the British and Soviet embassies. I agreed to transmit his note to my government.

The communication, which was signed by Mikolajczyk and by Wojcik, secretary general, and which was supported by twenty-six annexes giving names, dates and places, protested the following actions by the "State machinery":

Arrests of party members without warrants from the competent prosecutor or legal tribunal;

Compulsory enrollment of Polish Peasant Party members in the government parties;

Compulsory collaboration of Polish Peasant Party members with the U.B. under the threat of arrest;

Expulsion of Polish Peasant Party members from their farms in the western territories;

Dismissal of Polish Peasant Party members from their jobs;

Illegal searches of homes of Polish Peasant Party members;

The planting of arms and illegal leaflets in homes of Polish Peasant Party members to justify their arrest;

Forcible confiscation of party membership cards and other party documents, thereby hampering activities of party;

Wrecking of the party premises in August and September 1946 in Warsaw, Tarnowskie Góry, Bedzin, Sosnowiec, Plock, Gdansk-Wrzeszcz, Klodzko, Katowice, Szczecin, Nysa, Raciborz and elsewhere;

Attacks on meetings of the Polish Peasant Party at Plock, Klodzko and Kochanów, and issuance of orders by the State authorities to prevent meetings from taking place;

The suspension of Polish Peasant Party branches in certain parts of the country (about twenty-five per cent);

Beating party members to force resignation or collaboration (in many cases beatings were so severe as to cause loss of consciousness, permanent injury and even mental derangement);

One hundred ten murders of party members (in some cases admittedly by U.B. officials);

Restriction of the activity of the Polish Peasant Party press, through denial of printing facilities, limitation of newsprint, and censorship (because of publication of Polish Peasant Party bulletin, distributed only among party members, members of editorial staff were arrested and premises of editorial office sealed).

The party complained further that Provincial National Councils at Olsztyn, Katowice, Lódz, Poznan and Warsaw had adopted resolutions excluding its members from holding positions in the district and local commissions; and that in the states of Kraków and Lublin areas of electoral districts had been enlarged, contrary to the provisions of the electoral law, so that even if weather and road conditions were favorable, many voters in country districts would not be able to register their votes within the twelve hours provided.

Even the Army had been sent out into country sections to carry on political agitation and a slanderous campaign against the Polish Peasant Party through the distribution of a booklet entitled *The Voice of the Soldier,* published by the Central Committee for Political Education of the Polish Army.

Summing up, the note said that the assurances of the Provisional Government of National Unity on freedom of elections and the rights of democratic parties had not been fulfilled with respect to the Polish

Peasant Party; through the postponement of the elections until January 19, 1947, far distant from the time limit fixed by the Yalta and Potsdam agreements, the Security Police authorities had been employing all possible measures to exterminate the party. Appeals to the President and Prime Minister had brought no relief; on the contrary, terrorism had increased.

In conclusion, the party stated it was approaching me as the representative of one of three governments responsible for carrying out the decisions taken at Yalta. It was informing my government, through me, of the conditions under which the elections would be held.

As soon as I could study a translation of Mikolajczyk's communication I appreciated more than ever what an empty term "freedom of speech" is in Poland today. The suppression of the Polish Peasant Party's printed bulletin had obliterated the last chance of imparting freely the views of its central committee to the members. And I well knew that, though undoubtedly the substance of Mikolajczyk's complaints would reach a few members by word of mouth, the bulk of the Polish nation would never be permitted by the government to know that the Yalta Powers had been approached because of its nonfulfillment of a solemn international pledge.

An American would appreciate that no such suppression of fact could take place in the United States, where a free press would assuredly inform every voter that charges of so grave a nature were being made. It was indeed saddening to reflect that, although Mikolajczyk's party might number millions, no more than a comparative handful could be told what was going on.

Several Polish citizens, who felt that our Embassy should be informed of developments in violation of the Yalta agreement, notified us orally during the last week of December 1946 that seventy-five out of the eight hundred fifty-four Polish Peasant Party candidates for election to the Sejm had been arrested and the names of forty more candidates had been stricken from the electoral list. One of these informants reported that he had seen the orders issued by the government to the electoral officials to disqualify at least thirty per cent of the Peasant Party candidates.

A foreign embassy in Warsaw with which we maintained very cordial relations had close contacts with Communist members of the Polish Government because of the strong Communist movement in its own country. It often received valuable information about the intentions of the Polish Government.

According to this embassy the Communists of the Polish Government had admitted to close friends that the present government would fall if fair elections were held. In that event the Russians would march in and take over the country. The Polish Communists felt that they were justified in employing any means to keep the government in power. They admitted that a deliberate policy had been adopted to reject as many Polish Peasant Party candidates as possible, on the false ground that they were pro-Nazi.

During the Christmas holidays petitions were circulated by hand throughout Poland by Security Police officials. These U.B. members went from house to house in the cities and villages endeavoring to obtain the signatures of as many voters as possible, indicating their support for the candidates on the government list.

We received reports from the larger cities—Kraków, Poznan, Gdansk, Katowice and Lublin—that those persons who refused to sign the manifesto were told they would probably lose their living quarters and their jobs unless they reconsidered their attitude. The housing shortage was critical all over the country, especially in cities such as Warsaw and Gdansk where the destruction made it almost impossible to find shelter. Many persons signed the manifesto out of sheer necessity. One head of a family whom I knew in Warsaw told me that he had finally agreed to sign it because he did not feel he had the right to endanger the health and perhaps the lives of his wife and children.

The U.B. went farther than merely threatening. Many cases of physical torture were reported to the Embassy. The U.B. were not far behind the Gestapo in inventing refined brutalities. We learned of persons forced to remain during that unusually cold winter in icy water up to their knees for two or three whole days in attempts to drive them to sign the manifesto. An unfortunate man stood this torture for seventy-two hours rather than agree to support the government ticket. Gangrene set in. Both his feet were amputated.

The circulation of the manifesto had a dual purpose: it served to compel supporters of the opposition to vote the government ticket against their will; it would serve as evidence that the government had the support of many thousand peasants, in the event that charge of rigged elections should be made.

A Polish woman who had been known to the Embassy for years came to us with her story: She and all the other persons quartered in the same building in Warsaw were visited by the U.B. and asked to sign up that they would vote the government "democratic bloc." She had told the U.B. that she knew nothing of politics and did not wish to sign a statement that had no meaning to her. The U.B. officer left her room, threatening, "We will be back." In cases of persons with children these tactics of menace had the desired results.

I had of course immediately cabled the State Department Mikolajczyk's impressive arraignment of the Polish Government's repressive measures against the Polish Peasant Party. Little more than a week later I was heartened by word from Washington that his charges had been made the effective basis for a communication addressed by the United States Government on January 5, 1947, to its co-partners in the Yalta agreement: Great Britain and the Soviet Union. This took the form of identical notes. One had been delivered to the British Ambassador in Washington; the other by Ambassador W. Bedell Smith in Moscow to Mr. Andrei Vishinsky, Deputy Minister for Foreign Affairs. The note said sharply that the United States Government was "especially perturbed" by the increasingly frequent reports of repressive measures which the Polish Provisional Government had seen fit to employ against those democratic elements in Poland which had not aligned themselves with the "bloc" parties; authoritative reports from other quarters in Poland had served to substantiate the weighty charges brought by Mr. Mikolajczyk.

After emphasizing that the sanctity of international agreements was involved, the Department of State said it meant again to approach the Polish Government in the immediate future with a reminder of its obligations and to call on it to provide those conditions of security which could enable all democratic and anti-Nazi parties to take full part in the elections. We hoped that the British and Soviet governments as parties to the Yalta and Potsdam agreements would associate themselves with the United States Government in this approach to the Polish Provisional Government of National Unity.*

When Ambassador Smith delivered this note he informed Mr. Vishinsky orally of the United States' position on the forthcoming Polish elections. Vishinsky indicated what his government's reply would be when he gave it to General Smith as his personal opinion that the Polish Provisional Government had complied in all respects with the requirements of the Yalta and Potsdam agreements; therefore any interference in "this purely Polish affair" was unwarranted.

The official reply of the Soviet Government dated January 13, 1947,** belittled the basis of our argument on the score that it came from a sole source—Mikolajczyk. (This was untrue. As our note stated, our information came from many independent sources.) The Soviet Government charged that certain members of Mikolajczyk's party had been implicated in the activities of underground organizations and had resorted "to every kind of threat, violence and murder in order to interfere with the normal conduct of the electoral campaign for the Sejm." The Polish Government would not be fulfilling its duty to the Polish people if it did not take measures against "these criminal elements"; and it would be inadmissible to interfere with the carrying out of such measures "particularly on the part of foreign governments." The Soviet Government saw no basis for approaching

---

* For full text of note, see Appendix.
** For translation of note, see Appendix.

the Polish Government on the impending elections, as it would constitute an "interference in the internal affairs of Poland on the part of the powers which had signed the Yalta and Berlin agreements."

The Soviet Government had resorted to its familiar stratagem, accusing Mikolajczyk and his followers of the same charges that he had leveled against the Polish Provisional Government in his letter of December 18.

On January 9, under instructions from the Department of State, the Embassy in Warsaw delivered a note to the Foreign Office.* I had planned to deliver it personally, so that I might reinforce its language with oral arguments. But I was told that Olszewski and Zebrowski were both so busy preparing the Polish thesis on the frontier question for presentation to the deputies of the Foreign Ministers of the United States, United Kingdom, Soviet Union and France, then meeting in London, that neither would be able to receive me. More probably, however, they would not see me because they knew (through the Department's January 7 publication of the text of the January 5 notes to the British and Soviet governments) that a note to the Polish Government was coming soon. So Dillon left the note with a minor functionary of the Foreign Office, and no oral explanation accompanied its delivery.

Our note did not refer to Mikolajczyk's letter but repeated our perturbation over the increasingly frequent reports of repressive measures which the Polish Provisional Government had seen fit to employ. We mentioned that our notes of August 19 and November 22, 1946, had not been answered, and repeated that unless the repressive measures ceased forthwith, there was little likelihood that free and unfettered elections could be held in accordance with the terms of the Potsdam agreement. After alluding, as we did in our notes to the British and Soviet governments, to the sanctity of international agreements being involved, we ended:

My Government would be failing in its duty if it did not again point out that the continuation of the present policy of suppression, coer-

---

* For full text of note, see Appendix.

cion and intimidation, as applied to the political opposition in Poland, constitutes a violation of the letter, as well as the spirit, of the Yalta and Potsdam agreements.

To me it seemed very significant that the United States Government had addressed notes to the Polish Government, as well as to the British and Soviet governments, before the elections, rather than after. Their timing demonstrated that even should the elections be fairly held and the ballots honestly tabulated and reported, we still could not feel that they could correctly represent the will of the electorate, because of the repressive measures employed during the pre-election campaign.

The Polish Government's reply, dated January 14* (the Soviet reply, dated January 13, was received by our Embassy in Moscow on the same day) was signed by Olszewski, Rzymowski being reported ill and Modzelewski in Moscow. It brushed aside our objections to the repressive measures. Our fears were based "on distorted facts and unfounded reproaches which are raised by the antidemocratic elements working in Poland." The elections we were blandly told would take place on January 19, "in accordance with the tradition of Polish democracy and with the will of the Polish nation." Hence, there was no justification for any further consideration of the question!

In diplomatic language we had been informed that the election was none of our business. The reply ignored our insistence that the sanctity of international agreements was involved—agreements assumed by the Soviet, British and United States governments at Yalta and Potsdam and subsequently assumed and often reiterated by the Polish Government.

It was painfully significant that the notes of the Polish and Soviet governments discarded the principles of those agreements, which from their point of view were no longer to be invoked. It was equally significant that although the Polish Government published its note of January 14, none of the other communications, although released to

---

* For translation of note, see Appendix.

the press by the Department of State, was permitted publication in the Polish press.

The hypocrisy of the phrase "free and unfettered elections" was tragically obvious.

At a press conference in Washington in November 1946 I had urged the representatives of the various press associations and newspapers who were covering activities of the Department of State to send trained observers to Poland so that the forthcoming elections would be fully and accurately reported. Gratifyingly, at least fifteen correspondents were in Warsaw at election time. Among the well-known writers who came were Dorothy Thompson, Ralph Ingersoll, formerly editor of *PM,* and Liston M. Oak, managing editor of the *New Leader.* These were in addition to the correspondents regularly assigned to Warsaw.

As I had done at the time of the referendum, I arranged to send out fifteen teams of observers from our Embassy staff and invited the correspondents to accompany them to whatever parts of Poland they considered particularly interesting.

I gave general instructions to our various teams on the nature of information which we desired—intimidation, if any, prior to the elections, the procedure adopted in voting and in counting ballots, the general reaction to the elections in the different districts, and any other data that they might consider pertinent. I suggested that election officials, members of the various parties, including the opposition, should be interviewed, but I made one reservation: contact with the underground should be scrupulously avoided. Although it represented a political element of importance, we felt that the Embassy should have no contact with it, because of the danger of our being accused of connections with an element which presumably was planning—or at least hoping for—the overthrow of the Polish Provisional Government, and because of the danger to the persons interviewed.

I had good reason to be apprehensive, because of a case involving the British Ambassador, Mr. V. Cavendish-Bentinck. His family had known the aristocratic Grocholski family of Warsaw for over thirty-five years. During his first assignment to Warsaw in 1919 he and Count Grocholski had become warm friends, and a cordial relationship had continued over the years. When Bentinck returned to Poland in 1945, it was natural that he should seek out his old friend and invite him to the British Embassy from time to time. Undoubtedly they discussed topics of the day, including the intolerable conditions existing in Poland. On one occasion while the Ambassador was paying a visit at Count Grocholski's country house, the villa was surrounded by the U.B., and the inmates, including Mr. Bentinck, were prohibited from leaving. By insisting on his diplomatic prerogative of immunity from arrest, Bentinck was finally able to get away. Grocholski was arrested, charged with association with the underground and with having communicated information to a foreign ambassador. (Like all patriotic Poles who had been forced to remain in Poland as a result of the war, he had been connected with the underground Home Army during the Nazi occupation.)

At the public trial Grocholski "confessed" to guilt on the two charges. Then, on January 14, 1947, five days before the elections, the verdict in his case was announced: death. The sentence was immediately executed.

The severity of his sentence was the government's brutal way of warning the Polish people of the risk they ran if they talked to foreign emissaries about existing conditions. The announcement of the verdict on the very eve of the elections had a sinister connotation: the government would probably consider treasonable the imparting to the American and British embassies information about frauds and repressive measures in connection with the elections. Had not the Polish Government's note of January 14 said that no further consideration by us of the election question was warranted?

The elections were held on January 19, 1947, in bitterly cold weather. On that Sunday afternoon my wife and I, accompanied by some of the correspondents, visited polls on the outskirts of Warsaw. At one of them, Lieutenant Rulski, a member of the Foreign Office who had acted as an interpreter when I interviewed Mrs. Dmochowska in the U.B. headquarters, recognized us and was kind enough to arrange for us to observe the procedure. Seats were provided in the building where the voting took place.

Voters coming into the booth picked up their choice of one of six ballots—plain, square pieces of paper, marked only with the number of the list, from one to six. The government bloc list was number three in all election districts throughout the country; but the list of the Polish Peasant Party had, by directions of the government, been given numerical designations which were not the same in all. The ruse made it impossible for Mikolajczyk to give directions to his followers as to the list which they should vote. Of course, this made for confusion, and was intended to diminish the total of the Polish Peasant Party's votes.

As the electoral law provided for secrecy in the casting of the ballots, I was at first surprised to note that many of the voters conspicuously showed their choice of the ballot which displayed the large black numeral 3—the single designation of the government list—before inserting it in the envelope furnished for the purpose. But soon I discovered that the election officials made a special note against the names of all voters who placed their ballots secretly in the envelopes and who consequently did not display the number of the list they chose. Nuns and priests invariably voted secretly, as the law prescribed.

Many of our observers returned to Warsaw that evening, reporting general calm throughout the country and considerable apathy as to the election. It was the same story over again—the peasants had learned from their experience in the referendum the preceding June that the results would be in harmony with the government's wishes, regardless of the voters' opinions.

Because of the pre-election measures of intimidation and repression, the government might even be able to claim a victory on the basis of the ballots cast, without resorting to fraud in the tabulation and reporting.

The next day, as the returns were announced, it was not surprising to find that the government list had scored an overwhelming victory over its only opponent—the Polish Peasant Party, which still, in the estimate of unbiased observers, represented sixty per cent of the electorate!

As was to be expected, the Polish press heralded the result as a great blessing for Poland and a vote of confidence in the government. Demonstrations were at once organized in Warsaw to simulate public satisfaction. A half holiday was decreed for the afternoon of January 22. All government offices were closed at 1:00 P.M. and all government employees had to take part in the parade that afternoon. The parade failed of its objective because of the unenthusiastic attitude of the marchers. Their demeanor was in fact so morose that passers-by openly laughed at the spectacle. All realized it was staged by the government as propaganda.

The government desired to make it appear that the Roman Catholic Church approved the election outcome. Even though most of the officials were not communicants, they well realized that over ninety per cent of the population were Catholics.

I learned from Church sources that the government had asked for a solemn Mass in the Warsaw Cathedral to celebrate its victory, and as it was the Church's practice never to refuse a request for a Mass it would be held. Cardinal Hlond, the Archbishop of Warsaw, however, did not attend.

Certain Catholics of the diplomatic corps were resentful because members of the government, present as a political gesture, openly showed their disrespect for the Church. They alternated between tossing their hats in the air and lounging in unmistakable boredom!

When the bishop of another important city in Poland was approached with the same request, his answer was: "I shall offer Mass next Sunday as I would on any other Sunday. If any of my communicants wish to give thanks for any event, it will be a matter for their own conscience." Another leading bishop was asked to ring the church bells for the "victory." He replied that there were very few church bells in his city. The Nazis had removed most of them to be melted for cannon. The few that were left would be rung as usual.

As I weighed in my mind the situation we were facing, I thought of my experience in Yugoslavia whence I had seen Hitler conquer country after country. I could see no difference between Hitler's and Stalin's aims. Both were after world domination. I could not see the difference, which so-called liberals in the United States often claim to see, between the methods of the two tyrants. They were exactly the same—suppression of personal liberty; terrorism by the police; sickening propaganda that the totalitarian state is democratic.

I had felt in 1940 and 1941 that the United States was in danger of being brought into a war because of the imperialist ambition of a country seeking to dominate the world. I felt this now; only the name of the country was changed. The position I had supported about the elections having been definitely rejected by the Soviet and Polish governments, my usefulness as Ambassador was ended. It would be more effective if my successor were appointed at once, a man not associated in the Polish mind with the loss of political prestige which the United States had suffered because the Soviet and Polish governments refused to live up to their international obligations. I felt, with all humility, that out of my experience in Poland, I might accomplish some good by bringing the facts before the American people.

My course was clear. I decided to resign.

CHAPTER TWENTY

Betrayal Legalized

ON JANUARY 23 I asked to be relieved. My telegram to Secretary of State Marshall summed up the situation and my convictions about it. In spite of the customary restraint of diplomatic correspondence I believe the strong feeling which actuated me is apparent in the message.

As anticipated, the election was a mere formality in implementing the decision which had been previously reached between the government bloc parties and the Soviet Government: to retain in power the Communist-controlled minority. Mikolajczyk's note of December 18, 1946, to the representatives in Warsaw of the Yalta Powers amply described the steps which have now been confirmed by our staff observers as well as by most of the American press correspondents now in Poland. Similar to the so-called vote of confidence given to Hitler following the German-Austrian Anschluss in 1938, the election itself was merely a mechanical routine to indicate a legal justification for the puppet regime to continue in power.

All the Poles with whom we have been in contact are asking: what is the United States going to do?

In my letter of March 1, 1946, to Matthews I expressed the opinion, which I still hold, that only through the exercise of American public opinion can the Soviet Government be prevailed upon to ease its policy of domination of European countries and to refrain from further imperialistic expansion.

I, therefore, urge the Department to make public our position, namely, that the United States Government cannot acquiesce in the result of the elections in which, regardless of what is stated in the Soviet note of January 13 and Polish note of January 14, we had a direct international obligation as a result of the Yalta and Potsdam decisions.

I believe that it would be most inadvisable to break diplomatic relations to indicate our dissatisfaction; for nothing would be more satisfactory to the Communist clique than for us to withdraw our influence and prestige from Poland.

For all practical purposes my mission to Poland is ended. I believe I could do more by educating American public opinion as a private citizen than I can by remaining in Poland, where my continued presence would be considered as tacit acquiescence in the recent fraudulent elections. I should, therefore, appreciate it if the Department would permit me to retire from the Foreign Service.

I believe that now is the time to state our policy clearly and emphatically and without diplomatic evasion or reserve, for I feel that the situation which has just culminated in the elections is potentially one of the most far-reaching in its implications in so far as American foreign policy and the possible subsequent creation of military hostilities are concerned.

A few days after the elections, my wife and I went by automobile to Kraków, not realizing at the time that it was to be our last journey to that beautiful city. I wished to learn at first hand the reaction of the people in this center of intellectual life, famed for its independence and culture, and to ascertain whether they accepted the verdict of the elections as final.

I found them very resentful. My friends in Kraków, whether Socialists, Peasants or members of the Christian Labor Party, were bitter in their denunciation of the methods used in the elections to prevent the opposition from obtaining victory. They firmly believed that the outcome had been prearranged.

The melancholy concensus of opinion, as expressed by those to whom I talked, was that whether the result had been obtained through use of military force, liquidation of members of the Polish Peasant Party or fraudulent count, there was nothing the Polish people could do. The Soviet Government and its puppet Polish regime had determined that the latter must remain in power. The Soviets desired a regime completely acquiescent. The puppet government obviously did not wish to give up its enjoyment of power and comfort. The result was inevitable, just as it had been inevitable in Yugoslavia, in Bulgaria and in Rumania.

My friends in Kraków, while bitterly regretting that the United States had not been able to give effective assistance to the people of Poland by insuring that they have a government of their choice, realized that it was out of the question to suppose that we would go to war with Russia because of the Polish elections. They hoped, however, that we would not continue to follow a policy of appeasement but would make known clearly and openly our indignation over the way international agreements had been violated.

On January 26, while I was in Kraków, an urgent message was brought to me from Warsaw by Reginald Kazanjan, secretary of our Embassy, from Secretary Marshall in answer to my telegram of the twenty-third. It showed complete understanding of my wish to leave Poland and said that I would soon be called to Washington for consultation.

At the same time the Department declared its intention of giving the press a statement condemning the manner in which the elections had been held and the pre-election activities witnessed by many unbiased American correspondents.

My views having been asked, I heartily approved such a statement as signifying our disapproval of the flouting of solemn international obligations.

The statement was issued on January 28. After recounting the unsuccessful steps which it had taken with the Soviet and Polish governments to ensure the holding of free and unfettered elections, the Department said:

The reports received from the United States Embassy in Poland in the period immediately prior to the elections, as well as its subsequent reports based upon the observations of American officials who visited a number of Polish voting centers, confirmed the fears which this Government had expressed that the elections would not be free. These reports were corroborated by the general tenor of the despatches from foreign correspondents in Poland. It is clear that the provisional government did not confine itself to the suppression of the so-called "underground" but employed widespread measures of coercion and intimidation against elements which were loyal to Poland although not partisans of the government "bloc." In these circumstances, the United States Government cannot consider that the provisions of the Yalta and Potsdam agreements have been fulfilled. . . .

The United States Government considers that the Polish Provisional Government has failed to carry out its solemn pledges. . . .

The United States Government firmly intends to maintain its interest in the welfare of the Polish people. While retaining full liberty of action to determine its future attitude toward the Government of Poland, this Government will continue to keep itself informed of developments in Poland through its diplomatic mission in Warsaw.

This strong declaration drew a meaningful distinction between the Polish Provisional Government and the Polish people, and manifested that the United States would maintain an Embassy in Warsaw. But its force was not felt in Poland, as no mention of it appeared in the press there. The Embassy, however, made copies available to any visitors who wanted to know how we felt about the election returns.

Equally significant were the remarks which President Truman made to the newly appointed Polish Ambassador to the United States, Mr. Jozef Winiewicz, when he presented his credentials at the White House on February 4. The President ended:

The Government of the United States gave expression to this interest in the Polish people when it joined with the British and Soviet Governments on the important decisions concerning Poland that were taken at the Yalta and Potsdam Conferences. One of these decisions provided for the holding of a free election and the Polish Provisional Government of National Unity pledged itself to carry out this decision. It is a cause of deep concern to me and to the American people that the Polish Provisional Government has failed to fulfill that pledge.

The Government of the United States has not lost interest in the welfare of the Polish people. It is with this in mind that I offer to you the co-operation of the officials of this Government.

President Truman made the same sharp distinction between the Polish Government and the Polish people as did the Department's release of October 28. And never in the memory of Department officials had a President of the United States used such blunt and forceful language in receiving a newly accredited foreign envoy.

But Mr. Truman's remarks were not published in the Polish press. Instead, the press editorialized on the unprecedented rapidity with which he acted on Mr. Winiewicz's request to be received!

The new Sejm, or Diet, the members of which had been elected on January 19, was to hold its first meeting on February 4. On that day, with snow falling heavily, President Bierut, accompanied by Prime Minister Osóbka-Morawski, drove in an open automobile to the new Diet building, a few blocks from the American Embassy. All chiefs of diplomatic missions in Poland were invited and were expected to attend; but the British Ambassador and I, who had, under the instructions of our respective governments, protested the manner in which the electorate had been intimidated through arrests, physical tortures and murders, considered it would be most inconsistent if we gave our blessing, through our presence, to an assembly which had been chosen by fraudulent means. We therefore stayed away.

Polish Government employees in Warsaw lined the streets between the President's palace and the Sejm, marshaled by members of the Security Police. The police had indicated, as we in the Embassy could well see from our offices on the Aleja Ujazdowskie, the places where they were to stand and the type of applause which they were to give to the President and the Prime Minister when they drove by. It was a farce.

The Sejm, which now supplanted the National Council of the Homeland, dutifully elected the former Minister of Arts and Culture,

Kowalski—a Communist and a member of the original Lublin Committee of Liberation—as its Marshal, or Speaker. Bierut was elected President of the Republic.

To celebrate the transition on paper of the Provisional Government of National Unity into the Government of the Republic of Poland, the diplomatic corps was invited to attend a reception at the Belvedere Palace on February 6. In the Pompeiian Room, where I had presented my credentials, I was to witness the formal celebration of the flouting of the Yalta and Potsdam decisions.

The Chief of Protocol, Gubrynowicz, unctuous and officious, herded the chiefs of mission into line in accordance with the rule of seniority—date of presentation of credentials. Behind each Ambassador the members of his staff grouped themselves in single file.

Soon President Bierut entered the room. The Soviet Ambassador who, like all his staff, was attired in his diplomatic uniform ornately decorated with golf leaf, made an address in his capacity as Dean of the Diplomatic Corps, congratulating Mr. Bierut on his election as President of Poland and on the accomplishments of the Provisional Government since its formation. In his reply Bierut thanked the Soviet Government for its invaluable assistance in contributing to the reconstruction of Poland; understandingly, no reference was made to the United States.

Bierut shook hands with all the guests; he spoke amiably with me on matters of trifling importance. It was my last conversation with him. He had refused to receive me the previous June, and I did not propose to risk another snub. Yet the press stated that I had asked for an audience. The implication was that the United States had recognized the validity of the elections.

Members of the diplomatic corps were amused by the fact that although formerly the President and other members of the government had dressed in the simplest style, as was fitting under Poland's difficult conditions, on this state occasion Bierut, Rzymowski, Modzelewski, Olszewski and Berman all appeared in cutaway coats and striped trousers.

Just as children are proud when they come to man's estate and wear long trousers for the first time, so the naïve officials displayed evident pride at this reception, where, on their assumed coming of age politically, they strutted in formal morning clothes!

The next day Bierut appointed Jozef Cyrankiewicz President of the Council of Ministers, to succeed Osóbka-Morawski. A left-wing Socialist, Cyrankiewicz had been a bitter fighter against the Nazis. He had also at one time written articles condemning Soviet policy toward Poland. Some political observers felt that those articles were now being used by the Communists as a lever to keep him in line. A tall, spare figure, with a completely bald head, he was of far more impressive appearance than Osóbka-Morawski. His expression was inscrutable, but his mouth was hard. As one of his Socialist Party colleagues said to me, "He is really tough."

But it was soon apparent from Cyrankiewicz' own appointments that he was no more head of the government than Osóbka had been. Modzelewski replaced Rzymowski as Minister for Foreign Affairs; and Skrzeszewski, another Communist, succeeded Wycech, a Polish Peasant Party member, as Minister of Education. In addition to these ministries which they acquired, the Communists retained control of the key posts of National Defense (through the two Communist undersecretaries, General Spychalski and General Swieczynski), Industry (Minc), Regained Lands (Gomulka) and Public Security (Radkiewicz). Osóbka was given the innocuous Ministry of Public Administration, which had neither control over the police nor jurisdiction over the western territories or former East Prussia. The Polish Socialist Party which had expected to gain power as a reward for agreeing to enter the single government list had indeed fared badly. Some of its members told me they wondered how soon would come their turn to be liquidated politically.

The Polish Peasant Party was not represented at all in the new government. Out of four hundred forty-four seats in the Sejm, it was allotted only twenty-eight. Of this number Mikolajczyk and Zygmunt Zulawski, the eloquent Socialist leader from Kraków, who had been elected on the Peasant Party ticket, still stood for independent thought.

When Mikolajczyk arose to protest the elections, Marshal Kowalski banged the gavel, calling him out of order, while the Communist members booed vociferously.

Zulawski, in an impassioned speech in the Sejm, attacked the police-state methods which had been used in the pre-election days. He was allowed to continue, but part of his remarks were expunged from the Congressional record. On the next day he objected to the excision, but no mention of his criticism was permitted in the minutes.

Yet the *Gazeta Ludowa,* though it could not publish Zulawski's speeches, continued to appear on the newsstands. It was generally believed that the government, having consolidated its position as a result of the elections, could now afford to adopt a more lenient attitude to its defeated opponents and thus ingratiate itself with foreign public opinion.

On February 15 I called on Mr. Cyrankiewicz, to establish official relations with the new Prime Minister and to notify him of my imminent departure. I outlined to him the developments since my appointment as Ambassador in 1944: the efforts which the United States Government had made to prevent Lwów from being taken away from Poland; the stand which we had taken in the meetings at Moscow in 1945 to ensure that non-Communists would be invited to consult on the composition of the Provisional Government of National Unity; the restrained hope which I had had on my arrival that friendly relations could be maintained between our two governments; the great assistance which the United States had rendered Poland through UNRRA, the American Red Cross, American Relief for Poland, the Joint Distribution Committee, the Quakers, the National Catholic Welfare Conference, the Paderewski Fund, the Y.M.C.A. and the

HERBERT HOOVER MEETS THE REAL POLAND

Little girl shows gratitude toward United States in an unrehearsed gesture.

PREMIER CYRANKIEWICZ TAKES HIS ORDERS

His meeting with Stalin took place shortly after Cyrankiewicz's appointment as Polish Prime Minister.

VOTERS AT THE ELECTIONS OF JANUARY 19, 1947

CHECKING THE VOTERS' LIST

Committee for American Relief for Europe (C.A.R.E.), not to mention the extension of ninety million dollars of credits to the Polish Government.

Yet the Polish Government had shown no public appreciation of our action. On the contrary, the United States had been continually attacked in the press from the moment of our arrival. And the Polish Government had done nothing, except one thing, to better our relations. (The one exception, which I did not specify to the Premier, was the granting of permission to establish consulates and of free entry to American consular officials, on a reciprocal basis.) The United States had not been allowed to give protection to American citizens or to American property in Poland. And we had been put off by various excuses in our efforts to conclude an aviation agreement.

But, I told Cyrankiewicz, the Polish Government's policy was indeed a shortsighted one. I did not feel that the people of the United States would approve the granting of further assistance to the Polish Government once they knew the facts.

In conclusion I said that as Mr. Cyrankiewicz had not been previously in the government and as I was leaving Poland for good, in consequence of the way the elections had been held, I had used the greatest candor with him.

The Premier, who spoke in a very low voice, but carefully and earnestly, replied that he was sorry my visit was one of farewell, for he knew, because of my frankness, that we would have got on well together. As Prime Minister, he wished to have Poland's relations tied up with the West, as well as with the East, for the Poles did not want to be dependent on any single country for support. Besides, Poland wanted to raise its standard of living, if not to that of the United States and Great Britain, at least to that of Czechoslovakia. If the Poles should be dependent only on the East they would, through the physical law of connected vessels, be obliged to accept the Eastern standard of living, much against their will.

Cyrankiewicz said that when the United States declined to give aid to Poland, the cry immediately rose that this was evidence of American unwillingness to help and hence Poland's only salvation would lie in applying to the U.S.S.R.

At this juncture I interjected, "But the United States has not declined to give aid to Poland."

He made no acknowledgment of my interruption, but went on to generalize about Poland's desire to obtain as much democracy as possible under existing conditions.

From my talk with Cyrankiewicz, which was cordial throughout and at which Keith and Zagorski were present, I had the impression that he was trying to apologize for Poland's subservience to the Soviet Union and at the same time was striving to retain the friendship of the United States so that our material assistance would not be cut off. But he made no excuses for the fraudulent election results. Nor could he well have done so, when he had been his party's chief advocate of the single electoral list.

On February 19, 1947, the Sejm took a step of profound importance. It approved a temporary constitution creating the Sejm as the sole legislative organ of the nation, and the President of the Republic, the Council of State and the Government as the executive authorities. The significant feature of this constitutional law was the setting up of the Council of State which virtually delivered the control of the country to the persons who formerly composed the Presidium of the National Council of the Homeland. According to Article 15, the Council of State was to be composed of the President of the Republic (Bierut) as chairman, the Marshal and Vice-Marshals of the Constituent Sejm (Marshal Kowalski, Vice-Marshals Zambrowski and Waclaw Barcikowski, all Communists, with Vice-Marshal Schwalbe, a Communistically inclined Socialist), and the Chairman of the Supreme Control Chamber (Henryk Kolodjieski—without party affiliation).* As Article 16(a) entrusted to the Council of

---

* In spite of its impressive title, the Supreme Control Chamber's chief function, as set forth in the temporary constitution, appears to be that of a bureau to audit the government's finances, corresponding to our Office of the Comptroller General.

State "supervision over local national councils within the limits of authority granted to the National Council of the Homeland and to its presidium on the basis of the law of September 11, 1944" (prior to the formation of the Provisional Government of National Unity), it was evident that government by hand-picked officials would continue. Furthermore, the Sejm was to be convoked for only two ordinary sessions each year (Article 7). The Council of State would, even on paper, be the ruling power in Poland throughout almost the entire year by its sole authority to issue decrees with the force of legislation. It meant in effect that from the Council of State in Warsaw to the national council in the smallest village, the will of the Communists in power would be carried out. It meant, without employing the term, that the sovietization of Poland had been prepared under the guise of constitutional legality.

On Washington's Birthday February 22 I held a reception for the American colony but invited also the officers of the British Embassy, not only on the historical ground that George Washington had at one time been a British subject, but also to show our appreciation of the very effective co-operation which we had received from Ambassador Bentinck and his staff. The British Government had pursued a course parallel to that of the United States in almost all matters dealing with Poland.

I made a very informal talk to our guests, among whom were included the Polish members of our staff. As they would all have surmised from my wife's activity in packing our effects, we were leaving for Washington and did not plan to return. My departure should not be interpreted as a lessening of our government's interest in Poland. What we had all experienced in our eighteen months together was only the first chapter of the volume of Poland's postwar history. There were other chapters to follow.

I voiced my deep appreciation to all our official family for their loyalty and their devotion to duty under very difficult and often unpleasant circumstances, and my feeling that I could accomplish more in the United States for Poland and the Polish people than I could in Poland.

On the bright, cold morning of February 24, my wife and I left for London from Okecie airport—now equipped with asphalt runways, a modern administration building and a highly active Security Police service. Sorrowfully we took leave of all our staff and of the officers of the British Embassy who had kindly come to say farewell.

Gubrynowicz and Cieplak, the Chief of the American Section of the Polish Foreign Office, also came to the airport, but excused themselves after waiting only a few minutes.

By telephone from London I confirmed with the Department of State an appointment with the Secretary of State who was due to leave Washington on March 7 for the Moscow conference of the Foreign Ministers of the United States, United Kingdom, U.S.S.R. and France. I wanted to discuss with General Marshall my personal plans, but I also wished to put before him orally my views on the Polish-German frontier, a subject to come up before the Council of Foreign Ministers. I had written him on this matter January 13, 1947, immediately after he had assumed his duties as Secretary of State. But I knew only too well from experience that the views of an ambassador, unless expressed in person, may often be mollified, and hence virtually annulled, by the influence of those who enjoy the confidence of the Secretary, whoever he may be.

I arrived in Washington on March 6. Secretary Marshall had, to my regret, left the previous morning for the Moscow Conference, earlier than was planned. I saw Acting Secretary Acheson and obtained his approval of the course which I now proposed: to retire and to devote myself to informing the American public on the situation in Poland.

President Truman received me in the Executive Offices of the White House on March 21. I showed him the draft of my proposed letter to him:

I have the honor to request you to be good enough to accept my resignation as American Ambassador to Poland on the termination of my present period of consultation with the Department of State, that is, on March 31, 1947.

My reasons for asking you to relieve me of the post with which I was entrusted by you and by President Roosevelt are the following: My principal duty in Poland, outside of the protection of American interests, was under the terms of the Yalta decision, to report to my Government regarding conditions in Poland in connection with the elections which were held on January 19, 1947. As you know, these elections were not "free and unfettered" as the Polish Provisional Government of National Unity had previously pledged, in keeping with the Yalta and Potsdam agreements. Quite the contrary, the pre-election period was characterized by coercion, intimidation and violence—thus rendering the elections a farce and indicating on the part of the Polish Government a cynical disregard of its international obligations.

Under the circumstances I feel that I can do far more for the cause of the relations between the peoples of the United States and Poland if I should revert to the status of a private citizen and thus be enabled to speak and write openly, without being hampered by diplomatic convention, regarding the present tragedy of Poland.

May I take this occasion to express to you my gratitude for your unfailing support of my efforts, however unsuccessful, to persuade the Polish authorities, in their own interests, to fulfill their solemn international obligations? I wish at the same time to assure you that my services are at your disposal, should you require them in the future.

The President approved my course.

Before leaving, I recommended that my successor be appointed as soon as possible; otherwise, the Polish people might feel that we were lessening our interest in their welfare.

On March 25, President Truman sent me the following reply to my letter of resignation:

I have received your letter of March 21, 1947, in which you submit your resignation as American Ambassador to Poland to take effect on March 31 of this year.

I am well aware of the difficulties which confronted you in the performance of your mission to Poland and appreciate the vigorous efforts which you made to persuade the Polish Provisional Government to fulfill its pledges with respect to the holding of free elections in Poland. I regret that your able presentation of the views of this Government did not achieve its purpose.

You have had a long and distinguished career in the American Foreign Service, and while I appreciate the reasons which have prompted you to sever your connection with that Service at this time, I wish to assure you that I accept your resignation with great reluctance. In this connection I am pleased to note that I may feel free to call upon you should I require your services in the future.

Mr. Stanton Griffis, a prominent New York businessman, was appointed Ambassador to Poland on March 31, 1947.

That same day my retirement from the Foreign Service became effective. On the next day, a private citizen for the first time in thirty years, I held a press conference and made it clear that I intended to publicize the knowledge which I had gained during my assignment to Warsaw.

My mission to Poland had ended.

CHAPTER TWENTY-ONE

To All Free Peoples

IF THE primary responsibility for the present tragic condition of Poland should be placed on Hitler, who planned its conquest as a part of his scheme for world domination, it is evident from the events recorded in the foregoing chapters that almost equal responsibility must be placed on the Soviet Government. Had not the conclusion of the nonaggression pact of August 23, 1939, by Stalin and Hitler, made it possible for Hitler to start a world war without risking the encirclement of Germany?

Should there have remained any uncertainty as to Stalin's policy toward Poland, it was dispelled by the Russian invasion of Poland from the east on September 17, 1939, followed by the fourth partition of Poland eleven days later, "legalized" in the joint declaration of the Soviet and German governments that the Polish state no longer existed. In 1941, after the Nazi occupation of Yugoslavia, the Soviet Government also broke relations with that country on the same ground. In both instances the Nazi-Soviet co-operation in the partition of Europe was in full force.

Surely the Soviet Government must be called on to assume responsibility for having deported hundreds of thousands of Poles to Siberia during the Soviet occupation of the territory east of the Molotov-Ribbentrop line, from 1939 until after the German attack upon the Soviet Union on June 22, 1941. This was action calculated to remove Polish nationalistic and non-Communistic elements and to extinguish the flower of the Polish Army. Even though the Soviet Government has tried to avoid responsibility for the Katyn incident, with violent protestations of innocence, the accusing finger of public opinion in Poland is still pointed at the Kremlin; for that liquidation of ten

303

thousand Polish officers would be consistent with the Soviet policy of systematically destroying all elements representative of Polish nationalism. Not only were the Nazis and the Soviets in agreement on the annihilation of the Polish state, but they employed similar police-state measures to snuff out the spirit of Polish independence.

Fortunately that spirit still lives and will continue to live!

The Soviet Government's long-range policy to subjugate Poland had been logically and systematically planned since the setting up in 1941 of the Union of Polish Patriots in Moscow under the direct control of the Kremlin—a group which to this day is the core of the Polish regime. The Soviet Government's acquiescence in the quelling of the Warsaw insurrection of 1944, with its loss of two hundred fifty thousand Polish lives, was the most decisive and the most savage blow against Polish nationalism. As a Communist member of the present Polish Government explained in 1946 to a prominent American visitor to Warsaw:

Had General Bór-Komorowski and his underground army succeeded in liberating Warsaw, they would have been the heroes of Poland and would have formed the nucleus of the government within Poland. It would have been most difficult under such circumstances for the Soviet Government to maintain in power the Lublin Committee of National Liberation.

With the surrender of the Home Army forces to the Germans on October 3, 1944, and with the subsequent Soviet advance throughout Poland, the Soviet Government adopted an increasingly arrogant attitude on the Polish question and at Yalta forced its co-partners, the United States and Great Britain, to agree to its wishes. Without the concurrence of Polish Government or Polish people, the permanent frontier was fixed on an approximation of the Curzon Line. Although it was agreed that democratic leaders from within Poland and from abroad should constitute the new Provisional Government of National Unity, the Communist embryo of that government-to-be was already functioning in Poland, backed by the Red Army and by the

Russian NKVD. In those circumstances the really democratic forces never had a chance to express themselves freely or to form a government clearly representative of the Polish people.

The arrest of the sixteen Polish leaders and their trial at Moscow in the spring of 1945 was another instance, carried out in defiance of Western public opinion, of the Soviet Government's determination to put an end politically to all Polish leaders who might furnish an element of nationalistic opposition to the Communist-dominated government. Next, with an efficiency and concentration on detail recalling the methods of the Gestapo, the NKVD and its Polish counterpart organized the police state so that all effective opposition would be quenched. Arrests, tortures and assassinations were as effective under the Soviet-directed police state as under the Nazi variety.

Finally, the *coup de grâce* to democracy in Poland was given when, following the fraudulent elections of January 19, 1947, the present government was formed without recognition of the Polish Peasant Party's popular majority.

The world must condemn the Soviet Government for its ruthless annexation of Polish territory in 1939, a shameless violation of its antiaggression treaty with Poland, and for its inhumane and repressive measures taken in the succeeding years. But the Soviet Union knows full well the value of a foreign policy, no matter how diabolical in method, that is conceived carefully and executed with meticulous thoroughness. Vigorously and relentlessly it has been carried on through the years. No public opinion, no elected congress stand in the way of its fulfillment.

Although the principal responsibility for Poland's fate must be placed on the Nazi and Soviet governments, certainly the United States and Great Britain cannot escape a share in the tragic betrayal. Both Prime Minister Churchill and President Roosevelt, undoubtedly to maintain close relations with Stalin in a critical period of the war, agreed at Tehran in December 1943 to the dismemberment of the eastern part of the country. This executive action on Mr. Roosevelt's part was never embodied in a treaty and hence did not receive the consent of the Senate, as required by the Constitution. It was not made public during his lifetime, and it is quite apparent from testimony now available why it was kept secret until after the presidential elections of 1944. An official of the State Department who was at Tehran told me some months after that he had tried to prevail on the President to take a firmer policy with Stalin on Poland. According to my informant, Mr. Roosevelt had replied, "You may know a lot about international affairs, but you do not understand American politics."

When he made essential concessions at Tehran, the die was cast. His strong representations in August 1944 for help to the Warsaw insurrectionists were unavailing, or at least too late. His vigorous request that the recognition of the Lublin Committee as the Provisional Government of Poland be deferred until consultation at Yalta was abruptly rejected by the Kremlin.

At Yalta again we lost an opportunity to stand firm. Perhaps the aid which the Soviet Union could contribute in winning the war was overestimated. I cannot pretend to judge. Yalta, however, was the deathblow to Poland's hopes for independence and for a democratic form of government.

Our own policy of appeasement toward Soviet Russia undoubtedly emboldened Stalin to go ahead with his plans for the complete domination of Poland, as of all other countries in Eastern Europe. It finally showed an encouraging change early in April 1945. President Roosevelt's message on April 1 to Stalin, to which Mr. Byrnes has referred,* shows that even the President, responsible for yielding so much at Tehran and Yalta, had at last seen through the Moscow disregard of international commitments. The Soviet Government had shown its hand: it did not intend to have "free and unfettered elections" in Poland or in any other nation covered by the Yalta decision.

---

* In *Speaking Frankly*. See pages 54, 55.

But the blame for appeasement cannot justly be placed entirely on Mr. Roosevelt. The Department of State must share the onus. The optimistic utterances of Secretary Stettinius in April 1945; the directive given orally to the United States delegates to the United Nations Conference in San Francisco—to take pains not to irritate the Soviet delegation—and the continued naïve belief in Soviet good intentions, even during the first year of Mr. Byrnes's tenure as Secretary of State, were all factors of encouragement to the Soviet Government and to its satellites to keep on flouting their international engagements.

In fact at the time when, over my repeated protests, the Department of State had approved credits to the Polish Provisional Government totaling ninety million dollars, a credit of one billion dollars for the Soviet Government was under serious consideration.

Mr. Byrnes himself put a stop to further assistance to Soviet satellites in May 1946 by cabling from Paris to Assistant Secretary Clayton in Washington that the United States Government did not propose to extend further financial aid to governments unfriendly to the United States. This change in our position was undoubtedly influenced by the hostile attitude taken by Soviet satellites at the hearings before the Council for Foreign Ministers.

What does the future hold for Poland?

I wish I could give an answer with a note of optimism for the immediate years to come. But with the present group in control, supported as they are by Moscow and by Soviet-dominated armed forces, the populace has no chance to establish a government of its own choice.

In my opinion, the most grievous error that the Polish people could commit would be to attempt to overthrow the regime by force. A revolt would undoubtedly be put down in most merciless fashion. It would bring upon the Polish people, who have already suffered far more than their share of cruelty, still further barbarities. And yet more important and more tragic: such an attempt, doomed to be abortive in the face of overwhelming physical power, would give justification to the Soviet Government to overrun Poland under the pretext of restoring order, and incorporate it into the Soviet Union, like Estonia, Latvia and Lithuania. This would render impossible, for many years, fulfillment of any hope for Polish independence.

If one looks beyond the immediate future one can, however, justify a more optimistic prospect for the Polish people. First, they are the most homogeneous in Europe today. They are, almost all, of one race, language and religion; they are closely knit by suffering and by tremendous devotion to their country. In the partitions of the eighteenth century they proved a most difficult people to subjugate. During the Nazi occupation they never lost their cohesion or their spirit.

As long as they maintain a relative degree of freedom of religion their moral strength cannot be downed.

There is great danger, however, that the indoctrination of Communism in the schools will influence coming generations against Western civilization and against the Four Freedoms for which it stands.

We can keep alive the association between the Polish people and the free peoples of the world, and especially with those of the United States, by the contribution of relief through the many humanitarian organizations now operating.

This is perhaps the most important way in which America may alleviate the plight of the Poles, a plight due in part to our having failed to keep our pledges in favor of a "strong, free and independent Poland."

The fate of Poland, the traditional friend of the United States, will always be of primary interest to Americans, among whom are millions of Polish descent. Yet in considering temporary loss of independence we should think in terms of world conditions, rather than in terms of Poland alone. What has happened to Poland has happened also to Albania, Bulgaria, Hungary, Rumania, Yugoslavia and, though in lesser degree, to Czechoslovakia. As I have tried to show, representations to the Polish Government under the Soviet shadow have been unavailing in matters affecting fulfillment of the Yalta and Potsdam promises; they have been unavailing too in all the other puppet states.

Today, only the will of the Soviet Government can improve the condition of the Polish people or of the peoples of the other nations under Soviet domination. Judging from the past ruthlessness of Communist policy in expanding its influence as far as physical forces will permit, there will be, in my opinion, no turning back on the part of Stalin. On the contrary, he will proceed on his policy, which was also that of Hitler, of seizing control, state by state, until he obtains world domination—the announced aim of the Third International (the Comintern) held in Switzerland in 1915—or until he meets the effective resistance of a stronger power—the United States of America.

The significance of the re-establishment in October 1947 of the Comintern in nine countries, with headquarters at Belgrade—the capital of the nation chosen as the center of Communist imperialism in Eastern Europe—is that it was done publicly. And it is noteworthy that the meeting of the Communist delegates of Bulgaria, Czechoslovakia, France, Hungary, Italy, Poland, Rumania, U.S.S.R. and Yugoslavia took place in Warsaw. There Gomulka and Minc—already proved loyal puppets of the Kremlin—represented Polish Communism.

As the *New Leader* of New York City said in an editorial on October 11, 1947:

Only to the utterly credulous and politically feeble-minded who believed that "Stalin has discarded Communism" and forever severed all ties with his puppet parties can the resurrection of the Communist International be astonishing. It was to be anticipated that the connection between Moscow and the other Communist parties, which had never been broken, would come into the open after the special reasons for the ostensible "abolition" of the Comintern had ceased to obtain. The rebirth of the Comintern comes, however, as the announcement of an imminent new offensive, elaborated and prepared in all its details. It is a concrete strategic plan for political attack, intermingled with military operations.

The military operations, the *New Leader* believes, will be inaugurated first in Italy, whence the American and British postwar occupation forces were withdrawing at the close of 1947. Civil war in Italy
could be provoked by the Italian Communist Party, with its two
million members, supported by the pro-Communists, and with Yugoslavia's army of four hundred thousand men—the largest in Europe,
next to the Red Army itself—ready to go to the aid. To the Communists of France would be assigned the role of intercepting the transportation of troops and munitions from overseas to put down the
insurrection. After the seizure of Italy, France would be next in line.

The day is undoubtedly coming when the Soviet Union will again
request our assistance, economic and financial. When that moment
arrives, the President and the Congress of the United States should
make it emphatically clear that no United States funds will be available to the U.S.S.R. until the violations of the Yalta agreement are
rectified. New elections, under supervision of the United Nations,
should be held in all the countries on which puppet regimes have been
imposed, without the pernicious control of the secret police or other
repressive measures.

We have a moral responsibility as a nation to put an end to terrorism by a police state. In Poland it has been intensified in the last
few months of 1947. In September nine Polish democratic leaders
were sentenced to death. Some were condemned on the charge of
having furnished me with information used in an article in *Life* Magazine, July 14, 1947, entitled, "How Russia Rules Poland." (The
charge was false; my article was based on actual happenings known
to many American press correspondents in Poland. There was no
need to employ secret agents, even had I had the unwise desire to do
so.) In October 1947 an employee of the United States Embassy,
Mrs. Wanda Sroka, an American citizen, was arrested, subjected to
rough handling and questioned by the Security Police, in violation of
the long-established rules of international law.

We have seen that a policy of appeasement toward the **Soviet**

Union has failed dismally, just as it failed toward Hitler at Munich.

The alternative is obviously a policy of firmness. It must be backed by the only element which dictators such as Hitler and Stalin understand: military strength. This is not talk in favor of war, but for peace. Unless we show clearly and strongly to the men who direct the policy of the Soviet Union that we are deeply earnest in our resolve to defend ourselves, and other nations which wish to preserve a democratic form of government, Russia will make further encroachments in Western Europe and the Near East. Eventually will come the turn of the American continent.

That Hitler was designing to dominate the world in 1939, when he and Stalin were partners in international crime, was a conception unthinkable to many. But his signing the Tripartite Pact with Fascist Italy and Japan in 1940 clearly revealed his purpose. In the light of history, can one honestly say that such a conception of Stalin's policy is unthinkable today?

In one respect the task will be greater than the task of combatting Hitler. Stalin possesses a more powerful "Fifth Column" in many countries than Hitler ever had. In some, Hitler had no considerable number of agents who were nationals. In Stalin's case, many nations find a body of their own citizens manifesting belief in Communism, which demands an allegiance transcending loyalty to the land of their citizenship.

It is obvious from events in Poland and in the other countries of Eastern Europe that our official notes of protest on the violations of the Yalta agreement, in which we sought to carry out the principles of the Atlantic Charter, have accomplished nothing positive. But they have served a purpose: they have put on the official record the United States Government's strong disapproval of the cynical disregard of international commitments by the Soviet Union.

The attitude of the Soviet Government toward our protests may perhaps be illustrated by Stalin's remark to a group of Polish Communists and Socialists who had been secretly summoned to Moscow in August 1946. They were there to discuss the policy to be adopted by the Polish Government in formulating an electoral law at the forthcoming meeting of the National Council of the Homeland. One of the participants told me that Stalin advised the Poles not to be disturbed by our protests. The United States often showed great consternation over some international happening; but, little by little, public interest in it would die down and some other matter would absorb our attention. All that these Poles needed was patience; in time, the United States Government would forget the past!

This estimate of our national psychology was reflected, shortly after my departure from Poland, by what Foreign Minister Modzelewski said to Gerald Keith, who had remained in Warsaw as American chargé d'affaires. Modzelewski had taken exception to public statements made by me on my arrival in the United States as to the fraudulent character of the elections of January 19, 1947. When Keith replied that I was merely reiterating the views of the Department of State, Modzelewski asked, with seeming astonishment, whether the United States would still be talking in 1948 about the Polish election results!

It was evident from this, as it was from the Polish note of January 14, 1947, that the Polish Government considered the matter of the elections closed, once and for all.

When I discussed with officials of the Department of State in 1945 and 1946 the advisability of our making a strong public statement on the deterioration of our relations with the Soviet Union and the reasons for it, I was told that the time was not propitious, as the American people were not yet sufficiently prepared. I contended that if the branch of our government dealing with foreign affairs does not acquaint the public with the official version of what has transpired in our foreign relations, the public has no other channel, except those of nonofficial character, on which to rely.

The very foundation of the United States, without which this nation could not survive as a democracy, is that its citizens shall be kept informed, so that on the truth, and the truth alone, they may build

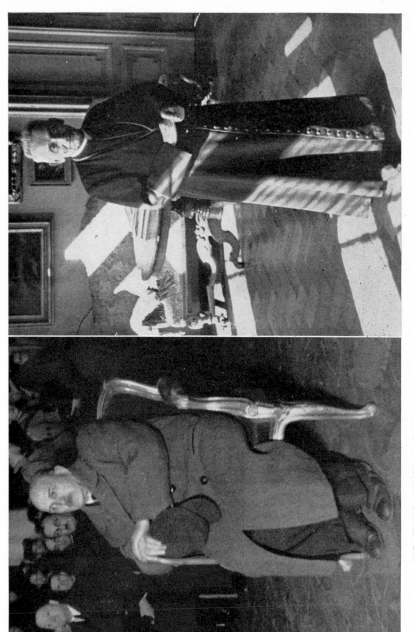

WLADYSLAW KOWALSKI
Marshal of the Sejm.

CARDINAL SAPIEHA
Archbishop of Kraków.

THE BRITISH AMBASSADOR TO POLAND

Mr. Victor Cavendish-Bentinck whose collaboration was invaluable to our Embassy.

their judgments. The public has a right to know when the executive branch of the government makes far-reaching commitments which affect millions of persons and which might seriously endanger the security of the United States. The support of the public is equally essential to our government in carrying out a policy toward other nations. The peace of the globe itself calls for the maintenance of a policy of firmness by the United States backed by military strength. History has already proved that such a policy is a far more effective deterrent of international aggression than a policy of inertia, vacillation or appeasement.

If a policy of appeasement is a fatal course for an individual nation, such as the United States, to pursue in its dealings with another nation, it would inevitably entail even more disastrous consequences were it adopted as a policy of the United Nations. Then it would directly affect not two nations only but all the nations of the world, bringing universal disaster in its train.

The United Nations Organization cannot conceivably accomplish its basic purpose—the maintenance of human rights in all lands, and therewith the maintenance of lasting peace on earth—as long as it contains within itself an irreconcilable element which fights against the principles that are the life, the very soul, of the organization.

As long as the democratic nations now joined together hold firmly to the principle of equal justice for all, they need fear no nation, or groups of nations, outside their number. Even though the Soviet Union and its satellites, angered by the refusal of the United Nations to compromise, where compromise would mean the sacrifice of its cardinal principle, should take the unfortunate step of withdrawing, the moral stature of the United Nations would not be diminished. Such a step would be but a public recognition of a condition which now actually exists: the cleavage of the globe into two worlds—one slave, one free.

I have just quoted the gloomy prediction that Italy would be the next country to fall before the advance of Sovietism, and that after

Italy would come France. There is no reason why this prediction should be allowed to become accomplished fact. The responsibility of preventing a Communist seizure of Italy, France or any other country, and of restoring freedom to Poland and to other nations, rests on the people of the United States and of all other democracies.

It is, therefore, the grave duty of the individual citizen, in every democratic nation, unceasingly to press upon his chosen representatives in all branches of government the folly of political opportunism and the wisdom of fearlessness based on moral integrity.

The people must not fail!

APPENDIX

Appendix

AIDE-MÉMOIRE

The President received in audience Mr. S. Mikolajczyk, Deputy Prime Minister of Poland, accompanied by Mr. J. Zoltowski, Chargé d'Affaires a.i. of Poland, on November 9, 1945.

In reply to the President's questions as to the present economic and food situation in Poland, as to the progress of the work of reconstruction and as to Poland's most urgent needs in connection with rehabilitation and reconstruction, Mr. Mikolajczyk pointed out that the most urgent requirements fall under several headings:

a) a deficit in grain, expected before the August 1946 harvest, will be felt more acutely in early summer;

b) livestock was terribly depleted by the German occupation: horses are reduced by two-thirds, milk cows by sixty per cent, hogs by seventy per cent, sheep by ninety per cent.

As the result thereof milk has become a luxury, fats and meat are almost totally lacking, fertilizers have to be imported in vast amounts.

Tractors are needed in large numbers before the next sowing season.

The President was glad to hear there would be no famine in Poland during the winter months, as he feared, and expressed his desire to help Poland both by supplying tractors and grain to cover the needs during the two months preceding the harvest.

The President stated he will bring the above to the attention of the Secretary of State with the view of action being taken and instructed the Polish Chargé d'Affaires a.i. to communicate with the Secretary of State on these matters.

Continuing, Mr. Mikolajczyk stressed the urgent need of a rapid rehabilitation of the transportation system. There is a most critical deficiency of locomotives and freight cars; trucks, road building and road repairing machinery, railroad and motor car repair shops, etc., are also needed.

Next in importance is the rebuilding of Polish ports, through which pass the UNRRA shipments and in the future will pass the bulk of imports of reconstruction supplies and of exports from Poland, especially coal. For this purpose dredges, scoops, cranes, etc., are urgently needed.

Third in urgency is the speediest possible rebuilding of cities, especially Warsaw, which is beyond question the world's worst ruined capital. For this work rubble and debris-removing machinery, bulldozers, steam-shovels, scoops, etc., are urgently needed.

Fourthly, essential industrial equipment is required to enable the staple industries of the country to resume production on a scale sufficient to cover the domestic needs of the country.

Mr. Mikolajczyk added in conclusion that Poland was not expecting to receive all the supplies she needs as a gift, or in the form of relief, but that she was anxious to purchase them on credit extended by the United States Government, on terms she could meet so as to be able to discharge her contractual obligations.

The President expressed great interest in Mr. Mikolajczyk's statement and declared that the United States will assist Poland as much as possible in her extremely difficult task of reconstruction, particularly by supplying on credit railroad rolling stock, motor trucks, tractors, harbor and road repairing machinery, and also equipment for clearing ruined cities and towns, especially "bulldozers."

The President reiterated his intention to discuss the matter with the Secretary of State and to request him to arrange for the extending of credits to Poland, so as to enable her to obtain supplies she urgently needs.

In concluding the audience, the President again instructed the Polish Chargé d'Affaires a.i. to call on the Secretary of State for the purpose of discussing with him the problem of credits and of supplies.

Washington, December 5, 1945.

Text of Notes from Polish Ambassador in Washington, Dr. Oskar Lange, to Secretary of State, dated April 24, 1946:

The receipt is acknowledged, on behalf of the Provisional Government of Poland of your note of April 24, 1946 reading as follows:

"The Government of the United States, desirous of aiding the people of Poland in their efforts to repair war damages and to reconstruct the Polish economy, expresses its satisfaction at the successful conclusion of the negotiations concerning the opening of credits of $40,000,000 to the Provisional Government of Poland by the Export-Import Bank of Washington, D.C., and the satisfactory conclusion of arrangements for extending credits up to $50,-000,000 for the purchase by Poland of United States surplus property held abroad.

"The Government of the United States hopes that these agreements will prove to be the first step toward durable and mutually beneficial economic and financial co-operation between the Governments of the two countries. It believes, however, that such co-operation can develop fully only if

"(1) a general framework is established within which economic relations between Poland and the United States can be effectively organized on the basis of principles set forth in Article VII of the Mutual Aid Agreement of July 1, 1942, so as to result in the elimination of all forms of discriminatory treatment in international commerce, and the reduction of tariffs and other trade barriers;

"(2) the Provisional Government of Poland is in accord with the general tenor of the 'Proposals for Expansion of World Trade and Employment' recently transmitted to the Provisional Government of Poland by the Government of the United States, and undertakes together with the Government of the United States to abstain, pending the participation of the two Governments in the general international conference on trade and employment contemplated by the 'Proposals,' from adopting new measures which would prejudice the objectives of the conference;

"(3) the Provisional Government of Poland will continue to accord to nationals and corporations of the United States the treatment provided for in the Treaty of Friendship, Commerce and Consular Rights between the United States and Poland, signed June 15, 1931;

"(4) the Government of the United States and the Provisional Government of Poland will make both adequate and effective compensation to nationals and corporations of the other country whose properties are requisitioned or nationalized;

"(5) the Provisional Government of Poland and the Government of the United States agree to afford each other adequate opportunity for consultation regarding the matters mentioned above, and the Provisional Government of Poland, recognizing that it is the normal practice of the Government of the United States to make public comprehensive information concerning its international economic relations, agrees to make available to the Government of the United States full information, similar in scope and character to that normally made public by the United States, concerning the international economic relations of Poland.

"The Government of the United States undertakes herewith to honor and to discharge faithfully the obligations which relate to the United States specified in points (1) through (5) above, and would be pleased to receive a parallel undertaking from the Provisional Government of Poland with respect to those obligations specified in points (1) through (5) above which relate to Poland."

Under instructions from my Government, I have the honor to communicate to you the following:

"The Provisional Government of Poland shares the views of the United States as expressed by the Secretary of State and undertakes herewith to honor and to discharge faithfully the obligations which relate to Poland specified in points (1) through (5) of the notes under reference."

Accept, Sir, the renewed assurances of my high consideration.

OSKAR LANGE

NOTE

Embassy of Poland
April 24, 1946

The Ambassador of Poland presents his compliments to His Excellency the Secretary of State and has the honor to communicate to him the following statement:

Certain information recently published in the press concerning the purpose of the Referendum proposed by the six Political Parties which support the Provisional Government of National Unity seems to imply that the Referendum is to be a substitute for the general elections. This is not the case. The Referendum is a measure preparatory to the election. The principal question to be submitted for decision must be clarified by popular vote before elections are held. This question is whether the future parliament is to be composed of one or two houses. This consultation is to take place this summer, by which time it is hoped that the major part of displaced citizens of Poland will be returned home. Thus, the Government will leave to the Electorate decisions on this basic constitutional issue.

The general elections will take place this year in accordance with the stipulations of Article IX: *A* of the Agreement of Potsdam of August 2, 1945, which notes that the Polish Provisional Government "has agreed to the holding of free and unfettered elections as soon as possible and on the basis of universal suffrage and secret ballot in which all democratic and anti-Nazi parties shall have the right to take part and to put forward candidates, and that representatives of the Allied Press shall enjoy full freedom to report to the World upon developments in Poland before and during the election."

OSKAR LANGE

Text of note delivered by the American Ambassador to Poland, Mr. Arthur Bliss Lane, to the Polish Foreign Office on August 19, 1946:

Under instructions from my Government I have the honor to inform Your Excellency that my Government has been glad to learn that the Polish Provisional Government intends to promulgate electoral laws during the month of August and to hold elections early in the month of November. My Government is deeply conscious of the grave responsibility which it assumed, together with the British and Soviet Governments, by the decisions taken at the Crimea and Potsdam conferences with respect to the holding of free and unfettered elections in Poland. During the conversations which were held in Moscow in June 1945 the Polish leaders agreed to the acceptance of the principles formulated at Yalta. Accordingly, the Polish Government which was then functioning in Poland was reorganized and there was created the Polish Provisional Government of National Unity, with which the Governments of the Soviet Union, Great Britain and the United States established diplomatic relations.

In departing from its traditional policy by assuming responsibilities in connection with the internal affairs of another State, my Government was motivated by the feeling that as one of the principal powers engaged in liberating the peoples of Europe from the yoke of Nazi aggression, it had a special responsibility to assist in giving the Polish people who had suffered so greatly from Nazi occupation an opportunity freely to choose the government under which they would live. My Government feels, therefore, that it has both the right and the duty to bring the following to the attention of the Polish Provisional Government of National Unity.

The United States Government considers that it had no responsibilities in connection with the referendum held in Poland on June 30. Nevertheless, as the Polish Ambassador in Washington informed my Government on April 24, 1946, this referendum was a measure preparatory to the election, and the methods by which it was held bear a relation to the preparations for holding the election itself. The official representatives of the United States Government in Poland have reported that the voting in the referendum appeared to have been generally carried out in a correct and fair manner but that the methods used in tabulating the ballots and reporting the vote have given rise to charges of serious irregularities, including removal of ballot boxes from polling places in contravention of the referendum law.

It has also been brought to the attention of my Government that the Polish Labor Party was not allowed to hold its party congress and that as a result of this and administrative persecution of the party by arrests, censorship restrictions, administrative interference and other oppressive acts which have prevented normal democratic political activity, and the Central Committee majority leadership of the Labor Party has requested the membership of that party to suspend all political activity until such time as the attitude of the Polish Provisional Government toward the Labor Party has changed. The Polish Provisional Government is, of course, aware that one of the essential elements in the agreement for the holding of free elections in Poland is that all democratic, anti-Nazi parties shall have the right to take part and to put forward candidates. To this end it is necessary that all democratic parties be free to engage in political activity in the period preceding the elections.

Furthermore, my Government has learned with great regret that steps have been taken depriving the Polish Peasant Party of its right to assemble and to perform normal party functions in numerous points within Poland. According to reliable information the facilities which other parties enjoy in publishing electoral or party material, in using the radio for propaganda purposes and the ability to make known the views of the party through public posters and other forms of advertisement are through censorship and other means either denied to the Polish Peasant Party or restricted to a degree less than that accorded the parties adhering to the so-called government bloc.

In view of the foregoing, my Government wishes to emphasize its belief that *inter alia* it is essential for the carrying out of free elections that (1) all democratic and anti-Nazi parties are allowed to conduct election campaigns freely without arrest or threat of arrest. The parties recognized as "democratic and anti-Nazi parties" include the following: The Polish Workers Party (PPR), the Democratic Party (SD), the Polish Socialist Party (PPS), the Polish Peasant Party (PSL), the Peasant Party (SL) and the Labor Party (SP) ; (2) all such parties are represented on all electoral commissions and ballots are counted in presence of representatives of all such parties; (3) results will be published immediately by local districts; and (4) there shall be an adequate system of appealing election disputes.

My Government is confident that the Polish Provisional Government of National Unity will take into account the views presented above in making arrangements for the election.

Text of identical (mutatis mutandis) notes delivered on January 5, 1947 to Mr. Andrei Vishinsky, Deputy Minister for Foreign Affairs of the Soviet Union, by Ambassador W. Bedell Smith, and to the British Ambassador in Washington:

The Government of the United States, (my Government) as a signatory of the Yalta and Potsdam Agreements, with particular regard to those sections of the two agreements which deal with the establishment of a representative government in Poland through the instrumentality of free and unfettered elections, wishes me to inform you of the concern with which it views the pre-election activities of the Polish Provisional Government of National Unity. My Government is especially perturbed by the increasingly frequent reports of repressive measures which the Polish Provisional Government has seen fit to employ against those democratic elements in Poland which have not aligned themselves with the "bloc" parties.

According to information reaching my Government from various authoritative sources, these repressive activities on the part of the Provisional Government have now increased in intensity to the point where, if they do not cease immediately, there is little likelihood that elections can be held in accordance with the terms of the Potsdam Agreement which call for free and unfettered elections "on the basis of universal suffrage and secret ballot in which all democratic and anti-Nazi parties shall have the right to take part and put forward candidates."

On December 18, 1946, Vice-Premier Stanislaw Mikolajczyk addressed a communication to the American Ambassador in Warsaw in which he called attention to the reprehensible methods employed by the Provisional Government in denying freedom of political action to the Polish Peasant Party. This communication pointed out *inter alia* that the methods used by the Government in its efforts to eliminate the participation by the Polish Peasant Party in the elections include political arrests and murders, compulsory enrollment of Polish Peasant Party members in the "bloc" political parties, dismissal of Polish Peasant Party members from their employment, searches of homes, attacks by secret police and members of the Communist Party on Polish Peasant Party premises and party congresses, suspension and restriction by government authorities of Polish Peasant Party meetings and suspension of party activities in 28 Powiats, suppression of the party press and limitation of circulation of party papers, and arrest of the editorial staff of the Party Bulletin and of the *Gazeta Ludowa*. Authoritative reports from other quarters in Poland serve to substantiate the charges brought by Mr. Mikolajczyk in the communication cited. It is understood that copies of this communication were also delivered to the Soviet and British Ambassadors at Warsaw as representatives of the other two Yalta powers.

In the view of my Government, what is involved here is the sanctity of international agreements, a principle upon which depends the establishment and maintenance of peace and the reign of justice under law. The obligations with respect to the Polish elections which my Government assumed at Yalta and reiterated at Potsdam, together with the Soviet and British Governments, and the obligations subsequently assumed by the Polish Government and frequently reiterated, provide for the conduct of free and unfettered elections of the type and in the manner described above. It is of no significance that the subject matter of this international agreement relates to elections in Poland. The essential fact is that it constitutes an international agreement on the basis of which all four nations concerned have acted. Therefore, my Government believes that, for any of the parties to this agreement to refrain from the most energetic efforts to see to its proper execution would be to fail in a most solemn obligation. For this reason, it is my Government's view that it is both a duty and a right for the three Powers who are parties to the Yalta and the Potsdam Agreements to call to the attention of the Polish Government in a most friendly but in a most insistent manner the failure of the Polish Government to perform its obligations.

It is a source of regret to my Government that its own efforts in this direction have not resulted in any change in the course which the Polish Provisional Government has pursued in connection with pre-election political activities. My Government feels that it would be failing in its duty if it did not make further efforts prior to the elections to ameliorate the conditions under which certain democratic elements of the Polish population are now struggling in an effort to take their rightful part in the national elections. It intends, therefore, in the immediate future again to approach the Polish Government with a reminder of its obligations in connection with the elections and again to call upon it to provide those conditions of security which will enable all democratic and anti-Nazi parties to take full part in the elections. I hardly need add that my Government is interested only in seeing that the Polish people have the opportunity to participate in a free and unfettered election and that my Government does not regard the results of such an election as being a proper concern of anyone other than the Polish people themselves.

It is the hope of my Government that the Soviet Government, as a party to the Yalta and Potsdam Agreements, will associate itself with the American Government in this approach to the Polish Provisional Government of National Unity.

A similar communication is being addressed simultaneously to the British Government. . . .

Text of Note of January 9, 1947, sent by American Ambassador at Warsaw to Polish Acting Minister for Foreign Affairs:

I have the honor to refer to the Embassy's notes of August 19 and November 22, 1946, regarding the Polish National elections, to which no reply has yet been received, and pursuant to instructions from my Government to inform Your Excellency, as a signatory of the Yalta and Potsdam Agreements, with particular regard to those sections of the two agreements which deal with the establishment of a government in Poland, through the instrumentality of free and unfettered elections, of my Government's continued concern over the pre-election activities of the Polish Provisional Government of National Unity. My Government is especially perturbed by the increasingly frequent reports of repressive measures which the Polish Provisional Government has seen fit to employ against those democratic elements in Poland which have not aligned themselves with the "bloc" parties.

It is a source of regret to my Government that its previous efforts to call the attention of the Polish Provisional Government to its failure to perform its obligations under the agreements cited have not resulted in any change in the course which that Government has pursued in connection with pre-election political activities. According to information reaching my Government from various authoritative sources, these repressive activities on the part of the Provisional Government have now increased in intensity to the point where, if they do not cease immediately, there is little likelihood that elections can be held in accordance with the terms of the Potsdam agreement which called for free and unfettered elections "on the basis of universal suffrage and secret ballot in which all democratic and anti-Nazi parties shall have the right to take part and put forward candidates."

It is the view of my Government that this matter involves the sanctity of international agreements, a principle upon which depends the establishment and maintenance of peace and the reign of justice under law. The obligations with respect to the Polish elections which my Government assumed at Yalta and reiterated at Potsdam, together with the Soviet and British Governments, and the obligations subsequently assumed by the Polish Government and frequently reiterated, provide for the conduct of free and unfettered elections of the type and in the manner described above. The fact that the subject matter of these agreements relates to elections in Poland is incidental. The essential fact is that they constitute an international agreement under which all four nations concerned have assumed obligations. I need hardly say that my Government is interested only in seeing that the Polish people have the opportunity to participate in a free and unfettered election and that my Government does not regard the results of such an election as being a proper concern of anyone other than the Polish people themselves.

My Government would be failing in its duty if it did not again point out that the continuation of the present policy of suppression, coercion and intimidation as applied to political opposition in Poland constitutes a violation of the letter as well as the spirit of the Yalta and Potsdam Agreements.

Translation of note, dated January 14, 1947, received by the American Ambassador at Warsaw from Acting Minister for Foreign Affairs, Mr. Olszewski:

In connection with Your Excellency's note of January 9 of this year and with the preceding notes regarding the elections in Poland I have the honor to communicate to Your Excellency in the name of my government that the elections to the national representation in Poland will be carried out in accordance with the principles of Polish constitutional law and declarations made in Potsdam by the Polish Government of National Unity.

The election law passed on September 27, 1946 and all of the subsequent executive orders by the legal authorities determine the manner of carrying out the elections in accordance with the above principles.

It is the objective and unchangeable concern of the Polish Government to have the widest will of the Polish citizen participate in the elections and to have the result of the elections be the expression of the will of the voting citizens. My government states regretfully that the fears raised in the notes of Your Excellency to the Minister for Foreign Affairs in connection with the elections apparently are based on distorted facts and unfounded reproaches which are raised by the anti-democratic elements which are working in Poland. I believe that the Government of the United States is aware that besides the lists of candidates of all Democratic and anti-Fascist parties there were also admitted lists of other political parties which were not registered, as for instance the groups of Polish Catholics.

In the light of the above decisions and executive orders there could not be any doubt that the elections to the national representative body which is a natural privilege of Polish sovereignty will take place on January 19 of the current year in accordance with the tradition of Polish democracy and of the will of the Polish nation.

Considering this state of affairs it does not seem to my government that there is any justification for further consideration of this question.

Translation of note, dated January 13, 1947, received by the American Ambassador at Moscow from People's Commissar for Foreign Affairs, Mr. Molotov:

In connection with your note of January 5, 1947, regarding the impending elections in Poland, I consider it necessary to inform you of the following:

The Soviet Government cannot agree with the accusations contained in the note under reference against the Polish Provisional Government of National Unity of violating the obligations imposed on it by the decisions of the Yalta and Berlin conferences envisaging the holding in Poland of free and unfettered elections on the basis of universal suffrage, by secret ballot, in which all democratic and anti-Nazi parties will have the right to take part and put forward candidates.

The Government of the United States of America advancing in its note of January 5, a series of accusations against the Polish Government, states that the basis therefor are reports coming to the American Government, and makes reference to the sole source of the information received—to the communication of the Vice-Premier of the Polish Government, S. Mikolajczyk, who transmitted to the American Ambassador in Warsaw reports of the above character, which the American Government considered possible to reproduce in its note.

In the note are repeated the accusations against the Polish Provisional Government contained in Mikolajczyk's statement of repressive measures directed against certain members of the party he represents. In this connection, however, there are completely ignored widely known facts concerning the participation of certain of the members of Mikolajczyk's party in the activities of underground organizations, who resort to every kind of threat, to violence, and to murder in order to interfere with the normal conduct of the electoral campaign for the Sejm.

Among other things, numerous facts are known concerning bandit attacks on electoral districts, terrorization of electors with threats in respect of adherents of the government and of the democratic bloc and even a whole series of murders of members of the electoral commissions.

In this situation, the Polish Government cannot remain indifferent and not undertake decisive measures with respect to the criminal elements who are endeavoring to disrupt the free and unfettered elections for the Sejm, even though certain members of Mikolajczyk's party should be guilty in this.

As is known, Poland suffered grievous years of German occupation, the consequences of which are still apparent at the present time both in the difficult economic conditions as well as in the difficulties in overcoming of the remnants of the banditry generated in the period of occupation of Polish territory by German troops.

It is impossible also to ignore the criminal activities of fascist emigré circles endeavoring to base themselves on their underground organization in Poland, particularly, having in view the connection of these underground organizations with the bandit elements who avail themselves of every kind of violence, even of murder of representatives of the Polish authorities and leaders of the democratic parties. In these circumstances the Polish Government would not be fulfilling its duty to the people if it did not take measures against these criminal elements to assure the conditions necessary for the holding of free democratic elections. To interfere with the carrying out of such measures would be inadmissible particularly on the part of foreign governments.

In view of the foregoing, the Soviet Government does not perceive any basis for the taking of any such steps as the Government of the United States of America proposes, with respect to the Polish Government in connection with the impending elections in Poland and thereby in this fashion bringing about interference in the internal affairs of Poland on the part of the powers who signed the Yalta and Berlin agreements.

INDEX

Index

NOTE ON PRONUNCIATION

PRONUNCIATION of many of the Polish names is indicated phonetically in parenthesis following each name. Consonants have generally the same sounds as in English, except for the symbol *zj*, which has the sound of the French *j* as in *je* or of the *z* in *azure* or the *s* in *fusion*. Vowels are generally marked long or short and the following symbols have been used: ē=the vowel sound in *same;* ĕ=the vowel sound in *get;* ee=the vowel sound in *eel;* i=the vowel sound in *it;* oi=the vowel sound in *oil;* y=the vowel sound in *my*.